T0292015

ADVANCED DATA MINING TOOLS AND METHODS FOR SOCIAL COMPUTING

Hybrid Computational Intelligence for Pattern Analysis and Understanding

ADVANCED DATA MINING TOOLS AND METHODS FOR SOCIAL COMPUTING

Edited by

SOURAV DE
Computer Science & Engineering, Cooch Behar Government
Engineering College, Cooch Behar, India

SANDIP DEY
Department of Computer Science, Sukanta Mahavidyalaya,
Jalpaiguri, India

SIDDHARTHA BHATTACHARYYA
Rajnagar Mahavidyalaya, Birbhum, India

SURBHI BHATIA
College of Computer Sciences and Information Technology,
King Faisal University, Riyadh, Saudi Arabia

Series editors

SIDDHARTHA BHATTACHARYYA AND NILANJAN DEY

ACADEMIC PRESS
An imprint of Elsevier

Academic Press is an imprint of Elsevier
125 London Wall, London EC2Y 5AS, United Kingdom
525 B Street, Suite 1650, San Diego, CA 92101, United States
50 Hampshire Street, 5th Floor, Cambridge, MA 02139, United States
The Boulevard, Langford Lane, Kidlington, Oxford OX5 1GB, United Kingdom

Notices

Knowledge and best practice in this field are constantly changing. As new research and experience
broaden our understanding, changes in research methods, professional practices, or medical
treatment may become necessary.

Practitioners and researchers must always rely on their own experience and knowledge in
evaluating and using any information, methods, compounds, or experiments described herein. In
using such information or methods they should be mindful of their own safety and the safety of
others, including parties for whom they have a professional responsibility.

To the fullest extent of the law, neither the Publisher nor the authors, contributors, or editors,
assume any liability for any injury and/or damage to persons or property as a matter of products
liability, negligence or otherwise, or from any use or operation of any methods, products,
instructions, or ideas contained in the material herein.

Library of Congress Cataloging-in-Publication Data
A catalog record for this book is available from the Library of Congress

British Library Cataloguing-in-Publication Data
A catalogue record for this book is available from the British Library

ISBN: 978-0-323-85708-6

For information on all Academic Press publications
visit our website at https://www.elsevier.com/books-and-journals

Publisher: Mara Conner
Editorial Project Manager: Regine A. Gandullas
Production Project Manager: Kiruthika Govindaraju
Designer: Christian J. Bilbow

Typeset by VTeX

Working together
to grow libraries in
developing countries

www.elsevier.com • www.bookaid.org

Dedication

Sourav De would like to dedicate this book to Satya Narayan De and Tapasi De, his loving wife Debolina Ghosh, his beloved son Aishik De, his sister Soumi De, and his in-laws.

Sandip Dey would like to dedicate this book to the memory of his father, Dhananjoy Dey, and to his mother Smt. Gita Dey, his wife Swagata Dey Sarkar, his children Sunishka and Shriaan, his siblings Kakali, Tanusree, and Sanjoy, his nephews Shreyash and Adrishaan, his brothers-in-law Chinmoy and Utpal, and his mother-in-law Smt. Manjushri Sarkar.

Siddhartha Bhattacharyya would like to dedicate this book to Late Nalini Bhusan Acharjee and Late Nirmala Acharjee, the parents-in-law of his elder sister.

Surbhi Bhatia would like to dedicate this book to her mother Smt Sushila, her beloved husband Mr. Sahil, and her daughter Inaya.

Contents

List of contributors

Ayan Banerjee
Department of Computer Science and Engineering, Jalpaiguri Government Engineering College, Jalpiguri, India

Haider Banka
Department of Computer Science and Engineering, IIT (ISM), Dhanbad, India

Surbhi Bhatia
Department of Information Systems, College of Computer Sciences and Information Technology, King Faisal University, Al Hasa, Saudi Arabia

Sutapa Bhattacharya
Siliguri Institute of Technology, Siliguri, India

Siddhartha Bhattacharyya
Rajnagar Mahavidyalaya, Birbhum, India

Avinash Bhute
Department of Information Technology Engineering, School of Computer Technology, MIT Academy of Engineering, Alandi, India

Rushikesh Borse
Department of Electronics and Telecommunication, School of Electrical Engineering, MIT Academy of Engineering, Alandi, India

Tej Bahadur Chandra
National Institute of Technology, Raipur, Chhattisgarh, India

Manisha Choudhary
Department of Electronics and Telecommunication, School of Electrical Engineering, MIT Academy of Engineering, Alandi, India

Ajanta Das
Amity Institute of Information Technology, Amity University, Kolkata, West Bengal, India

Sourav De
Department of Computer Science & Engineering, Cooch Behar Government Engineering College, Cooch Behar, India

Sandip Dey
Department of Computer Science, Sukanta Mahavidyalaya, Jalpaiguri, India

Paramartha Dutta
Department of Computer and System Sciences, Visva Bharati University, Santiniketan, India

Anuj Kumar Dwivedi
Govt. Vijay Bhushan Singh Deo Girls PG College, Jashpur Nagar, Chhattisgarh, India

Mousumi Halder
Amity Institute of Information Technology, Amity University, Kolkata, West Bengal, India

Pooja Jain
Department of Computer Engineering, Gokhle Education Society's, R.H. Sapat College of Engineering, Management Studies and Research, Nashik-5, India

Premananda Jana
Netaji Subhas Open University, Kalyani, India

V. Kakulapati
Sreenidhi Institute of Science and Technology, Hyderabad, Telangana, India

Harleen Kaur
Department of Computer Science and Engineering, Jamia Hamdard, New Delhi, India

Dipak K. Kole
Dept of CSE, Jalpaiguri Government Engineering College, Jalpaiguri, India

Monika Lokhande
Department of Electronics and Telecommunication, School of Electrical Engineering, MIT Academy of Engineering, Alandi, India

Mihir Narayan Mohanty
ITER (FET), Siksha 'O' Anusandhan (Deemed to be University), Bhubaneswar, India

Mohan Debarchan Mohanty
College of Engineering and Technology, Biju Pattnaik University of Technology, Bhubaneswar, India

Gaurav Mohindru
Department of Computer Science and Engineering, IIT (ISM), Dhanbad, India

Koushik Mondal
Computer Centre, IIT (ISM), Dhanbad, India

Rajendrani Mukherjee
Department of Computer Science and Engineering, University of Engineering and Management, Kolkata, India

Soumen Kumar Pati
Department of Bioinformatics, Maulana Abul Kalam Azad University, Kalyani, India

Poulomi Samanta
Amity Institute of Information Technology, Amity University, Kolkata, India

Dhrubasish Sarkar
Amity Institute of Information Technology, Amity University, Kolkata, India

Archana Vaidya
Department of Computer Engineering, Gokhle Education Society's, R.H. Sapat College of Engineering, Management Studies and Research, Nashik-5, India

Preface

Social networks have received increased attention since the 2010s, and they turned into an extraordinary region of computer science that involves a combination of social behavior and computational systems. Different kinds of social networks have been developed, like Google+, Facebook, Twitter, scientific cooperation networks, and airport networks. Social networks deal with huge volumes of heterogeneous and unstructured data that are very tough to handle. Due to the increasing volume and popularity, social network data analysis has become one of the most promising and attractive research areas. Data mining techniques aim to obtain information by finding patterns/correlations among data patterns. These data are applied in different applications like business, training, online life, the medical field, agriculture, and so on. Data mining algorithms and tools are efficiently and effectively applied to handle social media data. This book present an overview of different novel and hybrid high-quality data mining methodologies, techniques, algorithms, architectures, tools, and methods to deal with issues related to social network data analysis.

This volume presents major emerging trends in the field of social networks which support the current advancement of social networks with the help of data mining techniques and tools. It also aims to highlight advances in conventional approaches. This volume (i) reviews state-of-the-art techniques in the areas of data mining, machine learning, soft computing, etc., and their applications in the field of social networks and (ii) proposes novel techniques. We aim not only to put forward innovative technological ideas, but also to analyze their effects in the current context of social media analysis.

This volume, comprised of 10 well-versed chapters as well as introductory and concluding chapters, will serve as a treatise for the readers to explore the latest trends in mining of social network data as well as other data forms. This volume elaborates on the fundamentals and advances of conventional approaches in the field of data mining. This volume also reviews the state-of-the-art in the area of intelligent data mining techniques and opens a new arena for the researcher to propose new approaches.

Data mining is the procedure of uncovering patterns, correlations, and anomalies (if any) within big datasets to predict outcomes. In Chapter 1, a framework of the basic ideas and characteristics related to data mining in line with the theme of social networking is laid out. In this chapter, the details of data mining are explored in various directions. Thereafter, the concepts of modern social networks and their multiple features are provided. Furthermore, a brief discussion on clustering, multi-view clustering, and classification algorithms are presented to shed light on data mining techniques and social networks. Finally, various applications to data mining in the context of social networks are presented in this chapter.

Performance tuning of Android applications is a rarely explored issue as far as data clustering is concerned. The authors of Chapter 2 explore a new way of performance assessment of Android applications. Two benchmark Android applications (OmniNotes and Ringdroid) are chosen as objects of study. The k-means clustering technique is applied on the collected functional and non-functional requirements of these programs and the requirements are partitioned into clusters. Optimization of the number of requirements in a cluster will enhance the performance of the chosen Android application in terms of time as it is impossible to execute all requirements in a time-constrained environment. This study formulates a fitness objective which depends on the depth of inheritance tree (DIT) traversed per unit of execution time. The authors also explore the ant colony optimization method to compare the effectiveness with respect to knapsack solvers.

One of the most significant threats to today's global civilization is COVID-19. Due to the fear of the nCov-19 virus and increasing transmission and death rates, complete lockdowns are enforced in various countries throughout the whole world. Due to this contagious disease, physical communication is very risky, so the best communication option is connection via digital media. With the constantly growing number of media platforms, India has shrunk due to the increasing communication and exchange of information. These digital platforms turned out to be most effective as regards quicker communication during the pandemic. Chapter 3, on the usage of social media during a time of pandemic, addresses effective ways of usage of social media for public communication with emergency organizations, such as police, during lockdown. This information will help to identify people who are careless, cautious, and neutral towards this situation. Moreover, the authors discuss how to identify various emotions of people before, during, and after this crisis situation using naive Bayes and K-means clustering for clustering of tweets or comments on Twitter and Facebook and find trends using social media analytics.

Recent years have witnessed the application of statistical machine learning for different fields of research. To predict the future state of the process with observable characteristics, it is highly essential to analyze well. Time series analysis is an alternative that applies different statistical methods to explore different states and fluctuations. The main objective of Chapter 4 is to build a robust model that analyzes the worldwide COVID-19 outbreak and to predict the spread of the virus in the next 7 days using Prophet. This model is an additive regression model that produces excellent prediction results. It is well explained in the methodology section of this chapter. Through the proposed method, the authors analyze the total number of confirmed, death, and recovered cases. The authors also analyzed as to which countries have the highest numbers of cases. Prophet begins with a time series model using specified parameters, makes predictions, and evaluates them. The dataset includes 12,568 observations with 8 variables.

Sentiment analysis of human beings is a recent research area that is growing exponentially. Though certain works have been conducted in this area, much remains to be improved in terms of human attitude and accuracy. Sentiment analysis of text, sentiment analysis of speech, and visual sentiment analysis have been reported earlier. Though the task is difficult with only verbal statements, in Chapter 5, verbal data are considered to analyze the human sentiments using a deep recurrent neural network (RNN). First, the state-of-art of the field is discussed. Two major sentiments along with two submajor sentiments are worked out. Some of the versions are recorded from human subjects in different moods. These are deeply analyzed instead of only considering positive and negative options. Due to the efficacy of spectral features, different spectral techniques are used to derive features. Furthermore, the segmental features as parts of speech are considered along with Mel-frequency cepstral coefficients. Neural network-based models are tested for the task of classification. Finally, a deep RNN is used, evaluated, and found to be better than other methods that can lead to speech data mining. The training of RNN with these input features is performed using the stochastic gradient descent algorithm. The results show that the efficacy is higher than those reported in previous works.

Chapter 6 focuses on hand movement classification from electromyography (EMG) signals using machine learning algorithms. The use of EMG signals for the human–human interface to move a paralyzed person is discussed. EMG signals are generated when the electric potential of the muscles changes after receiving signals from the brain due to the contraction or expansion of muscles. EMG signals were collected by connecting electrodes to a person's arm and they were recorded using the BYB Spike Recorder App. Features were extracted from these signals and a dataset was obtained using these features. Hand movement of the person using this dataset was classified using various algorithms like k-nearest neighbor (KNN), support vector machine, naive Bayes, and decision tree. All algorithms offered a promising accuracy of around 90%, except KNN, whose accuracy was 60%. Thus, they can be used to control movements of people with disabilities by a human–human interface.

In the era of the 21st century, people cannot think of living without social network or social media. So, our daily life as well as social behavior is strongly influenced by social media or networks in urban areas. Due to the outbreak of COVID-19, people are living online mostly. It is observed from various studies that depression, loneliness, monotonousness, etc., can be overcome easily at home through social media. Human being never feel alone with good connectivity through social networking. Hence, it may be concluded that social media can stimulate people to be social, friendly, energetic, and also creative. Improvement of social behavior also depends on valuable vacation time and frequent traveling. Three different mental states, i.e., happy, normal or moderate, and depressed, can be easily detected through various exchanges of messages between close friends and the greater circle of friends. Even psychological behavior and various characteristics of people can also be identified through social media for the betterment of society and people. Therefore, the objective of Chapter 7 is to mine travel habits simultaneously through social networking and analyze social behavior based on the various blogs, photos, and comments related to the same post on social networking sites using machine learning techniques.

Social media is an example of a social network. In the 21st century social media sites have been gaining much attention. Many people are making steps on social media like Facebook, LinkedIn, Pinterest, and Twitter. Nowadays these platforms are taken very seriously for providing information and users' opinions on diverse subject matters. So, massive data are generated by the virtual network. The data are collected to understand the users' behavior. Additionally, it is necessary to simplify for further usage and related work. During the last few years, virtual platforms have become so popular and we have started to get involved it in in a different way in our daily life. However, in 2020, the use of technology has reached the top. Now, virtual platforms are used in every aspect of business, education, e-commerce, and entertainment. During the present pandemic, online platforms are needed globally. So, huge data are generated by individual users. These data are for future experiments, machine learning analysis, user examination, and so on. In order to do so, behavior analysis and data mining on online media platforms is very important. Chapter 8 addresses the basic concepts of behavior analysis techniques in social network system and it gives a brief idea of the usage of those techniques in the virtual environment to identify and understand the patterns in networks between nodes in different areas. It also explores recent related works about the topic.

With the rise of technology, anyone can easily share their sentiments through social media platforms like Facebook, Twitter, Wikipedia, LinkedIn, Google+, and Instagram. Sentiment analysis is a technique that categorizes opinions from pieces of text to determine a sentiment score (positive, negative, or neutral). Recommendation systems usually aim to match user patterns by finding similar users or different users according to their sentiment scores. Sentiment analysis is dependent on machine learning- or lexicon-based approaches. Chapter 9 attempts to enlighten how sentiment analysis can be used to improve the outcomes of recommender systems. The chapter describes the basic concepts and terms related to sentiment analysis and recommendation system. Different aspects of sentiment analysis are discussed, followed by an overview of recent developments and related works. The authors propose a combination of a BERT model and an S3VM classifier using a collaborative recommendation architecture to obtain good accuracy.

Data visualization has a strong footprint on today's scientific exploration, reasoning, hypothesis formation, and business data analysis. As an analytical tool for scientific or business forecasting, it has been accepted worldwide. Data visualization has an important role in making the massively accumulated data over the internet (shopping malls, data centers, etc.) usable for future prediction, strategic development, risk analysis, etc. Over time, data have become the essential competitive factor for businesses/enterprises to grow and develop. Selected businesses/enterprises such as industrial information businesses will put more focus on product innovation or technology for solving the challenges of gigantic data, i.e., capture, storage, analysis, and presentation/application. Enterprises/businesses like banking, manufacturing, and other enterprises will also benefit from analysis and management of huge data and provide more prospects for management/strategy/marketing innovations. For centuries, persons/societies have depended on visual illustrations such as maps and charts to grasp information quickly. Due to the way the human brain processes information, it is faster for people to grasp the meaning of many data points when they are displayed in charts and graphs rather than in piles of spreadsheets or long reports. Data visualization is the presentation of data in a graphical or pictorial format. Visual displays or presentations become more attractive with the use of computers for providing context or circumstances that enable to select a particular segment and to focus on changes. Over time, as data are collected, stored, and analyzed, decision makers at all stages rely on data visualization/presentation software that enables them to see and visually present fruitful analytical results, find significance among the heaps/millions of variables, communicate established concepts and hypotheses to others, and even forecast/predict the future. By exploring each aspect of existing tools and techniques related to data visualization, the primary objective of Chapter 10 is to present essential theoretical aspects in an analytical way with a profound focus on challenges to represent data in visual form and limits in terms of pros and cons of existing tools and techniques. This chapter presented 127 data visualization tools/techniques and several of their properties.

Nowadays, significant amounts of data are generated across almost all areas such as social networks, sensor networks, biological fields, etc., and useful information is retrieved from these data in the form of graphs. Using graphs, more frequent data are extracted by applying a frequent submining (FSM) algorithm. The FSM algorithm can get all subgraphs from a single large graph with a more significant number of edge connections. Graphs consist of vertices and edges, and sometimes these graphs are uncertain due to the higher number of vertices and the lower number of edges. Some vertices may have a considerable number of edges in uncertain graphs, fewer edges, and one aims to find frequent subgraphs from the uncertain graph. Chapter 11 utilizes two algorithms, i.e., an evaluation probabilistic algorithm and an evaluation estimate algorithm. The existing methods can perceive subgraphs but are unable to estimate whether they are frequent or infrequent. In this chapter, a method is proposed using the min support threshold value, which is able to prune out all sparse subgraphs and take only those subgraphs whose frequent count is greater than the user-given threshold value.

Chapter 13 draws the conclusion, discusses future aspects of research in this direction, and highlights limitations of the existing techniques.

This volume will benefit several categories of students and researchers. For students, this book can be useful as it refers to special papers and may inspire possible future researchers. PhD candidates may find the contents of this volume useful as far as their compulsory coursework is concerned. Researchers interested in interdisciplinary research will also benefit from the volume. After all, the rich interdisciplinary contents of this volume will always be a subject of interest to members of the existing research communities and new research aspirants from diverse disciplines across the globe.

June, 2021

Cooch Behar, India   Sourav De
Jalpaiguri, India   Sandip Dey
Birbhum, India   Siddhartha Bhattacharyya
Hofuf, Saudi Arabia   Surbhi Bhatia

CHAPTER 1

An introduction to data mining in social networks

Sourav De[a], Sandip Dey[b], Surbhi Bhatia[c], and
Siddhartha Bhattacharyya[d]

[a]Department of Computer Science & Engineering, Cooch Behar Government Engineering
College, Cooch Behar, India
[b]Department of Computer Science, Sukanta Mahavidyalaya, Jalpaiguri, India
[c]Department of Information Systems, College of Computer Sciences and Information Technology,
King Faisal University, Al Hasa, Saudi Arabia
[d]Rajnagar Mahavidyalaya, Birbhum, India

1.1 Introduction

In the current digital arena, the interdisciplinary research in the fields of
computer science, engineering, social sciences, art, and humanities has
evolved into a new research field, known as social computing. The rapid
development of some well-known social network applications, like instant
messaging, wikis, email, blogs, social bookmarking, etc., empowered the
social capability of computer networks. These urge individuals to take part
in aggregate asset building, activity, and work.

There is no doubt that today's world is contracting into a small village
inferable from the unmistakable impact of social media. It associates individuals with different backgrounds, nationalities, ages, and qualities and
permits them to impart their insights, encounters, emotions, interests, pictures, and recordings. For private and public organizations, a new avenue is
opened to advance, dissect, learn, and improve their organizations dependent on the information shared on social media. Hence, the meaning of
social media for the scholarly community and industry is very prominent
in the measure of exploration done by these two areas, looking for answers
to essential inquiries.

As social networks are developing endlessly and quickly, it is not an
easy task to handle the generous pool of unstructured data that have a
place within a large group of domains, including business, governments,
and wellbeing [1]. The unstructured social media data like text data, image
data, and audio and video data can be found in an unorganized way. Also,
social media provide a gigantic, persistent, and constant flow of informa-

tion that makes customary factual techniques inadmissible to examine this enormous amount of data. To overcome this situation, data mining can play a significant role.

In social networks, a group of Internet-based applications are employed to improvise the idea and innovation of web-based services, i.e., Web 2.0, that permit people to produce a public/semi-public profile inside a space to such an extent that they can informatively associate with different clients inside the network [2][3]. In the earlier days, the homepages of websites only shared information with most of the internet users. Nowadays, due to the social networks, the World Wide Web (www) has become a place for social communication as the information can be exchanged between users regardless of their location. Social networks can be followed by numerous organizations, people, and even legislature of nations. The organization empowers large associations, big names, government officials, and government bodies to get information on how their crowd responds to postings that worry them out of the huge information produced on social network. The powerful assortment of large-scale data which brings about major computational difficulties can be allowed by the network. However, the utilization of productive data mining procedures has made it feasible for clients to find important, precise, and valuable information from social network data.

Extraction of information and knowledge from immense amounts of data can be easily done by data mining. Finding data from a large database is an important step in data mining. Different types of databases, data warehouses, and data marts are present in this world. It is the responsibility of the data miners to find out the data patterns from the huge pile of data. Three main challenges to handle the social network data are size, noise, and dynamism. They can be handled efficiently by data mining. A reasonable time is required to analyze the voluminous nature of social network datasets with the help of automated data processing. Data mining tools are quite handy to mine the social network sites as data mining methods can handle huge datasets to mine noteworthy patterns from data [3]. Though much research has been conducted on data mining and social media, few studies have been conducted to compare different types of data mining techniques in respect of exactness, execution, and appropriateness [1]. For example, it was seen that the precision of certain machine learning strategies is different for different techniques, which makes it hard to characterize responses and applicability of the data mining methods. Injadat *et al.* [1] presented an in-depth survey of 19 data mining techniques applied on social media data to deal with nine different research objectives in six different industrial and service areas. The existing web mining techniques that are employed to mine social network data have been identified and analyzed in [4][5]. Commonly applied social media-based applications and different types of analysis techniques, like time series analysis, network analysis, sentiment analysis, and topic analysis, are discussed in [6].

Deep learning is also applied in the field of social media. Hayat *et al.* [7] discussed the state-of-the-art deep learning network architectures and how those networks are employed for social media analytics. The social media-based problems and their respective deep learning-based solutions are also illustrated. Batrinca and Treleaven [8] reviewed several research papers on the well-known software tools and their application to scratch, cleanse, and analyze the spectrum of social media.

1.2 Data mining concepts

Nowadays, the people live in the so-called modern age, called the information age. Information leads the way to success and power in this present society. Gigantic amounts of information can be accumulated by utilizing state-of-the-art technologies like satellites. With the advancement in computer technology, storage capacity became cheap and extensive. Various sorts of data are collected, used, and stored by different people for different purposes. Every day, the amount of data to be handled becomes more overwhelming. To deal with this chaotic situation, the concept of database management systems (DBMSs) has been amounted. DBMSs can create databases, manage data, and retrieve a very large collection of information from databases using efficient methodical approaches. The growth of DBMSs has recently led to a huge variety of many different kinds of information. These days, a much greater degree of information needs to be handled in separate sectors; some of the popular examples are business and scientific data, texts, satellite pictures, and data related to military intelligence. In contrast to the past, decision making is not restricted anymore to information retrieval. In line with massive assemblage of data, new requirements are being created to do someone a good turn in making preferable managerial choices. Some of the popular examples are instinctive data summarization, unsheathing of the gist of information, and the determination of patterns using raw data [9].

Data mining is a comparatively new and intelligent concept to sift through historical data to uncover relevant information. It is a potentially effective, implicit, and non-trivial technique to exact fascinating knowledge or trends or patterns from gigantic amounts of data. It may be greatly helpful for management personnel of any company to put their focus on the most apposite facts in their associated data warehouses [10].

1.2.1 Text mining

Text mining is referred to as the most significant method to analyze and process unstructured data. In today's world, a bulk of firms and institutions congregate and store huge volumes of data in their cloud platforms and data warehouses. The volume of data may become larger over a period of time, since data may be concurrently collected from multiple sources. As a result, it begins to be a challenging task for different organizations to process, store, and analyze these gigantic volumes of textual data with conventional tools. To deal with this critical scenario, several text mining tools and techniques have been introduced.

Text mining, also called text data mining, is the approach that is employed to derive high-quality textual information. It is used to examine and explore unstructured data for taking out meaningful patterns and textual data sources. Text mining assimilates and amalgamates the tools of data mining, information retrieval, statistics, machine learning, etc., and hence, it can be thought of as a multi-disciplinary field. It can handle natural language texts in any available format. A few basic steps involved in this method are presented below [11].

- Firstly, unstructured data are collected from various sources such as web pages and files in different formats like pdf, plain text, or emails.
- Thereafter, different anomalies are detected and removed from these collected data by performing pre-processing and cleansing tasks using a variety of text mining tools applications.
- Then, the extracted information is converted into a structured format.
- The patterns within the data are analyzed thoroughly using a management information system (MIS).
- All valuable and relevant information is stored in a secure database. This helps to guide trend analysis and improve the decision making procedure of the company.

1.2.2 Image mining and video mining

Nowadays, images are probably the most decent way to memorize past events. Images are actively used in a variety of fields, such as sports, medicine, and social networking, to name a few. Image processing has become a very popular and commonly used research field in these days. To start analyzing images, they need to be captured first using suitable cameras. This is known as image acquisition. In the last few years, there has been a significant growth in storage technology and image acquisition. Some useful information from these images can be retrieved, if analyzed properly. Image mining is a popular tool used for extracting implicit knowledge, relationships between images and data, or patterns. It can be defined as an extended part of data mining in the image domain. Image mining is an interdisciplinary research field. Several state-of-the-art techniques line up expertise in database management, machine learning, computer vision, image processing, data mining, and artificial intelligence (AI).

Video mining can also be defined as the extended research part of image mining. It is the process of bringing to light structures, knowledge, and patterns in the video data. Like image data, high-quality video data can also be captured in a simple manner. These days, several companies heavily rely on videos for marketing their services and products. In the era of information technology, users can acquire a large amount of multimedia data and use numerous multimedia systems. So, in line with the availability, the volume of video data is increasing exponentially in society. Videos can be categorized into the multimedia group that comprises various data including image, text, audio, visual, and meta-data. In the last few years, several researchers across the globe have been inspired by data mining and have expressed their profound interest in video mining. This is used to extract semantic information, knowledge, and implied patterns and dynamics from video data, which in turn intensifies the level of video applications. In today's life, video mining has a major role in a variety of applications across entertainment, sports, security and surveillance, medical science, and education, to name a few.

1.2.3 Web data mining

An application area of data mining is popularly known as web data mining. It is very useful to uncover patterns by utilizing web data mining techniques from the World Wide Web. Several automated techniques can be utilized for extracting data from web pages. Data can also be extracted from server logs and different link structures. Web mining can be categorized into the following subcategories [12,13].

- Web content mining: In this category, information is extracted within a web page.
- Web structure mining: In this category, documents in the web pages are thoroughly searched from hyperlinks and web pages. The comparability

and relationship between a variety of sites are also measured in web structure mining.

• Web usage mining: In this category, patterns of utilization of web pages are found to better understand and serve web-based applications.

1.2.4 Mining sequence patterns

Mining sequence patterns is a problem in which the association between distinct items in a database needs to be found. Mining sequence patterns are actually itemsets, substructures, or subsequences which appear within a set of data and have frequency not below a user-specified limit. For example, a collection of items, like bread and eggs, that are often present together in a transaction dataset can be called a frequent itemset [14]. A subsequence like the purchase of a laptop, followed by a camera and later an external hard drive, if it often occurs in the history of a shopping database, will be termed a frequent sequential pattern. Structural forms like subgraphs or subtrees, which can be joined with itemsets or subsequences, are referred to as substructures. The frequent occurrence of substructures within a graph database is known as a frequent structural pattern. Frequent pattern mining has been a requisite task in data mining, and many researchers are dedicated to this task since a couple of years. With its plentiful uses to data mining problems like classification and clustering, it has been broadly researched. The application of frequent pattern mining in real-world businesses can lead to increased sales, which results in increased profits. Frequent pattern mining has been applied in domains like recommender systems, bioinformatics, and decision making. The literature dedicated to this field of research is abundant and tremendous progress has been achieved such as the development of efficient and effective algorithms aimed at mining of frequent itemsets. Mining sequence patterns is of immense importance in many important data mining tasks like association and correlation analysis, analyzing patterns in spatiotemporal data, classification, and cluster analysis. The problem of pattern mining can be specified as follows. If we have a database DTB which contains transactions $T_1, T_2 \ldots T_n$, all the patterns P need to be determined which appear in no less than a fraction s of all the transactions [15]. Fraction s is usually referred to as the "minimum support." This was put forward first by Agrawal *et al.* [16] in 1993 for analyzing market basket as a kind of association rule mining (ARM). It analyzed the buying habits of customers by discovering the associations among the items which are being placed by customers in their respective baskets used for shopping. For example, for customers who buy bread, what are their chances of buying eggs? Information like this can help increase the sales because the owners will do marketing as per this information and shelf spaces will be arranged accordingly.

1.2.5 Mining time series data

In the last few years, mining of time series data has gained utmost popularity among data mining researchers. Many algorithms have been developed in different segments, which include clustering, classification, indexing, segmentation, bringing to light rules, and finding anomalies in time series [17]. Instead of using original raw data, these algorithms include high-level data representation as a feature extraction step. The other possible reason for data representation is that it helps to store, transmit, and compute huge datasets in a feasible manner. In the literature, plenty of representations have been introduced so far, which include wavelets transforms, spectral transforms, symbolic mappings, and eigenfunctions, to name few [17].

Time series data deliver a large portion of the world's data requirements. In line with the fast expanding sizes of databases, different researchers have recently expressed an explosion of interest in this field. In medical science, a large amount of data like gene expression data, gait analysis, electroencephalograms, and electrocardiograms are routinely used. In a similar way, large volumes of time series data are used in finance, entertainment, industry, meteorology, and practically every field of human pursuit. Some notable works using mining of time series data can be found in the literature [18].

1.2.5.1 Hidden community mining

Due to the fast growth of the internet sector and the World Wide Web, web-based social networks are gaining importance and more research is inclined towards the broader domain defined as "social network analysis" [19][20]. A social network is based on the graph structure with nodes as individuals and edges reflecting the relationship between the interconnected nodes. The modeling of a social network in the form of a graph network is rather interesting and challenging [21][22]. The challenges include identifying the groups of individuals with identical characteristics and methods to evaluate the significance of individuals with respect to each other [23]. The link analysis plays an important role in discriminating relationships and a lot of research has been conducted in this area [24][25][26]. Different algorithms related to graph partitioning are used to determine the communities by constructing the graph. There may be existing relations in a typical human community, like individuals working in a common place, with common interests, etc. The model can be structured mathematically also by representing it as a big graph where the nodes and edges are taken. The edges, also called links, measure the strength of the connections or relations drawn. The nodes are taken as the people. To evaluate the existing relations between the nodes treated as individuals is considered as extracting insightful information called community mining.

1.2.6 Association rule mining

ARM, presented by Srikant *et al.* [27][28] in 1996, is an important data mining model. At the initial stage, it used for market basket analysis to detect how items are purchased by customers. It assumes all data are categorical. In ARM, simple IF/THEN statements are the backbone of association rules and these are applied to define the relationships between apparently free relational databases or other information stores. Determination of the patterns in the dataset, like non-numeric, categorical data, is done by ARM. It is a methodology which means to notice correlations, frequently repeating patterns, or relationships from datasets found in different sorts of databases and different kinds of repositories. Basically, any association rule is based on an *IF-THEN* condition, i.e., an antecedent and a consequence. The effectiveness of the rule is measured on the basis of **support** and **confidence**. The frequency of the appearance of the *IF-THEN* relationship is indicated by the **support** and **confidence** talks about the occasions these connections have been discovered to be true. Shaukat *et al.* [29] presented an elaborate review of ARM applications and discussed the different aspects of the association rules that are used to extract the interesting patterns and relationships among the set of items in data repositories.

1.2.7 Sequential pattern mining

Sequential pattern mining (SPM), another area of data mining, is applied to discover the statistically relevant patterns between information models where the qualities are conveyed in a grouping. The relationships between happenings of sequential events to get if there exist any special order is determined by SPM [30]. SPM is also known as a special kind of structured data mining. Mooney and Roddick presented different approaches and algorithms related to SPM [31].

1.2.8 Data warehouse and OLAP

A data warehouse [32][33] is a physically stored dataset kept separate from the organization's operational database. It contains secure historical data to aid in the analysis of the organization's business; for example it assists executives to realize and organize the data to choose strategic business decisions. It also helps to merge diverse application systems. No frequent updating is done in data warehouses. When new data are added to the warehouse, previous data are not erased. Data warehouses are mainly applied in retail, banking, and financial services and for controlled manufacturing of consumer goods.

It is subject-based as it gives information around a subject rather than the organization's functionalities. The subjects can range from products, sales, and revenue to customers and suppliers. It is retraced by combining data from sources such as relational databases, flat files, etc., which help to analyze the data effectively. A data warehouse unlike operational datasets does not involve transaction processing, recovery, and concurrency controls. An online analytical processing server (OLAP) query allows the user to access data in read-only mode whereas an operational dataset query gives access to both read and modify operations.

1.2.8.1 OLAP

OLAP [34] is dependent on the multi-dimensional data model. It helps to get fast, consistent, and interactive access to information. There are four types of OLAP servers, i.e., multi-dimensional OLAP (MOLAP), relational OLAP (ROLAP), hybrid OLAP (HOLAP), and specialized SQL servers.

1.2.8.2 Classification of data warehouses

- **Information processing** – A data warehouse gives the permission to operate the data stored in it. Different methods like statistical analysis and reporting using crosstabs, tables, charts, or graphs or by querying are employed to handle those data [35].
- **Analytical processing** – The analytical processing of the data which are stored is done with the help of the data warehouse. Different basic OLAP operations like slice-and-dice, pivoting, drill down, and drill up are applied to analyze those data.
- **Data mining** – Data mining is used to find information by finding hidden patterns and associations, constructing analytical models, and performing classification and prediction [35]. Visualization tools are used to present these mining results.

1.3 Social computing

Social computing is concerned with the intersection of social behavior and computational systems. The way the people connect with the computational systems by identifying and responding to several queries like responding to how and why the online content is created by the population also explains the mechanism of developing and designing the dynamic information retrieval systems for enabling them to complete the task [36]. Examples include collective intelligence, prediction markets, and crowdsourcing markets. Social computing is more to the tune of what Facebook, Twitter, etc., do. They provide a computing platform for social interaction. Computational social science, on the other hand, is making sense of these social connections and activities [36]. Social media sites such as Facebook and Twitter analyze their data, identifying the populations based on their actions using computational science. In the future, virtually all computing will be "social" in various ways. It depends on different research questions such as (i) solving existing problems, (ii) innovating applications, and (iii) extending the boundaries of the field into new areas. The convergence of social computing and the older ideas of the semantic web may make both of them take off. Users do not like to be directly aware of semantic meta–data so it must be inferred from implicit behavior and from what can be gleaned from their "contexts" of computing activity. Context modeling needs work to extend from the business focus of context analysis and "consumers" toward more diverse models of individuals and groups such as toward a social semantic web to social machines, collective knowledge systems, where the social web meets the semantic web. This requires work on user interfaces, visualization, and natural language generation and will support a shift from a dominant emphasis on data mining and information retrieval towards semantic social authoring and curation. Gamification will also play a role in raising the social intelligence of our interactions with computing media.

One of the biggest issues with social media is the dependency on static categorization and constructs. Some social media platforms are now beginning to draw real links between adjacent subject matter. On a similar vein, consumer and site visitor trends can be seen that show much more predictable patterns. With all the anonymous user data that are collected by some sites, all the raw information is there but the systems to make use of the data are lacking.

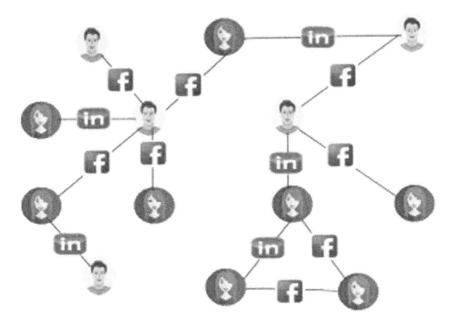

Figure 1.1 Social network.

1.3.1 Social networks

A network can be represented as the group of entities and their connections [37]. In the social network characterized as a graph, the nodes and edges are considered to represent the set of connections between the nodes taken as edges. An example of a social network is shown in Fig. 1.1, in which the nodes represent people and there are two types of links: friendship (Facebook) and professional (LinkedIn).

Social networks differ based on the types of nodes and edges as explained below. Homogeneous network contains nodes and edges of the same type [38]. An example of a homogeneous network and a heterogeneous network is shown in Fig. 1.2. The heterogeneous network has multiple types of nodes and multiple types of edges. The multi-relational (MR) network and the bipartite network are special types of heterogeneous networks [39]. An MR network contains a single type of nodes and multiple types of edges, whereas a bipartite network contains exactly two types of nodes and edges exist between two different types of nodes. Social networks are dynamic in nature. New interactions may be established between nodes, leading to the addition of new edges to the network, causing growth

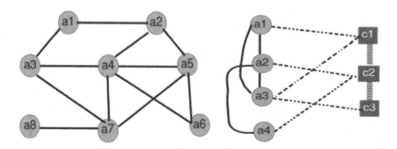

Figure 1.2 Homogeneous and heterogeneous graphs.

in networks. The growth of the social graphs has been exponential in the past decade [40][41].

1.3.2 Social network representation

Social networks can be represented using nodes and edges. Nodes represent individuals and edges represent relationships between individuals. The edges can be considered as homogeneous graphs or heterogeneous graphs. For instance, like in the COVID-19 pandemic, unprecedented pressures have been placed on hospitals. Now, we try to find those most likely infected. Here, existing relationships among people will not play the same role; rather, at such situations, people staying at one place or working in close contacts will be considered critical. Here a reasonable research question will be based on finding the relation that most strongly affects spread of the disease. Also, we are required to extract the hidden relations to discover the path by which the disease spreads. These research questions need to be modeled using the mathematical relations in the social network analysis. Extracting the relation requires to evaluate the importance of different relations considered as a heterogeneous social network. The importance of evaluating the relations needs to be monitored. The combination of the present existing relations also needs to be identified in order to match the relation of labeled examples.

1.3.3 Network representation learning

In network representation learning, low-dimensional vectors are represented in the form of nodes in a network. This is also called network embedding. Applications where network analysis plays an important role include predicting links [42], community detection [43], classifying nodes [44], and tasks done through visualization [45]. Challenges appear when representing data with a heterogeneous nature, sparse data, nodes with varying degrees, and other issues that actually make mining tasks difficult. For resolving these problems, encoding is done by the network embedding and every node is characterized in a unified low-dimensional space. This further aids in improving our understanding of semantic relationships and enables the application of classical machine learning algorithms for network mining tasks [45]. For example, with the learned network representations, the community detection problem is reduced to a classical clustering algorithm and K-means can be applied. Network embedding has attracted increasing attention in recent years and various network embedding algorithms have been proposed [45][46][47]. For example, in [47], spectral analysis is performed on a Laplacian matrix where eigenvalues are computed and the vectors are used for representing the nodes in the network. t-Distributed stochastic neighbor embedding (t-SNE), proposed in [48], embeds the weighted network to a low dimension for visualization by using SNE. SocDim [49] exploits network modularity to learn the latent social dimensions as the node representation. The state-of-the-art network representation learning algorithms borrow the idea from word2vec [50] techniques. The essential idea is to first extract the node proximity from the network structure and then train the embedding to preserve the node proximity [50]. For example, DeepWalk [51] introduces the idea of Skip-gram, which is a novel method introduced in natural language processing (NLP) and taken as a word representation model, to learn node representations by extracting node proximity using random-walk sequences. Node2Vec [52] extends DeepWalk by introducing second-order random walk to extract node proximity [52]. LINE [53] exploits first-order proximity and second-order proximity to learn network embedding. Deep learning is effective in representation learning, which has achieved great success in many domains such as computer vision [54], NLP [55], and speech recognition [56]. Therefore, more and more effort is dedicated to the investigation of deep learning models for network representation learning. For example, Wang et al. [57] propose structural deep network embedding (SDNE), which utilizes deep networks to learn highly non-linear features. The graph attention network [58] adopts the attention mechanism to learn a network representation, where the attention mechanism is widely used in deep learning models. Graph convolutional networks try to extend the concept of convolution in signal processing to learn a network representation. However, the majority of the aforementioned network representation learning algorithms are designed for plain networks, i.e., networks with fixed nodes and links, while in social media, networks can be present in different formats, such as attributed networks, signed networks, dynamic networks, and document networks. Different types of social networks contain rich information that can help to alleviate the network sparsity problem. For example, negative links in a signed social network usually mean distrust or a foe relationship, which have different semantic meaning from positive links and can be used to learn a better network representation.

1.3.4 Influence analysis

With the proliferation and rapid spread of applications related to social media, (i) various chat applications like Jabber, Skype, Botim, and IMO, (ii) social network sites such as Facebook, Twittter, and Instagram, (iii) blogs such as Blogger, WordPress, and LiveJournal, (iv) wikis such as Wikipedia and PBWik, and (v) collaborations such as IEEE and Xplore DBLP affect and influence our personal and social lives across the globe. Thus, influence analysis has become an unstoppable, prevalent subtle force that is ruling the dynamics of all social networks. It is the need of the hour to prioritize the techniques and designs to analyze and quantify the social influences. There are different parameters to discuss how the influence is spreading through social networks so rapidly. In particular, the primary issues are whether the social networks are of heterogeneous nature with varying objects such as users, blogs, and objects and how the influence is affected by different types of objects on different topics, e.g., entertainment, marketing, and research. Apart from this, the user-generated content spreading on the media and social networks through microblogs, tweets, and retweets and other stories through which users enjoy sharing their opinions is closely interconnected because of these many heterogeneous networks. One of the examples is that the supervisors greatly influence their research scholars, though their interests are influenced by their siblings or their close ones. Thus influence strength varies with topic. The second reason may be different in aspects related to topic-level influence in the problem of jointly learning topic distributions associated with each other. The friends also have some kind of influence on their friends' behavior. For example, Fowler [59] and Christakis and Whitfield [60] demonstrated different case studies including the influence of happiness, and stated that happiness can be distributed among people depending upon the three degrees of separation in a social network. The different models, named microscopic and macroscopic models, can be studied for considering the interconnection process in influence analysis. The human interactions and the structure of the influence process are studied using microscopic models and the probability of transmission to identify the effects on all users is considered in the macroscopic model. Different methods for analyzing the influence methods such as influence maximization, influence minimization, flow of influence, and individual influence can be studied. Different metrics can be evaluated for justifying and claiming the results. This process will help in understanding peoples' social behaviors, provide theoretical support for making public decisions and influencing public opinion, and promote exchanges and dissemination of various activities.

1.3.5 Sentiment analysis

Sentiment analysis, also known as opinion mining, is a machine learning and NLP technique [61]. It can, as the name implies, examine the emotional tone conveyed by the author in any piece of text. Businesses use sentiment analysis tools to assess the sentiment value of their brands, goods, or services. Customer feedback analysis is one of the most widespread applications of sentiment analysis. Customers' emotions/sentiments can be analyzed and evaluated using sentiment analysis software. Sentiment analysis is used by data analysts in large companies to measure public opinion, track brand and product images, evaluate consumer experiences, and perform market research. There are many advantages of sentiment analysis such as recognizing your consumer base, developing and accessing a marketing campaign, improving customer service, crisis management, and increasing revenue from sales.

Sentiment analysis (or opinion mining) is a mechanized method used by businesses to detect positive sentiments or negative sentiments in a text to understand the customers better and keep an eye on its reputation. Sentiment analysis helps us to identify the motive and emotions behind a purchase, gain many more insights, and eventually predict the future response.

Sentiment analysis is a research area of text mining and machine learning. Often, we are interested to analyze the influence of some text [62]. In that case, we need an approach to describe what exactly is the intention of that text. So, we can say that "I love that music" is a positive sentiment. So in an algorithmic way, we can say that these sentiments are based on a set of polarities, i.e., positive, negative, or even neutral. As such, one can quantify the positivity or negativity of the text.

To understand how opinion mining can help, an example is given. In a television manufacturing company, suppose a business problem is discussed to analyze the sentiment from reviews. They wanted to understand the contentment of users in product pricing and features. A very thorough analysis of the reviews was conducted and the features most liked, features most disliked, views on pricing, and segments of users with which priorities (for example, certain users were more concerned about the pricing than the quality, some just need bare minimal features in TV) were identified. After this study, the manufacturer was able to understand how they need to pitch what type of television to which type of users. Also, the most commonly features liked were upgraded permanently and the most commonly disliked features were removed.

There are different types of sentimental analysis.

- **Aspect-based sentiment analysis**: A text analysis technique that divides the text data and defines its sentiment based on its aspects. It analyzes consumer feedback data by correlating emotions to different aspects of a product or service.

- **Fine-grained sentiment analysis**: This sentiment analysis model contributes to the advancement of polarity accuracy. Sentiment analysis can be done in the different categories discussed in the above section based on polarity.

- **Emotion detection**: Emotion analysis is the method of defining and evaluating the emotions conveyed in textual data. Emotion detection and classification are straightforward tasks that can be completed based on the emotions conveyed in the text, such as fear, rage, happiness, sorrow, affection, motivation, or neutral.

- **Intent analysis**: The method of analyzing text data to determine the author's intent is known as intent detection. Many human behaviors and actions are motivated by motives, and knowing intentions will help you perceive these behaviors.

Some of the major hurdles for sentiment analysis are the following:

- sentences taken out of context,
- irony and sarcasm in sentences,
- sentences that include a negation, such as "this will be his first and last masterpiece,"
- sentences of ambiguity.

1.4 Clustering and classification

Several companies make suitable devices that can be effectively used to collect valuable data. Nowadays, a large collection of data needs to be generated and collected to serve different purposes. Classification is the procedure to find a model that outlines and differentiates classes and ideas. Classification extracts models illustrating main data classes. Researchers have introduced several classification techniques in pattern recognition, machine learning, and statistics. Classification has a variety of application areas, which may include manufacturing, fraud detection, medical diagnosis, target marketing, and prediction. The learning step is known as the training phase. A classification algorithm produces the classifier using tuples from the given database. In the classification step, the class label of given data is predicted using the model. Numerous modern approaches have been introduced for classification that can be easily and effectively applied to discover patterns in datasets. A labeled training points set from each category is necessary in classification. Here, the grouping structure can be learned in a supervised manner [63]. Classification is fundamentally applied as a supervised learning mechanism, whereas clustering is used for unsupervised learning, in general. The objectives of classification and clustering can be defined as descriptive and predictive, respectively [64].

Clustering can be defined as the process to organize objects into a number of groups on the basis of similarity by some means. A cluster is an assemblage of similar objects, which are dissimilar to other objects in any other clusters. The idea of clustering is to find a new set of categories, based on which the new groups are formed. The assessment in clustering is performed intrinsically, whereas it is extrinsically carried out in the case of classification. Data clustering is a popular technique to identify groups of clusters within multi-dimensional data on the basis of some similar attribute [65]. Euclidean distance is a popular measure that can be used in data clustering. It can be widely used in modern technology like machine learning, AI, and pattern recognition [66]. Usually, a cluster is recognized by a cluster center, called centroid. There are numerous classification methods available in the literature. One popular method of this category is support vector machine. Nowadays, clustering is used in a variety of fields like information retrieval, medicine, and taking out relevant information from spatial cells, to name a few [67]. The popularity of classification algorithms has increased since the last few years.

Clustering and classification are two basic parts of data mining. In data mining, it may be a very typical task to classify data by applying several classification methods. There exist a variety of classification methods in data mining like functions, Bayes, trees, rules, etc. The foremost objective of classification is to precisely compute the value of each existing class variable [68]. This classification method can be split up into two fundamental steps. Firstly, the classification model is built from the training dataset; in other words, sample data are selected at random from the dataset (learning step). Thereafter, the model's accuracy is verified after assigning the data values to the model (classification step) [69].

Unlike classification, clustering is an unsupervised method. The classes are defined beforehand in classification, whereas based on the class variables, classes are divided in clustering. There exist several clustering algorithms. Some popular examples of this category are hierarchical cluster, K-means, OPTICS, DBSCAN, Cobwebm, and EM. Out of them, the K-means algorithm is easy to use and outperforms others [70].

1.4.1 Clustering algorithms

Clustering algorithms can be successfully and effectively used to process a wide variety of data. The objective of clustering is to bring down the volume of data by segregating similar data together. One of the prime motivations of designing a variety of clustering algorithms is that efficient automated tools can be designed that can help in establishing taxonomies or categories [11]. The methods minimize the human interference in the process.

Clustering is broadly grouped into two categories, viz. hard clustering and soft clustering. The former keeps the data point only in one cluster. That means each data point is either completely placed into a cluster or not placed. In soft clustering, instead of putting each data point into a separate cluster, a probability or likelihood of that data point in those clusters is assigned. Clustering algorithms are broadly used in several applications, like grayscale and color image segmentation, machine learning, data mining, color image and vector quantization, and compression, to name a few [71–73].

Clustering algorithms are generally classified as follows.

1. Exclusive clustering: As the name suggests, this type of clustering algorithm congregates data in an exclusive manner. Here, a certain datum is owned by a single specific cluster. This means that if a particular data item is part of a cluster, it cannot be added to any another clusters. One popular example of exclusive clustering is K-means clustering algorithms.

2. Overlapping clustering: This type of clustering algorithm employs fuzzy sets to cluster data. Hence, the degree of membership is introduced here, based on whose value each data point may be added in multiple clusters simultaneously. In this type of clustering algorithm, data will be closely associated with an apposite membership value. A popular example of overlapping clustering algorithm is fuzzy K-means.

3. Hierarchical clustering: This clustering method is an unsupervised machine learning clustering in nature. This method uses a pre-defined top-down hierarchy of clusters. The data objects are then decomposed on the basis of this hierarchy to obtain the clusters. One approach among two different approaches (top-down or bottom-up) is followed to create clusters. The different versions are the divisive approach and the agglomerative approach. In divisive clustering, one cluster that contains all data items is chosen to start. Initially, clusters are broken down into a number of smaller clusters in succession based on some dissimilar features. It is basically a top-down approach. Agglomerative clustering is a bottom-up approach. This type of clustering is based on association between two nearby clusters. The initial criteria are to be satisfied for every datum to be a cluster. This task needs to be continued for a number of iterations to reach the final desired clusters.

4. Probabilistic clustering: In this clustering algorithm, an entirely probabilistic approach is taken. The Gaussian mixture model is an example of this type of algorithm.

1.4.2 Multi-view clustering

In this modern technological era (the Big Data era), data can be generated and gathered from various sources; at the same time, the data can be interpreted from different viewpoints. Modern datasets provide complementary and consistent information. For instance, when multi-lingual data are considered, each language has a separate view; in case of biomedical data, a clinical sample comprises patient information such as clinical traits and gene expression intensity. These types of data are known to be multi-view data. The power of knowledge is a key aspect in Big Data mining. This is also very important for analysis purposes. By exploiting the features of distinct views, it can be easily seen that multi-view learning generally procures better efficiency, more useful than single-view learning. There exist several information acquisition methods. As technology advances, multi-view data turned out to be ubiquitous. Multi-view learning has become the most useful approach in a variety of fields, such as data mining and machine learning. Both semi-supervised and supervised versions of multi-view learning have gained considerable attention.

In recent years, multi-view clustering (MvC), which exploits consensus and supportive information across multiple views, has received increasing attention. MvC is a natural way of forming clusters using multi-view data and has attracted significant attention among many researchers [74].

There exists numerous MvC methods, proposed by different researchers [74]. Amongst these methods, subspace clustering can perform better compared to others. This method has been widely studied in the literature. Details about this method can be found in the article by Mitra *et al.* [75]. Cao *et al.* [76] introduced diversity-induced multi-view subspace clustering (DiMSC), which can be used to exploit the complementary information from dissimilar views. The proposed method uses the Hilbert–Schmidt independence criterion (HSIC) to enforce diversity. Xie *et al.* [77] introduced a multi-view subspace clustering method based on a tensor-singular value decomposition (t-SVD) approach. This method applies tensor multi-rank minimization for capturing the interrelated information between the views. The proposed optimization method can be efficiently applied to deal with the MvC problems. Zhang *et al.* [78] developed two variants of the latent multi-view subspace clustering (LMSC) algorithm, viz. generalized LMSC (gLMSC) and linear LMSC (lLMSC). The former applies neural networks to get the generalized interrelation between the views, whereas the latter makes a linear correlation between every view and its latent representation.

1.4.3 Applications to data mining and social networking

A social network can be defined as a communal framework of people, who are directly or indirectly related to one another on the basis of a common connection of friendship, trust, etc. In these days, social networking is a widely spread concept that is generally analyzed for the purpose of understanding their behavior and structure. It has gained eminence owing to its usage in various applications in almost all fields. In recent times, a speedy increase in interest in social network analysis has been observed among data mining researchers. Nowadays, data mining-based approaches have been proved to be very useful to analyze social network data, particularly for large datasets.

Data mining can be popularly referred to "finding knowledge within databases." In line with the present scenario, this is more appropriate for social media data mining, since much larger databases are used in social media. Social media data mining is applied to discover current trends and hidden patterns from its popular platforms like Facebook, LinkedIn, Twitter, and many others. To perform this task, the mathematics, statistics, and machine learning methods are used. Social data need to be gathered first and then mined. The outcomes are sent to the relevant analytics software for explaining and visualizing the insights such that they can be interpreted further. There exist various data visualization tools. It is shown that social media analytics generally come up with their own visualization choices. Different data mining methods may be applied in this regard. Some methods may deploy machine learning for this purpose. The following points are very important in this aspect.

1. Trend analysis: This is a very powerful metric for businesses in which social listening is utilized. Sometimes, the relevant topics, keywords, etc., on social media that are currently trending must be discovered. After that, a few mining techniques are applied to uncover the reason for such trending.

2. Event detection: This may be also called social heat mapping. It is also a very important and powerful metric that is usually used by different agencies, for which social media monitoring is important.

3. Social spam detection: Social media platforms can benefit by utilizing data mining. That can be done applying a social spam detection mechanism. For example, in Twitter and Instagram, two things, called spammers and bots, are very eminent in this regard. Bots can find loopholes on some platforms, where infuriating, monotonous, and useless content is often posed by the users. It can take some time to detect bots and squeeze them. Spam detection can be better at these platforms with the use of social media data mining.

References

[1] M. Injadat, F. Salo, A. Nassif, Data mining techniques in social media: a survey, Neurocomputing 214 (2016) 654–670.
[2] A.M. Kaplan, M. Haenlein, Users of the world, unite! The challenges and opportunities of social media, Business Horizons 53 (2010) 59–68.
[3] M. Adedoyin-Olowe, M.M. Gaber, F.T. Stahl, A survey of data mining techniques for social media analysis, CoRR, arXiv:1312.4617 [abs], 2013.
[4] I.-H. Ting, H.-J. Wu, Web Mining Techniques for On-Line Social Networks Analysis: An Overview, Springer Berlin Heidelberg, Berlin, Heidelberg, 2009, pp. 169–179.
[5] G. Barbier, H. Liu, Data Mining in Social Media, Springer US, Boston, MA, 2011, pp. 327–352.

[6] Q. Hou, M. Han, Z. Cai, Survey on data analysis in social media: a practical application aspect, Big Data Mining and Analytics 3 (2020) 259–279.

[7] M.K. Hayat, A. Daud, A.A. Alshdadi, A. Banjar, R.A. Abbasi, Y. Bao, H. Dawood, Towards deep learning prospects: insights for social media analytics, IEEE Access 7 (2019) 36958–36979.

[8] B. Batrinca, P.C. Treleaven, Social media analytics: a survey of techniques, tools and platforms, AI & SOCIETY 30 (2015) 89–116.

[9] D.L. Olson, Data mining in business services, Service Business 1 (2007) 181–193.

[10] D.M. Hawkins, The problem of overfitting, Journal of Chemical Information and Computer Sciences 44 (2004) 1–12.

[11] N. Jardine, R. Sibson, Mathematical Taxonomy, Wiley, London, 1971.

[12] R. Cooley, B. Mobasher, J. Srivastava, Data preparation for mining world wide web browsing patterns, Journal of Knowledge and Information System 1 (1999) 5–32.

[13] B. Mobasher, R. Cooley, J. Srivastava, Automatic personalization based on web usage mining, Communications of the ACM 43 (2000) 142–151.

[14] J. Han, H. Cheng, D. Xin, X. Yan, Frequent pattern mining: current status and future directions, Data Mining and Knowledge Discovery (2007), https://doi.org/10.1007/s10618-006-0059-1.

[15] C.C. Aggarwal, An introduction to frequent pattern mining, https://doi.org/10.1007/978-3-319-07821-2_1, 2014.

[16] R. Agrawal, T. Imielinski, A. Swami, Mining association rules between sets of items in large databases, ACM SIGMOD Record (1993), https://doi.org/10.1145/170036.170072.

[17] D. Berndt, J. Clifford, Finding patterns in time series: a dynamic programming approach, in: Advances in Knowledge Discovery and Data Mining, AAAI/MIT Press, Menlo Park, CA, 1996, pp. 229–248.

[18] E. Keogh, K. Chakrabarti, M. Pazzani, S. Mehrotra, Dimensionality reduction for fast similarity search in large time series databases, Knowledge and Information Systems 3 (2001) 263–286.

[19] S. Milgram, The small world problem, Psychology Today 2 (1967) 60–67.

[20] S. Wasserman, K. Faust, Social Network Analysis: Methods and Applications, Cambridge University Press, UK, 1994.

[21] P. Domingos, M. Richardson, Mining the network value of customers, in: Proceedings of the 5seventh ACM SIGKDD International Conference on Knowledge Discovery and Data Mining, ACM Press, 2001, pp. 57–66.

[22] H. Kautz, B. Selman, A. Milewski, Agent amplified communication, in: Proceedings of AAAI-96, 1996, pp. 3–9.

[23] M.F. Schwartz, D.C.M. Wood, Discovering shared interests using graph analysis, Communications of the ACM 36 (1993) 78–89.

[24] D. Cai, X. He, J.-R. Wen, W.-Y. Ma, Block-level link analysis, in: Proceedings of ACM SIGIR-2004, 2004.

[25] S. Chakrabarti, Integrating the document object model with hyperlinks for enhanced topic distillation and information extraction, in: Proceedings of the 10th International World Wide Web Conference, 2001.

[26] T. Haveliwala, Topic-sensitive pagerank, in: Proceedings of the 11th International World Wide Web Conference, ACM Press, 2002.

[27] R. Srikant, R. Agrawal, Mining sequential patterns: generalizations and performance improvements, in: P. Apers, M. Bouzeghoub, G. Gardarin (Eds.), Advances in Database Technology – EDBT '96, Springer Berlin Heidelberg, Berlin, Heidelberg, 1996, pp. 1–17.

[28] R. Srikant, R. Agrawal, Mining sequential patterns: generalizations and performance improvements, in: Proceedings of the 5th International Conference on Extending Database Technology: Advances in Database Technology, EDBT '96, Springer-Verlag, Berlin, Heidelberg, 1996, pp. 3–17.

[29] K. Shaukat Dar, S. Zaheer, I. Nawaz, Association rule mining: an application perspective, International Journal of Computer Science and Innovation 1 (2015) 29–38.

[30] N.R. Mabroukeh, C.I. Ezeife, A taxonomy of sequential pattern mining algorithms, ACM Computing Surveys 43 (2010).

[31] C. Mooney, J. Roddick, Sequential pattern mining: approaches and algorithms, ACM Computing Surveys 45 (2013) 1–47, https://doi.org/10.1145/2431211.2431218.

[32] F. Almeida, Concepts and Fundaments of Data Warehousing and OLAP, 2017.

[33] A. Vaisman, E. Zimányi, Introduction, Springer Berlin Heidelberg, Berlin, Heidelberg, 2014, pp. 3–11.

[34] S. Chaudhuri, U. Dayal, An overview of data warehousing and OLAP technology, SIGMOD Record 26 (1997) 65–74.

[35] Data warehousing - overview, https://www.tutorialspoint.com/dwh/dwh_overview.htm. (Accessed 30 April 2021).

[36] M. Parameswaran, A.B. Whinston, Social computing: an overview, Communications of the Association for Information Systems 19 (2007) 37.

[37] R. Kumar, J. Novak, A. Tomkins, Structure and Evolution of Online Social Networks, Springer, 2010.

[38] M.A. Porter, Nonlinearity + Networks: A 2020 Vision, Springer, 2020, pp. 131–159.

[39] T. Falkowski, J. Bartelheimer, M. Spiliopoulou, Mining and visualizing the evolution of subgroups in social networks, in: Proceedings of the 2006 IEEE/WIC/ACM International Conference on Web Intelligence, IEE Computer Society Press, 2006, pp. 52–58.

[40] Dblp publication statistics, https://dblp.uni-trier.de/, 2018.

[41] Facebook q1 2018 results, https://investor.fb.com/investor-events/event-details/2018/Facebook-Q1-2018-Earnings/default.aspx, 2018.

[42] D. Liben-Nowell, J. Kleinberg, The link-prediction problem for social networks, Journal of the Association for Information Science and Technology 58 (2007) 1019–1031.

[43] Y. Dong, J. Zhang, J. Tang, N.V. Chawla, B. Wang, Coupledlp: link prediction in coupled networks, in: Proceedings of the 21th ACM SIGKDD International Conference on Knowledge Discovery and Data Mining, ACM, 2015, pp. 199–208.

[44] S. Bhagat, G. Cormode, S. Muthukrishnan, Node Classification in Social Networks, Springer, 2011, pp. 115–148.

[45] B. Perozzi, R. Al-Rfou, S. Skiena, Deepwalk: online learning of social representations, in: Proceedings of the 20th ACM SIGKDD International Conference on Knowledge Discovery and Data Mining, ACM, 2014, pp. 701–710.

[46] S.T. Roweis, L.K. Saul, Nonlinear dimensionality reduction by locally linear embedding, Science 290 (2000) 2323–2326.

[47] M. Belkin, P. Niyogi, Laplacian eigenmaps and spectral techniques for embedding and clustering, Advances in Neural Information Processing Systems (2002) 585–591.

[48] L.V. der Maaten, G. Hinton, Visualizing data using t-SNE, Journal of Machine Learning Research 9 (2008) 2579–2605.

[49] L. Tang, H. Liu, Relational learning via latent social dimensions, in: Proceedings of the 15th ACM SIGKDD International Conference on Knowledge Discovery and Data Mining, ACM, 2009, pp. 817–826.

[50] T. Mikolov, K. Chen, G. Corrado, J. Dean, Efficient estimation of word representations in vector space, 2013.

[51] S. Papadopoulos, Y. Kompatsiaris, A. Vakali, P. Spyridonos, Community detection in social media, Data Mining and Knowledge Discovery 24 (2012) 515–554.

[52] A. Grover, J. Leskovec, node2vec: scalable feature learning for networks, in: Proceedings of the 22nd ACM SIGKDD International Conference on Knowledge Discovery and Data Mining, ACM, 2016, pp. 855–864.

[53] J. Tang, M. Qu, M. Wang, M. Zhang, J. Yan, Q. Mei, LINE: large-scale information network embedding, in: Proceedings of the 24th International Conference on World Wide Web, 2015, pp. 1067–1077.
[54] K. He, X. Zhang, S. Ren, J. Sun, Deep residual learning for image recognition, in: Proceedings of the IEEE Conference on Computer Vision and Pattern Recognition, 2016, pp. 770–778.
[55] J. Gehring, M. Auli, D. Grangier, D. Yarats, Y.N. Dauphin, Convolutional sequence to sequence learning, in: Proceedings of the 34th International Conference on Machine Learning (ICML 2017), 2017, pp. 1243–1252.
[56] I. Goodfellow, Y. Bengio, A. Courville, Deep Learning, MIT Press, 2016.
[57] D. Wang, P. Cui, W. Zhu, Structural deep network embedding, in: Proceedings of the 22nd ACM SIGKDD International Conference on Knowledge Discovery and Data Mining, ACM, 2016, pp. 1225–1234.
[58] A. Vaswani, N. Shazeer, N. Parmar, J. Uszkoreit, L. Jones, A.N. Gomez, L. Kaiser, I. Polosukhin, Attention is all you need, in: Advances in Neural Information Processing Systems 30: Annual Conference on Neural Information Processing Systems, 2017, pp. 6000–6010.
[59] J.H. Fowler, N.A. Christakis, Dynamic spread of happiness in a large social network: longitudinal analysis over 20 years in the Framingham Heart Study, BMJ 337 (2008).
[60] J.H. Hung, T.W. Whitfield, T.H. Yang, Z. Hu, Z. Weng, C. DeLisi, Identification of functional modules that correlate with phenotypic difference: the influence of network topology, Genome Biology 11 (2020) 1–16.
[61] K. Chakraborty, S. Bhatia, S. Bhattacharyya, J. Platos, R. Bag, A.E. Hassanien, Sentiment analysis of Covid-19 tweets by deep learning classifiers—a study to show how popularity is affecting accuracy in social media, Applied Soft Computing 97 (2020).
[62] S. Bhatia, M. Sharma, K.K. Bhatia, P. Das, Opinion target extraction with sentiment analysis, International Journal of Computing 17 (2018) 136–142.
[63] M. Kumar, N. Rathee, Knowledge discovery from database using an integration of clustering and classification, International Journal of Advanced Computer Science and Applications 2 (2011).
[64] M. Veyssieres, R. Plant, Identification of Vegetation State and Transition Domains in California's Hardwood Rangelands, University of California, 1998.
[65] A. Jain, M. Murty, P. Flynn, Data clustering: a review, ACM Computing Surveys 31 (1999) 264–323.
[66] G. Hamerly, C. Elkan, Alternatives to the k-means algorithm that find better clusterings, in: Proceedings of the ACM Conference on Information and Knowledge Management, CIKM-2002, 2002, pp. 600–607.
[67] J.A. Hartigan, M.A. Wong, A k-means clustering algorithm, Applied Statistics 28 (1979) 100–108.
[68] D. Grossman, P. Domingos, Learning Bayesian network classifiers by maximizing conditional likelihood, in: 21st International Conference on Machine Learning, Banff, Canada, 2004.
[69] J.-J. Aucouturier, F. Pachet, Improving timbre similarity: how high's the sky?, Journal of Negative Research Results in Speech and Audio Sciences (2004).
[70] N. Sharma, A. Bajpai, R. Litoriya, Comparison the various clustering algorithms of weka tools, International Journal of Emerging Technology and Advanced Engineering 2 (2012) 792–808.
[71] D. Goldberg, Genetic Algorithms in Search, Optimization and Machine Learning, Addison-Wesley, 1998.
[72] G. Coleman, H. Andrews, Image segmentation by clustering, Proceedings of the IEEE 67 (1979) 773–785.
[73] P. Frnti, J. Kivijrvi, O. Nevalainen, Tabu search algorithm for codebook generation in vector quantization, Pattern Recognition 31 (1998) 1139–1148.

[74] L. Fu, P. Lin, A. Vasilakos, S. Wang, An overview of recent multi-view clustering, Neurocomputing 402 (2020) 148–161.

[75] S. Mitra, S. Saha, M. Hasanuzzaman, Multi-view clustering for multi-omics data using unified embedding, Scientific Reports 10 (2020).

[76] X. Cao, C. Zhang, H. Fu, S. Liu, H. Zhang, Diversity-induced multi-view subspace clustering, in: 2015 IEEE Conference on in Computer Vision and Pattern Recognition (CVPR), 2015, pp. 586–594.

[77] Y. Xie, D. Tao, W. Zhang, L. Zhang, Y. Liu, Y. Qu, Ton unifying multi-view self-representations for clustering by tensor multi-rank minimization, International Journal of Computer Vision 126 (2018) 1157–1179.

[78] C. Zhang, H. Fu, Q. Hu, X. Cao, Y. Xie, D. Tao, D. Xu, Generalized latent multi-view subspace clustering, IEEE Transactions on Pattern Analysis and Machine Intelligence 42 (2020) 86–99.

CHAPTER 2

Performance tuning of Android applications using clustering and optimization heuristics

Rajendrani Mukherjee[a], Soumen Kumar Pati[b], and Ayan Banerjee[c]
[a]Department of Computer Science and Engineering, University of Engineering and Management, Kolkata, India
[b]Department of Bioinformatics, Maulana Abul Kalam Azad University, Kalyani, India
[c]Department of Computer Science and Engineering, Jalpaiguri Government Engineering College, Jalpiguri, India

2.1 Introduction

Building applications for Android platforms has gained momentum since the last decade and it has undergone several transformations [30,31]. Android software development focuses on building scalable applications which not only make social and business communication easier but also help in faster decision making [28,29]. However, performance analysis of Android applications is a challenging task and suffers many hindrances like resource constraints (lack of memory space, time scarcity), malware interferences [35], etc.

In this chapter, a novel methodology is proposed for tuning the performance of Android applications. Two open source applications, OmniNotes (a note taking application) and Ringdroid (free alarm, notifications, etc.), were investigated. Several functional requirements (technical aspects of the application) and non-functional requirements (speed, availability of the application) were noted initially. The unsupervised learning algorithm k-means [1–3] was applied on these sets of requirements and they were partitioned into clusters [12]. It is believed that while monitoring the performance of an Android application, execution of all scheduled requirements is non-beneficial in terms of time and money and hence optimizing the number of requirements in a cluster will reduce the time overhead. With the advent of agile software development, where coding-testing-delivery windows are critically time-bound and repeated in several sprints/episodes, it has become necessary to segregate the optimal requirements the Android application should execute in a stipulated time [32–34]. For example, as

Advanced Data Mining Tools and Methods for Social Computing
https://doi.org/10.1016/B978-0-32-385708-6.00009-6

100 requirements were run for the OmniNotes application, it took an average of 30 seconds or 1 minute for each requirement or scenario to run. Few use cases took 2 minutes while very few took 3 to 4 minutes. In total, it took 150 minutes to complete the run of all the 100 requirements in one shot. However, it is infeasible to devote 2 hours and 30 minutes for evaluating the performance of an Android application. So it is necessary to modularize these requirements into clusters and optimize their numbers. The requirement optimization problem was replicated with regard to the knapsack [22,26] problem. The genetic algorithm (GA) [19,25,27] was applied to optimize the number of requirements. Object-oriented metrics and the depth of inheritance tree (DIT) [20] were utilized to build the fitness function while executing the GA. Towards an effort to determine which optimization heuristics yield better results, ant colony optimization (ACO) [17] was also evaluated with the same fitness function.

The chapter is organized as follows. While the initial sections discuss some prominent related work regarding performance analysis of Android applications, describe the methodologies of the conducted research, and depict the implementation details using knapsack solvers and ACO, the remaining sections tabulate the results and scrutinize the findings. The chapter is concluded in the last section with a discussion of the future scope.

This chapter presents a unique study which presents the clustering technique along with the abovementioned optimization heuristics for performance tweaking of Android applications.

2.2 Related work

Several works have been conducted for analyzing the performance of Android applications. While some of them focused on highlighting important parameters (execution time, memory usage, response time, CPU usage, user satisfaction), other studies [32] [35] explored the security issues of the Android operating system (OS).

Azimzadeh *et al.* investigated the underlying Dalvik virtual machine (VM) of Android and concluded that 82% of total execution time is utilized for mainly five families (method invocation, read/write field, register movements) of instructions [29]. In 2012, Corral *et al.* conducted a study to understand the performance of mobile web applications and designed a multi-platform tool which is based on the strategy of "develop once and deploy everywhere" [30]. Wei *et al.* built ProfileDroid [31], which is useful for profiling Android applications. They evaluated multiple paid and free Android applications and profiled the applications in terms of resource usage, network data, cloud /third party server communication, etc.

A mobile sandbox [32] was developed by Spreitzenbarth *et al.* which will automate malware call detection to spot cybercriminals. With the increasing number of security threats, it is very important to protect mobile applications from malicious calls. Booz *et al.* devised deep learning methodologies for malware detection [35] of Android applications. They worked on to create an optimal environment setting for smooth running of Android applications.

In 2014, Lee *et al.* built a user interaction-based Android profiling system [33] which uses customer usage data. It is observed that the location of mobile users, network signal strength, and network type hugely affect the behavior of Android applications. This approach equips the researchers with an opportunity for real-time analysis of Android applications. Ongkosit *et al.* designed a static analysis tool to identify the potential defects of an Android application which are difficult to determine by common testing methods. The defects can lead to poor customer reviews and thus the app generates less revenue. The authors concluded that even though there are many reasons for unresponsiveness of an application like deadlock, improper termination, etc., the most common reason is lengthy operations [35].

Lee *et al.* researched efficient programming techniques (code refactoring, etc.) for better storage utilization of Android applications [34]. They compared Java and native C coding techniques to determine which one works best for Android programming. Fernandes *et al.* focused on the user experience of mobile applications [36]. The study focused on many nonfunctional requirements. They experimented on efficient usage of physical resources like battery and CPU time for two case study applications.

All these researches motivated us to explore the performance analysis of Android applications. As no studies leveraged optimization heuristics for managing Android application performance, we focused on the effects of several optimization heuristics on performance tuning of Android applications.

2.3 Research methodology

In the first step, functional and non-functional requirements were tabulated for both chosen applications. OmniNotes is freeware which helps to edit, delete, merge, and share notes, while Ringdroid can be used to create audio files for ringtones, alarms, notifications, etc. Both of these applications are open source and very popular among mobile users. At least 75 requirements were evaluated for each application.

After this, k-means clustering [4] [5] [6] was applied on these requirements where n requirements were partitioned into k clusters. Lines of code (LOC) and number of functions executed by a requirement were chosen as the similarity criteria/commonality measure while forming the clusters. As LOC and number of functions executed are considered as prominent software metrics when developing a software product, they were given due importance while choosing the clustering criteria [9] [10]. The elbow point method [7] [8] [11] was utilized to determine the optimal value of the number of clusters.

After setting up this background, several optimization heuristics were explored to optimize the number of requirements in a cluster. The optimization techniques are useful in finding the optimum solution of continuous and differentiable functions. While regulating the performance of an Android application, execution of all requirements is infeasible in time-constrained environments and optimizing the number of requirements will enhance the throughput of Android applications. For example, as 75 requirements were run for the Ringdroid application, it took an average of 45 seconds for each scenario to run. Few use cases took 1 or 2 minutes while very few took 3 to 5 minutes. In totality, it took 100 minutes to run all the 75 requirements. In modern agile software development methodologies, where coding-database handling-testing windows are repeated for every delivery window, it is impossible to contribute 1 hour and 40 minutes for judging the performance of an Android application. So the concept of clustering and optimization is lucrative from this point of view.

In this study, each cluster was treated as a knapsack [23] and each requirement was considered as a knapsack item. The requirement optimization problem was mapped with the knapsack problem. GA [15] [24] was utilized to reduce the number of requirements in a knapsack. We developed a fitness function while implementing the GA. The object-oriented software metric DIT [21] was utilized to build the fitness function. DIT refers to the maximum length from the class node to the root node in terms of number of ancestor classes. The DIT traversed per unit of execution time by a requirement is chosen as the fitness function for this research. As inheritance promotes reusability, it is a very useful object-oriented metric. Traversing more children in a stipulated time will ensure efficient execution of requirements of the Android applications in a time-constrained situation.

In order to do ensure the verifiability of the proposed approach and promote fair comparison, our investigation also applied ACO [13] [14] [16] [18] on the requirement clusters. A requirement is equivalent to a node, and the weight of each connector between two nodes is quantified by the deposited pheromone. The pheromone weight of an edge is equal to the DIT covered per unit of execution time by a requirement (same fitness function as knapsack solvers). The chapter shows the execution path after each iteration by several connected graphs.

The diagram in Fig. 2.1 summarizes the steps.

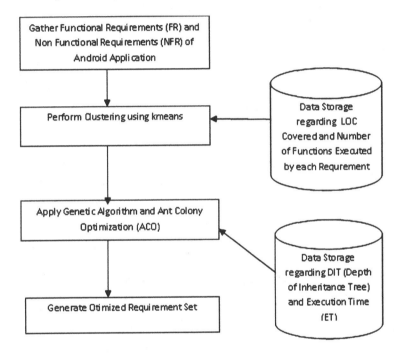

Figure 2.1 Basic steps of experimentation.

2.4 Subject applications

We used Android Studio 4.1 for running the chosen Android applications (Ringdroid and OmniNotes). Table 2.1 summarizes the applications with their details.

The Ringdroid application (version 2.7.4) was downloaded from Github. It is written in Java. It is a free utility which helps in creating

Table 2.1 Details of subject applications.

Subject freeware	Latest version	Release year	Size	Some prominent features
Ringdroid	2.7.4	2016	380 kB	Setting customized ringtones, setting alarms and notifications, recording audio files, setting up own start and end points
OmniNotes	6.0.5	2019	6.4 MB	Preparing notes, deleting them, merging notes, sharing them, putting an image or a to-do list in the note, archiving a note

customized ringtones, setting alarms or notifications. Ringdroid supports MP3, WAV, etc., file formats. The primary reason of choosing this application was its popularity, customer reviews, and useful features for day-to-day life.

The other subject of experimentation is OmniNotes, which is also freeware. Its latest version (6.0.5) was also downloaded from Github. The main reason for choosing OmniNotes was its extremely wide range of features, excellent customer ratings, and ease of use. OmniNotes helps in taking notes, merging or sharing them, inserting to-do lists, inserting image/audio in the note, etc.

2.5 Implementation phase 1 – clustering and knapsack solvers

2.5.1 Run requirement and gather clustering information

The latest versions of the chosen applications were downloaded from Github. Initially, functional and non-functional requirements were gathered for both applications. Then, 75 requirements were collected for Ringdroid while 100 requirements were summarized for OmniNotes. The functional requirements involved the functionalities of the application which are required by the customer (mainly technical aspects) while the non-functional requirements focused on availability, speed, etc.

As each requirement or use case was run in Android Studio 4.1, LOC covered by each requirement and the number of functions executed by each requirement were noted down. The information regarding LOC and number of executed functions will help in forming the clustering criteria while segregating the requirements into clusters. The codes of both Ringdroid and OmniNotes were written in Java and while counting the LOC, the comment lines and header lines were ignored. LOC is a useful metric to hint the project size. On the other hand, the number of executed functions is basically an indicator of number of supported features. Even though different requirements may take different efforts to develop, LOC and number of executed functions will give an approximate idea of that effort. Because of the importance of these two software metrics they were considered as commonality measure while clustering.

Table 2.2 lists the first 10 requirements that were run for the Ringdroid application along with information on clustering parameters. The requirements were tagged with identifiers like R1, R2, R3, etc.

Table 2.3 enumerates the first 10 requirements that were run for the OmniNotes application along with clustering parameters. The requirements were tagged with identifiers like O1, O2, O3, etc.

2.5.2 Formation of clusters

After collecting the requirements and the corresponding clustering parameter information as described in the previous section, the k-means clustering technique was applied on these requirements. So, n requirements were taken as input to the k-means clustering algorithm and they were divided into k clusters. k–Means is the simplest unsupervised learning algorithm. Requirements in the same cluster are as much alike as possible, whereas requirements in different clusters are as different as possible. LOC and the number of functions executed by a requirement were chosen as clustering attributes and the collected information in the previous step was utilized. The elbow point method was used to determine the optimal number of clusters (three in this case). According to this method, the value of k should be such that even if the k value is increased, the distortion/sum of squared errors (SSE) will stay constant (Fig. 2.2). The SSE is the sum of squared distances between each observation (requirement) and the group's mean. It resembles the dissimilarity within a cluster.

As 75 requirements were clustered into three clusters for Ringdroid, Cluster 1 contained 27 requirements, Cluster 2 contained 18 requirements, and Cluster 3 contained 30 requirements. Fig. 2.3 depicts the clustered requirements for Ringdroid, where the x-axis indicates the LOC attribute (Attribute 1) and the y-axis indicates the number of executed functions (Attribute 2). On the other hand, as 100 requirements were clustered into three clusters for the OmniNotes application, Cluster 1 contained

Table 2.2 Requirements (first 10) of the Ringdroid application with clustering attributes.

Requirement ID	Requirement description	Lines of code (LOC) covered	Number of functions executed
R1	Assign a ringtone to a desired contact from the contact list	55	3
R2	Creating a ringtone from an MP3 audio file	120	7
R3	Creating a ringtone from a WAV audio file	120	7
R4	Creating alarms from an audio file	77	5
R5	Creating alarms with personalized tones	200	12
R6	Setting songs for various notifications (for example, Facebook notifications, WhatsApp notifications, etc.)	135	9
R7	Record a live audio and set it as ringtone	180	10
R8	Change the start point and end point of a selected ringtone	95	8
R9	Save a ringtone with own choice of name	60	4
R10	Zoom in and zoom out the waveform when a ringtone is playing	85	5

28 requirements, Cluster 2 contained 35 requirements, and Cluster 3 contained 37 requirements. Fig. 2.4 portrays the clustered requirements for OmniNotes.

2.5.3 Knapsack solver replication

After the formation of clusters, the requirement optimization problem was mapped with the 0/1 knapsack problem.

While running 100 requirements for the OmniNotes application, approximately 30 seconds or 1 minute was taken for each scenario to run.

Table 2.3 Requirements (first seven) of the OmniNotes application with clustering attributes.

Requirement ID	Requirement description	Lines of code (LOC) covered	Number of functions executed
O1	Create and share a note	65	5
O2	Modify a note	45	3
O3	Merge several notes	55	2
O4	Archive a note and delete it	70	7
O5	Insert a to-do list in the note	102	5
O6	Insert photos and videos in the note	155	10
O7	Insert audio recordings and geographic locations in the note	200	12

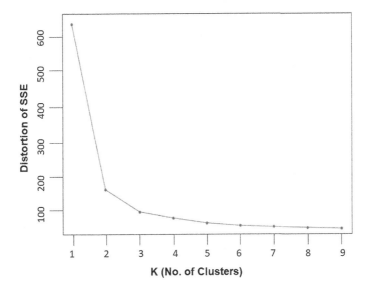

Figure 2.2 Elbow point method for determination of the number of clusters (k).

Only few use cases took 2 minutes while very few took 3 to 5 minutes. In whole, it took 150 minutes to run all the 100 requirements. On the other hand, while running 75 requirements for the Ringdroid application, approximately 45 seconds were required for each use case to run on average. In total, it took 100 minutes to run all 75 requirements. However, it is not possible to keep aside 100 or 150 minutes for running the requirements at

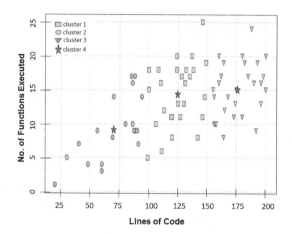

Figure 2.3 Clustered requirements for the Ringdroid application.

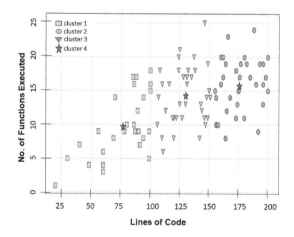

Figure 2.4 Clustered requirements for the OmniNotes application.

one shot to judge the performance potential of Android applications. From this point of view, the necessity to divide the requirements into clusters came into effect.

However, clustering alone is not sufficient for effective management of running the requirements. For example, as Cluster 3 of the OmniNotes application contained 37 requirements (Fig. 2.4), it took 70 minutes for all of them to complete. With the advent of an agile software development paradigm, where several sprints/delivery windows are assigned to the coding-database development-testing phase in a time-constrained fashion, it is impossible to dedicate 1 hour and 10 minutes to the determination of the performance of an Android application. Moreover, big applications may contain much more requirements. So the concept of optimization is beneficial from this point of view.

In this study, the requirement optimization problem was mapped to the 0/1 Knapsack problem. In this research, each cluster was treated as a sack and each requirement was considered as a knapsack item. The DIT covered by the requirement is considered as its value, the time of execution of each requirement is its weight, and the maximum amount of time allowed by the manager for performance evaluation is considered as the maximum capacity of the knapsack. DIT refers to the maximum length from a class to a root class in the inheritance hierarchy. It is measured by the number of superclasses affecting a class. As inheritance ensures reusability, it is an important object-oriented metric. Traversing more children in a fixed time will ensure competent execution of requirements of the Android applications under time-constrained circumstances. Tables 2.4 and 2.5 represent the collected data for DIT and the execution time for some requirements for both applications.

The following script was run to calculate the DIT, which basically counted the number of "extends" from a node. The following code snippet was utilized to measure the execution time.

```
long startTime = System.nanoTime()
/* Code for requirement execution */
long endTime = System.nanoTime()
long elapsedTime = endTime − startTime
```

2.5.4 Optimization using the genetic algorithm

After mapping the requirement optimization problem, GA was utilized. GA selects the fittest chromosome based on a fitness function (Fig. 2.5).

In this research, the chromosome is built of requirements. For example, Cluster 3 of the OmniNotes application contained 37 requirements and it took 70 minutes to run all of them. With the application of GA, Cluster 3 was reduced to a knapsack containing 12 requirements. It took just 15 minutes to run these 12 requirements. It is very easy and practical to run this optimized requirement sequence in between coding-database development-testing time windows in a time-constrained agile software development environment. Thus GA played a significant role in performance tuning of the OmniNotes application.

Table 2.4 DIT and execution time information for requirements (first 10) of the Ringdroid application.

Requirement ID	Requirement description	Depth of inheritance tree (DIT) covered	Execution time (in seconds)
R1	Assigning a ringtone to a desired contact from the contact list	3	55
R2	Creating a ringtone from an MP3 audio file	8	70
R3	Creating a ringtone from a WAV audio file	8	70
R4	Creating alarms from an audio file	5	65
R5	Creating alarms with personalized tones	12	90
R6	Setting songs for various notifications (for example, Facebook notifications, WhatsApp notifications, etc.)	10	95
R7	Recording a live audio and setting it as ringtone	15	120
R8	Changing the start point and end point of a selected ringtone	6	100
R9	Saving a ringtone with own choice of name	5	45
R10	Zooming in and zooming out the waveform when a ringtone is playing	7	45

2.5.4.1 GA implementation with example

In the first step, the chromosome was built using the requirements. For example, as Cluster 3 of OmniNotes contained 37 requirements, this 37-requirement sequence formed a chromosome. An initial population size of 300 (random population) was generated. Then each chromosome was evaluated using a fitness function. In this research, a novel fitness objective

Table 2.5 DIT and execution time information for requirements (first 10) of the OmniNotes application.

Requirement ID	Requirement description	Depth of inheritance tree (DIT) covered	Execution time (in seconds)
O1	Creating and sharing a note	4	30
O2	Modifying a note	5	45
O3	Merging several notes	4	40
O4	Archiving a note and deleting it	7	75
O5	Inserting a to-do list in the note	8	80
O6	Inserting photos and videos in the note	10	100
O7	Inserting audio recordings and geographic locations in the note	11	110
O8	Requesting confirmation when undoing changes in notes	8	90
O9	Placing the shortcuts of created notes on the homescreen	5	50
O10	Taking back up notes using the export option	5	40

was formulated which utilized the DIT traversed per unit of time. The objective function is presented by

$$f(x) = \sum_{i=1}^{n} \frac{DIT_i}{ET_i}, \tag{2.1}$$

where DIT_i is the number of superclasses affecting a class while running a requirement, ET_i is the time of execution of each requirement, and n is the requirement number. Traversing more children in a fixed time will promote the throughput of Android applications in time-restrained situations.

After this, the tournament selector was applied on the generated random initial population and chromosomes were selected based on the above fitness function. Then, the PMX technique was used for crossover. The crossover probability (p_c) was 0.25. The value of p_c was kept like this to

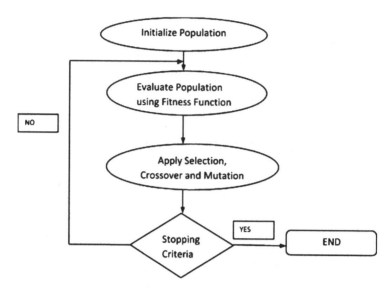

Figure 2.5 Overview of the genetic algorithm.

avoid the situation of premature convergence. Next, a swap mutator was applied to find the optimum requirement set (best phenotype) that will fit the knapsack and will get executed within $t_{m}ax$. Here, $t_{m}ax$ is the maximum amount of time allowed by the manager for performance checking (the knapsack's maximum capacity). In this case, it was chosen as 15 minutes. This time window was chosen empirically as the literature survey indicated that normally 15 minutes to 20 minutes [35,36] is allotted in between coding-database development-testing windows for Android user experience/performance evaluation. The chosen mutation probability p_{m} was 0.15. A low mutation probability value was chosen to avoid delayed convergence. In this experiment, a fixed generation number (50) was used as termination criterion.

Cluster 3 (Fig. 2.4) of the OmniNotes application contained requirements O2, O8, O9, O10, O16, O19, O21, O22, O27, O30, O31, O33, O36, O41, O42, O44, O46, O47, O55, O57, O58, O61, O68, O69, O71, O77, O78, O80, O81, O85, O87, O88, O90, O94, O95, O97, and O98. The requirements were tagged with identifiers like O1, O2, O3, etc., and the description, showing statistical information of some of the requirements, is presented in Table 2.3 and Table 2.5. However, it is not possible to put all these requirements in the knapsack. After running selection-crossover-mutation, the number of requirements for Cluster 3 of

OmniNotes was reduced to 12 from 37. As GA was applied with the above parameters, the resultant set of 12 requirements for Cluster 3 of OmniNotes contained O2, O10, O21, O22, O31, O47, O55, O61, O77, O81, O88, and O90. So basically the number of requirements that fit the knapsack to be executed within 15 minutes (tmax) was 12. Thus, instead of running the entire 37 requirements for 70 minutes, execution of only 12 requirements in 15 minutes will achieve the purpose because these 12 requirements formed the best phenotype/maximum fitness tuple/optimized solution obtained from GA.

Algorithm 1 sums up the followed steps.

Algorithm 1: GA to optimize requirements.

Input: Requirement set R, number of requirements (n),
number of superclasses affecting a class (DIT) while running a requirement, execution time (ET) of each requirement, crossover probability, mutation probability, j (number of iterations), $t_{m}ax$ as maximum capacity of knapsack

Output: Best phenotype

1: begin

2: Generate initial population (IPop)

3: for each iterations in j do

4: Derive fitness value as FValue where $FValue = \sum_{i=1}^{n} \frac{DIT_i}{ET_i}$

5: Apply ParentSelection (IPop, FValue) to produce SelectedParent

6: Apply Crossover (SelectedParent, p_c) to generate Offspring

7: Apply Mutation(Offspring, p_m) to generate maximum fitness tuple
    as $R_{optimized}$

8: end for

9: return $R_{optimized}$

10: end

2.6 Implementation phase 2 – Ant colony optimization

In this phase of research, ACO was used to optimize requirements. Usage of ACO will also help to investigate which optimization heuristics are better among knapsack solvers and ACO for performance tuning of Android applications.

As each ant moves, pheromone is deposited. The pheromone acts as a trail and makes it easy for other ants to find the target. As time passes by, the pheromone evaporates. The graph which is formed by the paths followed by ants is denoted $G(V, E)$, where V is set of vertices and E is set of edges.

When using ACO for requirement optimization,

- a requirement is equivalent to a node;
- the edge weight is the amount of deposited pheromone;
- pheromone is deposited at a rate of 100%;
- the evaporation rate is 10% in this study;
- the pheromone weight of an edge is equal to DIT covered per unit of execution time by a requirement (same fitness function as knapsack solvers); and
- the maximum time allotted to find the food is t_{max}.

2.6.1 Case study

For the Ringdroid application, Cluster 2 contained 18 requirements. Table 2.6 lists all the requirements that belong to Cluster 2 with their DIT and execution time information. For each requirement the calculated target function value (DIT/T) is also presented. The termination criterion for ACO run is tmax, which is kept at 15 minutes (to keep parity with the knapsack solver).

Table 2.7 shows the edges of the first iteration. The path R7 R12 R23 R35 R42 R71 R75 produced the highest pheromone levels (44.25) and the path R1 R5 R12 R35 R42 R71 R75 produced the second highest pheromone levels (43.04). These two paths are presented in Fig. 2.6. The deposition of pheromone is indicated by +1 and it evaporates at a rate of 10%. So, after the first iteration the pheromone weight of an edge is reduced to $(1 - 0.1) = 0.9$. The segment R35 R42 R71 R75 is traversed twice. So each edge in this segment becomes $((0.9 + 1) - (10\% of 1.9)) = 1.71$.

In the second iteration, path R1 R16 R20 R35 R42 R71 R75 is selected from all the traversed paths as it deposits the highest pheromone levels. Table 2.8 lists the covered paths in the second iteration. As the segment R35 R42 R71 R75 is traversed again in this iteration, each edge of R35–R42, R42–R71, and R71–R75 has a weight of $(1.71 - 0.17 + 1) = 2.54$. Fig. 2.7 portrays the second iteration. From the figure it becomes clear that the path R1 R16 R20 R35 R42 R71 R75 deposits the highest pheromone levels and thus it is the best path.

For Cluster 2 of Ringdroid, it took 33 minutes to run all 18 requirements. But with the application of ACO, the requirement set is reduced to 7 requirements R1 R16 R20 R35 R42 R71 R75 and it takes 14.91 minutes to run them. Thus ACO helps in executing the optimized requirements of Ringdroid within tmax (15 minutes).

Table 2.6 Requirement data for Cluster 2 of the Ringdroid application.

Requirement ID	Depth of inheritance tree (DIT)	Execution time (T) in minutes	Pheromone weight (DIT/T)
R1	3	0.91	3.29
R4	5	1.08	4.62
R5	12	1.50	8
R7	15	2	7.5
R12	15	2	7.5
R15	12	2	6
R16	3	1	3
R20	17	3	5.6
R22	3	0.75	4
R23	5	1	5
R35	14	2	7
R40	16	2	8
R42	21	4	5.25
R50	22	4	5.50
R55	5	1	5.00
R62	4	0.75	5.33
R71	12	2	6
R75	12	2	6

Table 2.7 Requirement execution in the first iteration.

Sequence	Pheromone weight
R7 R12 R23 R35 R42 R71 R75	44.25
R5 R20 R35 R42 R55 R62	36.18
R12 R22 R40 R71 R75	31.50
R1 R5 R12 R35 R42 R71 R75	43.04

Table 2.8 Requirement execution in the second iteration.

Sequence	Pheromone weight
R1 R5 R16 R20 R35	26.89
R1 R16 R20 R35 R42 R71 R75	36.14

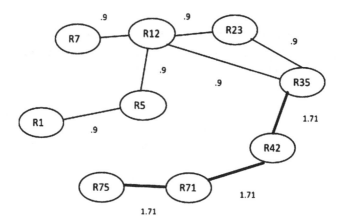

Figure 2.6 First iteration path.

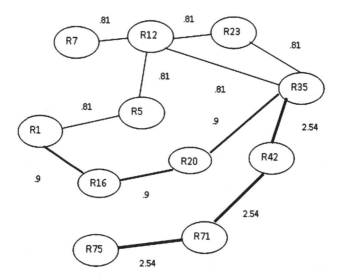

Figure 2.7 Second iteration path.

2.7 Results and findings

As 100 requirements were run for the OmniNotes application, on average 30 seconds or 1 minute was required to run each scenario. Some use cases required 2 minutes and a handful of them took 3 to 4 minutes. To complete the run of all 100 requirements in one attempt, 150 minutes were required. On the other hand, as 75 requirements were run for Ringdroid, it took an average of 45 seconds for each use case to run. Few scenarios took 1 to

2 minutes while very few took 3 to 5 minutes. In total, it took 100 minutes to run all 75 requirements.

However, with regard to the agile software development paradigm, it is infeasible to dedicate 100 or 150 minutes for judging the performance of an Android application. As agile methodology involves repetition of coding-database handling-testing windows in short sprints/delivery windows, it is necessary to divide these requirements into clusters and optimize their numbers. Thus, three clusters were formed for the Ringdroid application. Cluster 1 contained 27 requirements, Cluster 2 contained 18 requirements, and Cluster 3 contained 30 requirements. Three clusters were also formed for the OmniNotes application. Cluster 1 contained 28 requirements, Cluster 2 contained 35 requirements, and Cluster 3 contained 37 requirements.

Moreover, mere clustering is not sufficient for performance tuning of Android applications. For example, as Cluster 3 of the OmniNotes application contained 37 requirements, it took 70 minutes to run all of them. But with the help of GA, it was only necessary to run 12 requirements, which took 15 minutes. Furthermore, big applications may have huge numbers of requirements. So the perception of optimization is necessary from this point of view. Tables 2.9 and 2.10 list the effects of optimization (in terms of requirement number) for the Ringdroid and OmniNotes applications, respectively. Tables 2.11 and 2.12 present the effects of optimization (in terms of execution time) for the Ringdroid and OmniNotes applications, respectively.

To promote fair comparison with existing studies, the study conducted by Fernandes *et al.* was highlighted. As this study [36] focused on several non-functional requirements, for the Ringdroid and OmniNotes applications, similar non-functional requirements were chosen apart from some functional requirements.

Table 2.9 Effect of optimization (in terms of requirement number) for the Ringdroid application.

Cluster	Number of requirements before optimization	Number of requirements after optimization using GA	Number of requirements after optimization using ACO
Cluster 1	27	9	10
Cluster 2	18	9	7
Cluster 3	30	11	12

Table 2.10 Effects of optimization (in terms of requirement number) for the OmniNotes application.

Cluster	Number of requirements before optimization	Number of requirements after optimization using GA	Number of requirements after optimization using ACO
Cluster 1	28	9	10
Cluster 2	35	10	13
Cluster 3	37	12	9

Table 2.11 Effects of optimization (in terms of execution time) for the Ringdroid application.

Cluster	Execution time before optimization (in minutes)	Execution time after optimization using GA (in minutes)	Execution time after optimization using ACO (in minutes)
Cluster 1	35	14	12.5
Cluster 2	33	15	14.91
Cluster 3	32	9	10.5

Table 2.12 Effects of optimization (in terms of execution time) for the OmniNotes application.

Cluster	Execution time before optimization (in minutes)	Execution time after optimization using GA (in minutes)	Execution time after optimization using ACO (in minutes)
Cluster 1	30	7.5	5
Cluster 2	50	10.5	11
Cluster 3	70	15	10.5

From the obtained results it is evident that:

- In almost all the cases, GA caused a larger reduction in the number of requirements than ACO.
- Only in two cases (Cluster 2 of Ringdroid and Cluster 3 of OmniNotes) ACO caused a larger reduction in the number of requirements.
- In almost all cases ACO caused a larger reduction in time than GA.
- Only in two cases (Cluster 3 of Ringdroid and Cluster 2 of OmniNotes) GA caused a larger reduction in time than ACO.

- So basically, while GA is more effective for reducing the number of requirements, ACO is more effective in reducing execution time.
- In some cases, the number of requirements became half (Cluster 2 of Ringdroid) while in some cases it became almost one-third (Clusters 1 and 3 of Ringdroid, Clusters 1 and 2 of OmniNotes).
- In some cases, the number of requirements was reduced to close to one-fourth, like for Cluster 3 of OmniNotes (from 37 to 9 using ACO).
- The execution time of requirements became half (Cluster 2 of Ringdroid) in some cases, while in some cases it became almost one-fourth (Cluster 3 of Ringdroid, Cluster 1 of OmniNotes).

Thus clustering along with optimization heuristics can be very much effective for performance analysis of Android applications in a time-constrained environment.

2.8 Threats to validity

The conducted experimentation involved the following validation threats:
- Even though the chosen applications (Ringdroid and OmniNotes) are very popular and highly rated and host loads of features, some other applications (preferably from the industrial sector) might be used for implementation.
- k-Means is a very popular clustering method. However, the use of other clustering algorithms, like k-medoids, can also be explored. The effects of changing the number of clusters on the performance of Android applications can also be verified.
- GA and ACO are widely established optimization heuristics. But the usage of other optimization heuristics (multi-objective GA, two-archive evolutionary algorithm) could also be explored.

2.9 Conclusion

Building Android applications is a very popular activity nowadays. However, Android application development suffers several ongoing issues, like malware interference, lack of memory space, poor response time, compromised user experience, etc. This research work tries to bridge one of these gaps, and an attempt is made to optimize the performance of Android applications in time-controlled environments. Two open source applications (used for taking notes and for setting alarms, notifications, etc.) were examined and k-means clustering helped to cluster the functional and non-functional requirements of the applications. In agile software development, it has become necessary to separate the optimal requirements the Android application should execute in a stipulated time. GA and ACO techniques were used to optimize the number of requirements. DIT traversed per unit of execution time was chosen as the fitness function.

It appeared that GA caused a larger reduction in the number of requirements than ACO. On the other hand, ACO is more effective in reducing execution time. In some cases, the number of requirements became half while in some instances it was reduced to almost one-third. The execution time of requirements became half in many cases, while in multiple cases it was reduced to almost one-fourth. Thus clustering along with the usage of optimization heuristics made the performance evaluation of Android applications easier.

References

[1] L. Corral, A. Sillitti, G. Succi, Mobile multi platform development: an experiment for performance analysis, Procedia Computer Science 10 (2012) 736–743.

[2] X. Wei, C. Gurkok, ProfileDroid: multi-layer profiling of Android applications categories and subject descriptors, Network and System Security (2014) 137–148.

[3] S.S. Velan, Investigating the complexity of computational intelligence using the levels of inheritance in an AOP based software, in: Advances in Science and Engineering Technology International Conferences, ASET 2019, 2019, pp. 1–5.

[4] E. Azimzadeh, M. Sameki, M. Goudarzi, Performance analysis of Android underlying virtual machine in mobile phones, in: IEEE International Conference on Consumer Electronics, Berlin, ICCE-Berlin, 2012, pp. 292–295.

[5] J. Booz, J. McGiff, W.G. Hatcher, W. Yu, J. Nguyen, C. Lu, Tuning deep learning performance for Android malware detection, in: Proceedings – 2018 IEEE/ACIS 19th International Conference on Software Engineering, Artificial Intelligence, Networking and Parallel/Distributed Computing, SNPD 2018, 2018, pp. 140–145.

[6] S. Wang, A. Gittens, W.M. Mahoney, Scalable kernel K-means clustering with Nyström approximation: relative-error bounds, Journal of Machine Learning Research 20 (2019) 1–49.

[7] G. Gan, M. Kwok-PoNg, K-means clustering with outlier removal, Pattern Recognition Letters 90 (2017) 8–14.

[8] M.E. Celebi, H.A. Kingravi, P.A. Vela, A comparative study of efficient initialization methods for the k-means clustering algorithm, Expert Systems with Applications 40 (1) (2013) 200–210.

[9] N. Shi, X. Liu, Y. Guan, Research on k-means clustering algorithm: an improved k-means clustering algorithm, in: 3rd International Symposium on Intelligent Information Technology and Security Informatics, IITSI 2010, 2010, pp. 63–67.

[10] A.K. Jain, Data clustering: 50 years beyond K-means, Pattern Recognition Letters 31 (8) (2010) 651–666.

[11] W. Zhao, Q. He, Parallel K-Means Clustering Based on MapReduce, Springer-Verlag Berlin Heidelberg, 2009, pp. 674–679.

[12] K.R. Žalik, An efficient k-means clustering algorithm, Pattern Recognition Letters 29 (9) (2008) 1385–1391.

[13] D. Steinley, K-means clustering: a half-century synthesis, British Journal of Mathematical & Statistical Psychology 59 (1) (2006) 1–34.

[14] D.T. Pham, S.S. Dimov, C.D. Nguyen, Selection of K in K-means clustering, in: Proceedings of the Institution of Mechanical Engineers, Part C, Journal of Mechanical Engineering Science 219 (1) (2005) 103–119.

[15] A. Likas, N. Vlassis, J. Verbeek, The global k-means clustering algorithm, Pattern Recognition Letters 36 (2) (2003) 451–461.

[16] P.S. Bradley, U.M. Fayyad, Refining initial points for K-means clustering, in: 15th International Conference on Machine Learning (ICML' 98), 1998, pp. 91–99.

[17] F. Belli, M. Eminov, N. Gökçe, A fuzzy clustering approach and case study 1 introduction: motivation and related work, Dependable Computing (2007) 95–110.

[18] T. Stützle, Parallelization strategies for Ant Colony Optimization, 1998, pp. 722–731.

[19] R.S. Parpinelli, H.S. Lopes, A.A. Freitas, Data mining with an ant colony optimization algorithm, IEEE Transactions on Evolutionary Computation 6 (4) (2002) 321–332.

[20] D. Martens, M. De Backer, R. Haesen, J. Vanthienen, M. Snoeck, B. Baesens, Classification with ant colony optimization, IEEE Transactions on Evolutionary Computation 11 (5) (2007) 651–665.

[21] P. Guo, L. Zhu, Ant colony optimization for continuous domains, in: Proceedings – International Conference on Natural Computation, 2012, pp. 758–762.

[22] I. Alaya, C. Solnon, K. Ghédira, Ant colony optimization for multi-objective optimization problems, in: Proceedings – International Conference on Tools with Artificial Intelligence, ICTAI, 1, 2007, pp. 450–457.

[23] H.a. Abbas, B. McKay, Classification rule discovery with ant colony optimization, in: IEEE/WIC International Conference on Intelligent Agent Technology, IAT 2003, 2003, pp. 83–88.

[24] S.N. Sivanandam, S.N. Deepa, Principles of Soft Computing, John Wiley & Sons, ISBN 8126510757, 2007.

[25] N. Padhy, S. Satapathy, R.P. Singh, State-of-the-art object-oriented metrics and its reusability: a decade review, Smart Innovation, Systems and Technologies 77 (2018) 431–441.

[26] A.S. Nuñez-Varela, H.G. Pérez-Gonzalez, F.E. Martínez-Perez, C. Soubervielle-Montalvo, Source code metrics: a systematic mapping study, The Journal of Systems and Software 128 (2017) 164–197.

[27] N. Acevedo, C. Rey, C. Contreras-Bolton, V. Parada, Automatic design of specialized algorithms for the binary knapsack problem, Expert Systems with Applications 141 (2020).

[28] Y. Feng, G.G. Wang, S. Deb, M. Lu, X.J. Zhao, Solving 0–1 knapsack problem by a novel binary monarch butterfly optimization, Neural Computing & Applications 28 (7) (2017) 1619–1634.

[29] R.L. Kadri, F.F. Boctor, An efficient genetic algorithm to solve the resource-constrained project scheduling problem with transfer times: the single mode case, European Journal of Operational Research 265 (2) (2018) 454–462.

[30] B. Keshanchi, A. Souri, N.J. Navimipour, An improved genetic algorithm for task scheduling in the cloud environments using the priority queues: formal verification, simulation, and statistical testing, The Journal of Systems and Software 124 (2017) 1–21.

[31] A.J. Kulkarni, H. Shabir, Solving 0–1 knapsack problem using cohort intelligence algorithm, International Journal of Machine Learning and Cybernetics 7 (3) (2016) 427–441.

[32] S. Mirjalili, Genetic algorithm, in: Evolutionary Algorithms and Neural Networks, 2018, pp. 43–55.

[33] M. Spreitzenbarth, F. Freiling, F. Echtler, T. Schreck, J. Hoffmann, Mobile-sandbox: having a deeper look into Android applications, in: Proceedings of the ACM Symposium on Applied Computing, 2013, pp. 1808–1815.
[34] S. Lee, C. Yoon, H. Cha, User interaction-based profiling system for Android application tuning, in: UBICOMP '14, September 13–17, Seattle, WA, 2014, pp. 289–299.
[35] T. Ongkosit, S. Takada, Responsiveness analysis tool for Android application, in: 2nd International Workshop on Software Development Lifecycle for Mobile, DeMobile 2014 – Proceedings, 2014, pp. 1–4.
[36] T.S. Fernandes, É. Cota, Á. Freitas, Performance evaluation of Android applications: a case study, in: European Signal Processing Conference, 1998–January, 2014, pp. 79–84.

CHAPTER 3

Sentiment analysis of social media data evolved from COVID-19 cases – Maharashtra

Pooja Jain and Archana Vaidya

Department of Computer Engineering, Gokhle Education Society's, R.H. Sapat College of Engineering, Management Studies and Research, Nashik-5, India

3.1 Introduction

"Coronavirus" is derived from the Latin word "corona," meaning "wreath" or "crown." It was initially used in the 1930 when respiratory infection of chicken was found to be caused by infectious bronchitis virus (IBV). It is related to a group of RNA viruses which cause diseases in birds and mammals. Coronaviruses primarily cause infections of the respiratory tract ranging from moderate to lethal [1]. nCoV-19 originates from Wuhan, China, and has spread all over the world in very little time, causing a worldwide pandemic. Most communication has become digital-only. Social media is a new constant of our lives. It is helpful to individuals as well as the government. As of 2020, the global population is around 7.82 billion people, of whom more than 1 billion people are internet users. Due to the continuous increase in the use of social media platforms, the gap in communication and exchange of information has been abridged, rendering the world smaller. Furthermore, such media play a significant role in crisis situations. It is urgently needed to understand how to implement social media for public communication because only this source has been working everywhere for rapid communication since lockdown. Through social media, we are connected all over the world. It would not be an exaggeration to state that social media is omnipresent in all aspects of daily life, like tourism, healthcare, business, education, disaster management, and politics [2–5]. It can also effectively serve in the military and in unforeseen situations such as those discussed in [6]. Figs. 3.1 and 3.2 show the time evolution of the term "coronavirus" on Facebook and Twitter in India per region.

With the increasing usage of platforms like Facebook, Instagram, LinkedIn, Twitter, and Youtube, there are various other platforms coming

Advanced Data Mining Tools and Methods for Social Computing
https://doi.org/10.1016/B978-0-32-385708-6.00010-2
51

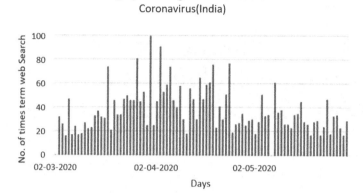

Figure 3.1 Use of the term "coronavirus" on Facebook in India (analyzed using Google trends).

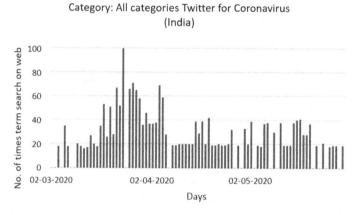

Figure 3.2 Use of the term "coronavirus" on Twitter in India (analyzed using Google trends).

to the market and establishing their foothold on the grounds of the digital era. It is very important to manage safety and peace measures. Therefore, the present work collects all recent relevant works about the use of social media during the COVID-19 pandemic and conducts sentiment analysis and trend analysis on coronavirus in Maharashtra with a view on the following issues:

1. How could we manage social media especially public communication with emergency organizations like the police or military during a pandemic?

2. How could we detect emotion or behavior of the public using social media analytics?

3.1.1 Cases

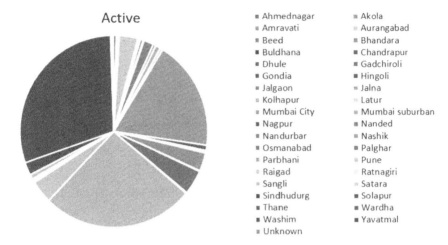

Active

- Ahmednagar
- Amravati
- Beed
- Buldhana
- Dhule
- Gondia
- Jalgaon
- Kolhapur
- Mumbai City
- Nagpur
- Nandurbar
- Osmanabad
- Parbhani
- Raigad
- Sangli
- Sindhudurg
- Thane
- Washim
- Unknown
- Akola
- Aurangabad
- Bhandara
- Chandrapur
- Gadchiroli
- Hingoli
- Jalna
- Latur
- Mumbai suburban
- Nanded
- Nashik
- Palghar
- Pune
- Ratnagiri
- Satara
- Solapur
- Wardha
- Yavatmal

Figure 3.3 Districtwise active patient statistics of June 2020 in Maharashtra (India).

Fig. 3.3 shows a districtwise graph of active patients in June 2020 in Maharashtra, India. From global point of view, China tops the list, followed by Spain, Germany, Italy, Iran, and the USA. Fig. 3.4 shows the number of recovered patients in Maharashtra after taking proper care and medications. These cases are increasing after the unlock 1.0 mission begins in mid-May, when the market opens due to a very strong global economic recession and as per e-pass people can travel from one place to another. The non-availability of a trusted universal vaccine worsens the situation for the already inadequate healthcare system of India. People are facing losses in many aspects like economical, psychological etc., as shown in Fig. 3.5. Many schoolchildren and students lost their lives, as it was not possible to follow the rules of social distancing. Districtwise cases of death in Maharashtra are shown in Fig. 3.6, and the total numbers of cases of active patients, recovered patients, and death in Maharashtra are shown in Fig. 3.7.

3.1.2 Structure of the virus

Coronaviruses are approximately spherical, large balls with projections on the surface. The mean radius is 62.5 nm. The casing radius is 42.5 nm

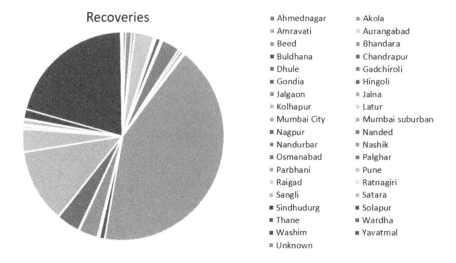

Figure 3.4 Districtwise recoveries of patients in June 2020 in Maharashtra (India).

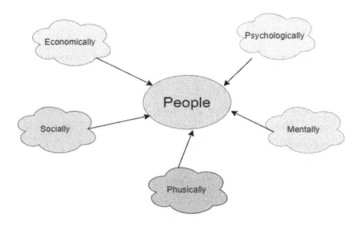

Figure 3.5 Psychological effects of lockdown on people.

and the projections are 20 nm in length. The virus as a whole looks like a distinct pair of electron-dense shells in electron micrographs. A coronavirus cross-section is shown in Fig. 3.8 [7].

3.1.3 Life of coronavirus

COVID-19 is spread from person to person. When someone who is infected sneezes or coughs, droplets containing the virus are transferred through the air [8]. A healthy human being can then inhale such droplets.

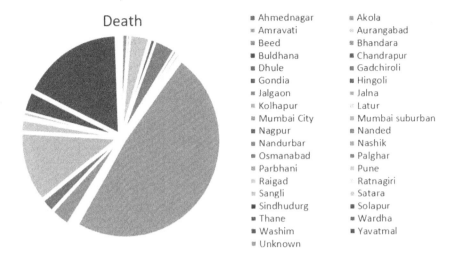

Figure 3.6 Districtwise deaths of COVID-19 patients in June 2020 in Maharashtra, India.

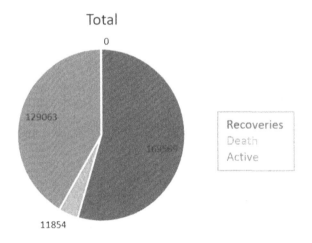

Figure 3.7 Districtwise total cases of coronavirus in June 2020 in Maharashtra, India.

One can also be infected by the virus if he/she comes in contact with an infected surface or object. The lifespan of coronavirus on different surfaces is shown in Table 3.1.

3.2 Literature review

To start with, [9] attempted to reach out to the citizens of Pune in lockdown to understand people's psychology. They followed non-doctrinal as

Table 3.1 Lifespan of coronavirus on different surfaces.

Sr. No.	Type of surface	Example	Lifespan
1	Metal	Doorknobs, jewels, silverware	5 days
2	Wood	Furniture, decking	4 days
3	Plastics	Milk containers and detergent bottles, subway and bus seats, backpacks, elevator buttons	2 to 3 days
4	Stainless steel	Refrigerators, pots and pans, sinks, some water bottles	2 to 3 days
5	Cardboard	Shipping boxes	24 hours
6	Copper	Coins, teakettles, cookware	4 hours
7	Aluminum	Soda cans, tinfoil, water bottles	2 to 8 hours
8	Glass	Drinking glasses, measuring cups, mirrors, windows	Up to 5 days
9	Ceramics	Dishes, pottery, mugs	5 days
10	Paper	Mail, newspapers	The length of time varies. Some strains of coronavirus live for only a few minutes on paper, while others live for up to 5 days.
11	Food	Coronavirus does not seem to be spread through food.	–
12	Water	Coronavirus has not been found in drinking water. If it does get into the water supply, your local water treatment plant filters and disinfects the water, which should kill any germs.	–
13	Fabrics	Clothes, linens	There's not much research about how long the virus lives on fabric, but it is probably not as long as on hard surfaces.

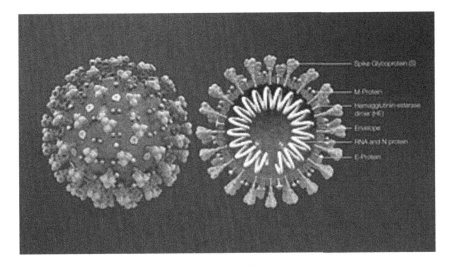

Figure 3.8 Cross-sectional model of a coronavirus [7].

well as doctrinal research. A cross-sectional, web-based study was carried out by the HealthCare Workers (HCWs) [10] regarding COVID-19 in the first half of March 2020. In [11], the sentiment analysis of India's post-lockdown announcements was reported. They used Twitter for analysis using R software. Similarly, [12] used the epidemiological SIR to estimate the fundamental reproduction number R/0 at both state and national levels. They went on to develop a statistical machine learning model to predict the cases ahead of time. Their analysis suggests that Punjab urgently requires attention. On the similar lines, [13] reports several patterns and trends which answer half a dozen distinct questions comprehensively. They suggested that national lockdown curbed the infected cases growth rate; however, certain unforeseen mass-level events adversely affected the infected cases with poly-nomial and exponential regression modeling. A novel mathematical model has been proposed by [14] to identify total infected cases or new cases in an actual situation. It is pertinent to organize medical facilities and design a future plan-of-action. Furthermore, [15] has reported the psychological effect of the said virus on people with a specific focus centered towards India's population. An interesting study was reported by [16], who stud-ied the Janta curfew using data related to both phase lockdown to relate between environmental and geological areas and its substantial suppressive effect on the pollution level in India's nationwide lockdown. Several lockdown strategies have been suggested to control the emission of greenhouse gas to a minimum.

3.3 Proposed design

3.3.1 Problem statement

Classification and clustering of tweets and Facebook comments related to COVID-19 can be performed by trend analysis or sentiment analysis. The proposed problem statement is a prediction of sentiments related to coronavirus with the help of machine learning.

3.3.2 Architecture

The main goal and challenge of the system are analyzing Twitter/Facebook data related to coronavirus to see (i) the impact of Twitter on people in Maharashtra or a particular place or situation and (ii) how people think about or react to the pandemic. Our proposed system is an analysis system which is based on a mechanism that analyzes user tweets using hashtags and keywords. The general public orientation toward the pandemic can be studied using the tweets that people have posted on Twitter. Twitter/Facebook are generally admired by academicians, journalists, and politicians. The proposed system mainly focuses on the collection of tweets to conduct a trend analysis for trending factors or persons and a sentiment analysis to actually divide the positive and negative tweets related to the COVID-19 situation so that performing trend analysis on these tweets can help the government obtain a clear picture of the public opinion about the pandemic. This is conducted in three phases.

1. Phase one is connecting with Twitter/Facebook and downloading the tweets.
2. The second phase is about loading these tweets on the dataset for further analysis.
3. The third phase is the actual trend analysis and sentiment analysis.

Fig. 3.9 shows the proposed system architecture of sentiment and trend analysis.

3.3.3 Algorithm

For implementation of this system the following algorithms will be used:
*   Step 1: Tweet processing
    Let T be the set of downloaded tweets.

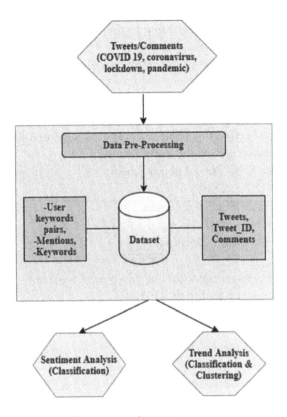

Figure 3.9 Block diagram of the proposed system.

- Input: T
- Output: Processed tweets with all unwanted words, spaces, and special characters removed
- Step 2: Trend analysis
  Let T be the set of pre-processed tweets.
- Input: T
- Output: Top trending hashtags, top active users, and top trends
  Steps:
- Pre-process all tweets to remove unrecognized unicode, garbage numbers, etc. Transfer all tweets from the local file system to the dataset.
- All tweets are split into words with whitespace as a separator.
- All similar words are counted and written to the dataset.
- All tweets of the output are transferred to the local file system.

- All tweets are sorted according to the count and filtered with hashtags, users, and trends.
- All top hashtags, users, and trends are visualized to obtain a better overview.

• Step 3: K-Means clustering algorithm

The tweets in the dataset are given as input to the K-means algorithm. The distance between centroid and tweet is measured in terms of the difference between x- and y-coordinates.

- Input: Let X be a set of points where
  $X = \{X1,X2,....,Xn\}$
  Let V be a set of centers where
  $V = \{V1,V2,...,Vn\}$
- Output: Formation of clusters
- Steps:
  - Pre-processing: Pre-process all tweets separately and find out unique terms and their TF-IDF.
  - Create a set of tweet vectors by using a dictionary of unique terms and provide the numbers of clusters to be quantified.
  - For initial Centroids of the clusters, provide the TF-IDF values for centroids from vectors randomly.
  - Transfer clusters and vectors from the Local file system to the dataset.
  - Repeat the following steps.
  - Determine closeness by Euclidean distance in terms of TF-IDF of each vector with every cluster centroid. Apply the Euclidean distance between two points: If p = (p1, p2) and q = (q1,q2), then the distance of a cluster is given by

$$d(p, q) = \sqrt{(q_1 - p_1)^2 + (q_2 - p_2)^2}. \tag{3.1}$$

  - Assign a vector to the cluster which is closest to the centroid of the cluster. Assign each point to the nearest cluster. If each cluster centroid is denoted by ci, then each data point x is assigned to a cluster based on

$$arg\ min_{(c_i \in C)} dist(c_i, x)^2, \tag{3.2}$$

where dist() is the Euclidean distance.
  - Until no more changes occur in the center of clusters.
  - The cluster's object is not changed further.

- Step 4: Naive Bayes classifier
  The orientation of users towards the coronavirus situation can be analyzed from tweets. The naive Bayes algorithm can be used to classify tweets or comments into positive, negative, and neutral classes. This will help to produce a safety tool, preventive measures, and post-pandemic examination on social media.
  Steps:
  - Create data for the classifier: Creation of a list of positive words and negative words.
  - Provide a dataset which has to be analyzed.
  - Design a classifier to classify the tweets/comments.
  - Extract the word feature list from the list with its frequency count.
  - Train the classifier using the training dataset.
  - Generate a label of positive probability which contains the total number of positive words in the input file.
  - Generate a label of negative probability which contains the total number of negative words in the input file.
  - Calculate the score probability for the positive and negative words for an individual tweet as follows:

$$p(t) = \sum_{k=1}^{m} score(w), \qquad (3.3)$$

  where t represents tweets, m is the length of t, w is the weight of t, and $p(t)$ is polarity of tweets (positive, negative, or neutral).
  - Calculate the score of positive tweets by divided the total number of positive words in the tweet by the positive probability.
  - Calculate the score of negative tweets by dividing the total number of negative words in the tweet by the negative probability.
  - Compare this probability to identify the tweet category as positive, negative, or neutral, that is, joy, anger, or neither of both related to coronavirus.

3.3.4 Analysis of tweets as per sentiments

1. Tokenize the tweet, i.e., split words from body of text.
2. Remove stopwords from the tokens (stopwords are the commonly used words which are irrelevant in text analysis like I, am, you, are, etc.).
3. Do part of speech (POS) tagging of the tokens and select only significant features/tokens like adjectives, adverbs, etc.

4. Pass the tokens to a sentiment classifier which classifies the tweet sentiment as positive, negative, or neutral by assigning it a polarity between −1.0 and 1.0.

3.4 Analysis and predictions

3.4.1 Dataset

Fig. 3.10 shows steps of how to download the tweets or comments from social media platforms like Twitter/Facebook and real-time tweets by the Twitter 4J tool. The system is able to download the tweets and upload them in the system for further analysis. The total number of tweets of Maharashtra is about 10,000, which were collected by a twitter development account. Using these tweets, the system is able to identify trending topics as well as total counts of sentiments of total tweets and top hashtags.

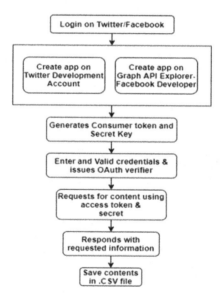

Figure 3.10 Procedure of the tweet/comment downloading process.

3.4.2 Accuracy comparison graph

Accuracy and precision values were computed based on the confusion matrix generated from the naive Bayes classifier model. The proposed system has better accuracy up to 97%.

- True positive (TP): correctly predicted number of instances.

- False positive (FP): incorrectly predicted number of instances.
- True negative (TN): correctly predicted number of instances as not required.
- False negative (FN): incorrectly predicted number of instances as not required. Based on this parameter, we can calculate the subsequent measurements.
  - Precision classifier: Precision measures the exactness of a classifier. A better precision means fewer false positives, while a lower precision means more false positives. This is often at odds with recall, as a simple way to improve precision is to decrease recall. It is calculated as follows:

$$Precision = \frac{T_{Pos}}{T_{Pos} + T_{Neg} + T_{Neu}}. \tag{3.4}$$

  - Recall classifier: Recall measures the sensitivity or completeness of a classifier. Higher recall means fewer false negatives, while lower recall means more false negatives. Improving recall can often decrease precision because it gets increasingly harder to be precise because the sample space increases. It is calculated as follows:

$$Recall = \frac{T_{Pos}}{T_{Pos} + F_{Neg} + F_{Neu}}. \tag{3.5}$$

  - Scalability: As we implement this technique on the platform its scalability increases.
  - Efficiency: The tasks are often divided into multiple nodes and hence the efficiency of the system increases.
  - Accuracy: We have used a user-defined function alongside the Porter stemmer. We have

$$Accuracy = \frac{(All_{True})}{(All_{Data})}, \tag{3.6}$$

$$F1\,Measure = \frac{2 \times precision \times recall}{precision + recall}. \tag{3.7}$$

3.4.3 Tweet analysis graph

Different sentiments and their tweet counts are analyzed by sentiment analysis classification using the naive Bayes algorithm shown in Fig. 3.11, and various emotions are captured from tweets shown in Fig. 3.12. Here, the number of tweets related to tension is about 2600, which is the highest

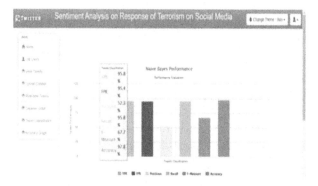

Figure 3.11 Comparison of accuracy, precision, and recall of existing algorithms and the proposed algorithm.

among people of Maharashtra. So we can verify whether people are happy or not with this lockdown and unlock phase and whether they follow the safety rules of social distancing and wearing the mask by their comments or tweets.

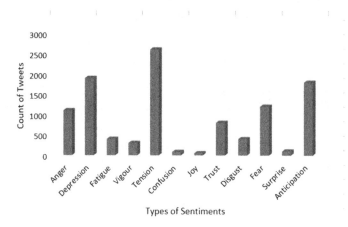

Figure 3.12 Analysis of tweets as per various sentiments.

3.5 Conclusion

With the increased use of social media, as a way to validate the proposed method, we analyze the tweets related to the novel coronavirus to predict the sentiments using machine learning. Training datasets were taken from a developer account of Twitter and Facebook and real-time data were obtained using the twitter 4J tool. Our approach uses the naive Bayes classifier, which is a competitive method for classification. It is possible to verify the sentiments of the users before and after a pandemic. This model can be implemented not only to identify the sentiments of people on social media but also as a safety tool, for implementing preventive measures, and for post-pandemic examination. The study also includes a machine learning approach to train a system to automatically classify the tweets and conduct a sentiment analysis on the tweets/comments. This study has a strong social aspect that relies on the idea that the predicted model could be helpful to the government and police to manage the situation after a lockdown or unlock phase and propose precautionary measures to stay safe.

3.6 Acknowledgment

We wish to express our gratitude to all those who have been helpful to us in the makings of this project. In the first place, we wish to thank Prof. A.S. Vaidya (PG coordinator), for having a genuine spirit of research and intellect. Immeasurable appreciation goes to Dr. D.V. Patil (Head of Department) for his prompt inspiration and administrative support which helped us to focus on our work with greater enthusiasm. Also, thanks go to all the teaching as well as non-teaching staff of the Computer Engineering Department and our librarian, GESCOE Nashik. It is a privilege and a matter of honor to express our overwhelming gratitude to all the soldiers of our country for sacrificing a lot for our safety.

References

[1] T. Estola, Coronaviruses, a New Group of Animal RNA Viruses, Avian Diseases (ISSN 0005-2086) 14 (2) (1970) 330–336, https://doi.org/10.2307/1588476, JSTOR 1588476, PMID 4316767.

[2] H. Chen, C.C. Yang, Special issue on social media analytics: understanding the pulse of the society, IEEE Transactions on Systems, Man, and Cybernetics - Part A: Systems and Humans 41 (5) (2011) 826–827.

[3] P.N. Jain, N.V. Alone, Importance of Social Media Analytics during elections: a review, International Journal of Computer Sciences and Engineering 6 (9) (Sep 2018), E-ISSN: 2347–2693.

[4] R.M. Medina, Social network analysis: a case study of the Islamist terrorist network, Security Journal 27 (1) (2014) 97121.

[5] S. Borau, S.F. Wamba, Social media, evolutionary psychology, and ISIS: a literature review and future research directions, in: World Conference on Information Systems and Technologies, April 2019, pp. 143–154.

[6] H.N. Teodorescu, Using analytics and social media for monitoring and mitigation of social disasters, Procedia Engineering 107 (2015) 325–334.

[7] C.S. Goldsmith, K.M. Tatti, W.W. Lee, et al., Ultrastructural characterization of SARS coronavirus, Emerging Infectious Diseases 10 (2) (February 2004) 320–326.

[8] C. Sohrabi, Z. Alsafi, N. O'Neill, M. Khan, A. Kerwan, A. Al-Jabir, C. Iosifidis, R. Agha, World Health Organization declares global, emergency: a review of the 2019 novel coronavirus (COVID-19), International Journal of Surgery (2020 Feb 26).

[9] R. Suryawanshi, V. More, A study of effect of Corona Virus Covid-19 and lock down on human psychology of Pune City region, Studies in Indian Place Names 40 (70) (2020 Mar 30) 984–994.

[10] Akshaya Srikanth Bhagavathula, Wafa Ali Aldhaleei, Novel Coronavirus (COVID-19) Knowledge and Perceptions: a Survey of Healthcare Workers, medRxiv pre-print, 9 March 2020.

[11] Gopalkrishna Barkur Vibha, Giridhar B. Kamath, Sentiment Analysis of Nationwide Lockdown due to COVID-19 outbreak: evidence from India, Asian Journal of Psychiatry (6 April 2020).

[12] Sourish Das, Prediction of COVID-19 disease progression in India under the effect of National Lockdown, arXiv:2004.03147v1 [q-bio.PE], 7 April 2020.

[13] R. Gupta, S.K. Pal, G. Pandey, A Comprehensive Analysis of COVID-19 Outbreak situation in India, medRxiv, 2020 Jan 1.

[14] M.K. Arti, K. Bhatnagar, Modeling and Predictions for COVID 19 Spread in India, ResearchGate.

[15] N.M. Patnaik, S. Maji, Psychological Issues and Stress on People in the Purview of COVID-19 Pandemic Lockdown.

[16] S. Kumar, S. Bhardwaj, A. Singh, H.K. Singh, P. Singh, U.K. Sharma, Environmental Impact of Corona Virus (COVID-19) and Nationwide Lockdown in India: an Alarm to Future Lockdown Strategies.

CHAPTER 4

COVID-19 outbreak analysis and prediction using statistical learning

Harleen Kaur[a] and Mihir Narayan Mohanty[b]

[a]Department of Computer Science and Engineering, Jamia Hamdard, New Delhi, India
[b]ITER (FET), Siksha 'O' Anusandhan (Deemed to be University), Bhubaneswar, India

4.1 Introduction

The field of statistical machine learning for application in time series data prediction is growing exponentially. It is a challenging aspect of current machine learning research for academia and researchers. Time series prediction can be used to study the behavior of the process and provides the future estimation from present and past data along with possible warnings and malfunction notifications. Successful utilization of time series data would lead to monitoring of the health of the system over time. Time series data analysis aims to utilize such data for several purposes that can be broadly categorized as understanding and interpreting the underlying techniques that produce the observed state of a system or process time-to-time. Several mathematical techniques and programming tools exist to effectively design computer programs that can explore, visualize, and model patterns in time series data. A similar application of it is in chaos theory in the field of engineering, medicine, science, finance, meteorology, and sunspot prediction. Prediction of time series uses the historical data to develop a model for the prediction of the future. The exact prediction will reduce the risk for decision making problems in different areas. A time series is a collection of data points that are generally sampled equally in time intervals. A mathematical model is used for prediction accuracy. Standard methods used for time series prediction seen in the literature are auto-regression (AR), moving average (MA), auto-regressive moving average (ARMA), auto-regressive integrated moving average (ARIMA), and Box–Jenkins models as statistical models, whereas neural network (NN)-based models are widely used as an intelligence-based approach. Out of many techniques in using neural networks, backpropagation is used mostly for updating the parameters of the model. In most cases, statistical methods are used like intelligent methods. However, hybrid models are used in specific applications to prove their robustness.

Currently, Prophet is used in many cases to mitigate the early problems. It is a robust technique with better accuracy results. COVID-19 is a major issue worldwide. Most research is focused on treatment and transmission. In this work, an attempt has been made to predict the global situation using the effective statistical tool Prophet. The early techniques in prediction application are provided in the literature section. The proposed method and results are discussed in the following sections.

4.2 Related literature

A practical form of fractional linear model was proposed in [1] that permits the extra covariates to develop a persistent way in the past to anticipate future estimations of the procedure. The main objective of their work was to introduce a model for creating a few estimates and to take a gander at their properties both from a hypothetical perspective by methods for asymptotic outcomes and from a reasonable viewpoint by treating some raw datasets. Authors have also presented literature about the use of the parametric and non-parametric models in their work. By applying multiple-output support vector regression (SVR) and a multiple-input multiple-output approach, the authors of [2] have proposed a new multi-step time series prediction model. Also, they have conducted a comparative analysis between three primary prediction models in their work. The model was validated with both simulated and real-world datasets. The quantitative and thorough appraisals were conducted based on the expectation accuracy and computational expense. For the prediction of time series data, different data analysis techniques were applied in different studies in the literature. An optimized monthly streamflow time series prediction model was designed by considering different data analysis techniques [3]. In the first stage of the proposed model, phase space reconstruction was conducted by applying the correlation integral and the false nearest neighbor (FNN) method. The result is compared with four types of models. The k-nearest neighbor (k-NN) model performed better as compared to other models, and in case of superiority, the ARMA model gave a better result. Also, the authors have used the MA of streamflow time series data as input to the artificial neural network (ANN) model. By using a polynomial architecture, the authors of [4] have proposed a novel neural network model for time series data analysis. They have used a regular aggregation function instead of using every higher-order factor. The proposed aggregation function is a combination of all linear functions within variations in the dimension space. The performance was also compared with the standard multi-layer neural network. An adaptive model selection algorithm was proposed in [5] for selecting a well-performing model from a set of candidate models. The experiment was conducted over 14 real-world sensor time series data, showing the effectiveness and flexibility of the model. The main objective of their work was to design an online lightweight framework for improving data communication. By using a non-stationary covariance function a Gaussian model was proposed in [6] for time series prediction. Their proposed model follows the Bayesian process and can be deployed in different time series predictions as well as for tracking of goods. Due to the simple concept and satisfactory performance factor, their proposed model can be easily applied to different types of problems. Support vector machines (SVMs), Elman recurrent neural networks (RNNs), and ARMA models were used for the prediction of time series in [7]. Based on the prediction ability of the model a comparison was also made among these three models. SVM performed better than other models for the prediction and regression of time series data. They have trained their SVM with a convex optimization algorithm that provides a better solution in prediction. To overcome the limitations of the traditional time series model, a novel neuro-fuzzy-based time series model was proposed in [8]. In their work, they have considered multiple membership functions for evaluating the ability of the fuzzy system with Sugeno interference. The results were compared with those of an AR model. The authors of [9] have designed an ensemble adaptive network-based fuzzy inference system (ANFIS) model for predicting the chaotic time series with minimum prediction error. Two types of integration models, i.e., average and weighted average integrators, were considered in their work. From the result, it was observed that their approach was capable of overcoming the limitations that occurred with the standard statistical and neural network-based models. For increasing the training complexity they have changed the membership function and the required error goal. In [10], authors have investigated the accuracy of various gray models like GM(1,1), the gray Verhulst model, and modified gray models using Fourier series. Profoundly boisterous information, the value of the United States dollar compared with the euro between 1 January 2005 and 30 December 2007, was utilized to look at the performances of the various models. From the results, it was observed that their proposed customized gray model exhibited better performance for both fittings of the model and forecasting. Authors have claimed that the modified GM(1,1) model with the Fourier series provided better results than the others. Particle swarm optimization (PSO), a popular optimization technique, was proposed for training a single neuron model in [11]. An improved form of the first PSO, cooperative random learning PSO (CRPSO), was considered to upgrade the presentation of the customary PSO. Proposed models were used for training three different types of time series models. Prediction of future events and behaviors by analyzing the input data is an important tool for various types of complicated system identification. These models can be deployed in different scientific and engineering applications such as signal processing, econometrics, and statistics. To improve the ability of the time series model, a hybrid model with ARIMA and a neural network framework was proposed in [12]. The proposed model is validated with water quality data that include different water characteristics. The neural network model was trained with the backpropagation algorithm with an optimized tarring approach. From the results, authors have claimed that their proposed hybrid approach provided better results than ARIMA and the neural network model. A recurrent radial basis function network (RRBFN)-based active monitoring and diagnosis model was proposed in [13]. The RRBFN architecture was based on the regular RBFN but in RRBFN the input node was configured with looped neurons with a sigmoid activation function. The dynamic memory of the RRBF was represented with looped neurons which were enabled to learn the patterns without disturbing the buffer. For testing the dynamic memory of the network, authors have considered two types of time series frameworks. The main benefit behind the use of the RRBF model was to mingle the learning flexibility of the regular RBF model with dynamic memory given by looped neurons. For non-stationary time series prediction, an online sequential extreme learning machine with kernels (OS-ELMK) model was proposed in [14]. The proposed algorithm was developed for modeling the non-stationary time series data. The authors have also compared the result obtained from the OS-ELMK algorithm and some other existing methods for both real and artificial non-stationary data. The learning performance of the proposed algorithm was better than that of others. By applying different SVR models, the authors of [15] predicted iterated time series data. Their proposed model was trained separately with various types of training data. Outputs generated from the previous layer were again taken as the input for further prediction. For reducing the prediction error, numerous SVR models performed better than single SVR models. For chaotic time series prediction problems, the authors of [16] have proposed a decomposition method for training Elman RNNs. Three time series models, Mackey–Glass, Lorenz, and sunspot time, were used to demonstrate the cooperative neuro-evolutionary methods' performances. The proposed method provided better results than other methods. For predicting the future value of the residual time series data, the authors of [17] have used a novel Elman neural network. The relationship between the predicted values of the residual and original time series data was captured by using the non-linear AR network with exogenous inputs (NARX) network. Mackey–Glass and Lorenz equations were considered for producing artificial and real-life time series data. From the numerical experimental result, it was confirmed that their proposed model more successfully predicted the time series expressions than other existing prediction techniques. By combining the filtering and wrapper techniques, the authors of [18] have proposed a complete data analysis technique for selecting, extracting, constructing, and transforming features. Their proposed method was capable of identifying the time series patterns, creating and transforming explanatory variables. Also, they have specified multi-layer perceptions for various sets of time series without proficient intercession. An investigation of the power system time series data was conducted in [19] by using an RBF network optimized with non-linear time-varying evolution PSO (NTVE-PSO) algorithm. For predicting the time series expressions the optimal RBFN structure was determined with the NTVE-PSO method. The inertia and acceleration coefficients were optimally adjusted with the non-linear time-varying evolutionary functions in the NTVE-PSO algorithm. In that modified PSO algorithm, the convergence was expedited towards the global optimum at the time of iteration. The Taiwan power system (Taipower) was used for predicting the time series with the proposed NTVE-PSO algorithm. For local and flexible adaption of margins, the authors of [20] have proposed a localized SVR (LSVR), model. The margin of the SVR model was fixed globally to improve the model efficiency. The hypothetical explanation and experimental calculation of their proposed model were provided. The advantage of the proposed LSVR model for predicting synthetic and financial data was provided and their model was compared with the generalized SVR model. For the easy and effective prediction of the unilabiate time series expression, the authors of [21] have used a NARX network in their work. Chaotic laser time series and variable bit rate (VBR) video traffic time series data were considered for evaluating the performance of the proposed approach. By using fuzzy logic, neural networks, and an evolutionary algorithm, the authors of [22] predicted the time series. The main goal of their work was to develop an automated model to identify the linear models. For obtaining better forecasting output, a hybrid approach was made by combining the ANN with the linear model. By combining the k-NN approximation method, mutual information (MI), and non-parametric noise estimation (NNE), a method for long-term time series prediction was proposed in [23]. By combining forward selection, backward elimination (or pruning), and forward-backward selection, a global input data selection methodology was introduced. The input selection method was optimized by using these three methods. The proposed method was validated with the Poland Electricity Load dataset. An RNN was trained with a hybrid methodology for predicting the absent values inside time series data [24]. PSO and an evolutionary algorithm were combined for improving the training ability of the RNN. The distinction among six basis function was validated for time series data in [25]. The validation was conducted over several types of data such as Mackey–Glass chaotic time series, Box–Jenkins furnace data, and flood prediction datasets for the Rivers Amber and Mole, UK. The training of every RBFN was done in two stages. In the first stage, the k-means clustering algorithm was used whereas singular value decomposition was conducted in the second stage. From the result, it was observed that by choosing the basis function all data points were predicted. By combining PSO and the gradient descent algorithm, a local linear wavelet neural network (LLWNN) was proposed in [26]. In the LLWNN the weights between the hidden and output layer were substituted with a local linear model. For the prediction of time series and related instability, the authors of [27] applied a Bayesian evidence strategy for designing a multi-layer perceptron (MLP). Again the MLP was also applied over an LS-SVM for designing a non-linear model to predict the time series. In the first stage of the work, a relation between the LS-SVM and a statistical framework was created for choosing an appropriate hyperparameter. By demoting the parameters of the model, the error bars of the model was obtained. Comparison of the model was conducted at the third stage of inference for automatic tuning of the kernel function parameters. A computationally efficient model for reducing the model criterion a novel method was presented in [28]. A coherence parameter was used for controlling the variable increment. The coherence parameter was an important factor that signifies the performance of lexica in sparse approximation problems. For addressing the issues in time series prediction, a dual-stage attention-based RNN (DA-RNN) was proposed [29]. For extracting useful input features, an input attention mechanism was introduced that extracts the features by following the earlier hidden nodes. After this step, an attention mechanism was used for selecting useful hidden states in every time step. By applying these double step attention mechanisms, an effective prediction model was proposed. For omitting the noise and estimating the parameters from the clean data, an RNN model was designed in [30]. The noise from both input and target data was removed by using the filtering approach. For providing the effectiveness of their robust neural network model they have applied the RNN model over synthetic data and on the Puget Power Electric Demand time series. For working with the non-stationary time series data, the authors of [31] have presented a modified RBFN framework. In their proposed RBFN, the hidden nodes were modified for detecting the gradient series. Their proposed model was named the gradient RBF (GRBF) model. In [32], the fractional dimension definition was modified which integrates the fuzzy set concept. The proposed definition was named fuzzy fractal dimension, which was more realistic compared to others. They have also combined the neural network, fuzzy logic, and fractional dimension for defining the definition. An effective RNN model was designed with a Bayesian framework in [33] that follows the echo state mechanism. Their proposed model was capable of handling the missing values in the training data and was defined with an efficient echo state network (ESN). Their model receives the fundamental concept of ESN learning with a Bayesian strategy and substitutes the Gaussian distributions. A bound optimization algorithm was proposed for training the robust ESN model. For predicting the time series a NARMAX model was designed with the fuzzy neural network in [34]. They have considered both feedforward and fuzzy network approaches in their proposed work. Authors have developed the NAMAX model with an effective algorithm that identifies parameters for producing the effective outputs. Some works were already conducted for analyzing X-ray images [35] and various sentiments of COVID-19 patients [36]

4.3 Proposed model

The COVID-19, which emerged in Wuhan (China) in December 2019, has now become a pandemic. India reported its first COVID-19 case on 30 January 2020, when a student arrived to Kerala from Wuhan. In this global pandemic situation, our model helps in analyzing the COVID-19 outbreak and in predicting the spread of the virus in the next 7 days using

Prophet. In this model, we use the predictive analytics approach of machine learning to predict future outcomes. This proposed model also analyzes the total number of cases worldwide and also which country has the maximum number of cases.

4.4 Prophet

Forecasting of time series is an ever-growing area in which various machine learning techniques have been used to predict and analyze the future based on the data gathered in the past. The "Prophet" forecasting model is the most recent development in forecasting the time series, developed by Facebook. Prophet is much faster and simpler to implement than previous forecasting models such as the ARIMA model. Prophet is open source software and we use it as a procedure for forecasting time series data, where non-linear trends are fit with yearly, weekly, and daily seasonality (https://facebook.github.io/prophet/). Prophet is robust to missing data and shifts in the trend and it can also handle outliers. Prophet finds applications across Facebook in producing reliable forecasts for planning and goal setting. We can make a reasonable forecast on messy data with no manual effort needed. The Prophet procedure is based on the additive regression model principles. It detects the changes automatically by choosing the points on a piecewise linear or logistic-based model. Also, for the seasonal model, it adopts the Fourier series. As a result, the forecasting can be automated. It begins with time series modeling by using analysts' parameters and predictions. Finally, it evaluates the model, so that the model can be understood well and adjusted according to the feedback. The model can be expressed as

$$y(t) = g(t) + s(t) + h(t) + \epsilon_t, \tag{4.1}$$

where:

$g(t)$ = the model trend that describes the increase or decrease in data for non-periodic changes in time series;

$s(t)$ = the Fourier series model seasonality that describes the impact of time factors in data;

$h(t)$ = the model to accommodate new data;

ϵ_t = the error accommodated by the model.

The evaluation is based on parameters like mean, drift, and seasonal naive that can be compared among the simple and advanced methods according to the variety of problems. It tries to fit the linear and non-linear functions by the method of regression. The problem is framed with the curve fitting technique and $s(t)$ are approximated by the following function:

$$s(t) = \sum_{n=1}^{N} \left(a_n \cos\left(\frac{2\pi nt}{P}\right) + b_n \sin\left(\frac{2\pi nt}{P}\right) \right), \qquad (4.2)$$

where P is the time period and parameters $[a_1, b_1, \ldots, a_N, b_N]$ need to be estimated for a given N to model seasonality.

The high-frequency components are considered as noise components and neglected. Else, N can be tuned and set using the forecast accuracy.

We will build the model for data analysis for the given dataset with dimensions of 12,568 rows and eight columns or variables. The analytic model in Fig. 4.1 shows the different stages of model building.

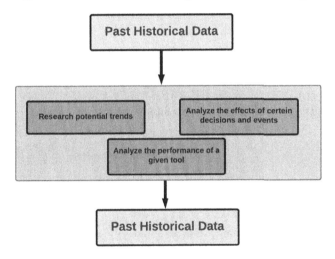

Figure 4.1 Flowchart of the model.

Firstly, in this model, we import the different libraries like NumPy, pandas, matplotlib, and seaborn to analyze the data. Next, we import the CSV file to import data and use the command "df.head()" to get the first five rows as output. A snapshot of the data is displayed in Fig. 4.2.

The next step is data processing or removal of all the missing values. A dataset may contain categorical and object data types and filling up all the missing values is done as shown in Fig. 4.3. We also use the "df.describe()" command to summarize statistics for numerical columns.

After this step, the total number of cases per day is analyzed as shown in Fig. 4.4. Fig. 4.5 shows the cases per country and state.

	SNo	Date	Province_State	Country_Region	Last Update	Confirmed	Deaths	Recovered
0	1	01/22/2020	Anhui	Mainland China	1/22/2020 17:00	1.0	0.0	0.0
1	2	01/22/2020	Beijing	Mainland China	1/22/2020 17:00	14.0	0.0	0.0
2	3	01/22/2020	Chongqing	Mainland China	1/22/2020 17:00	6.0	0.0	0.0
3	4	01/22/2020	Fujian	Mainland China	1/22/2020 17:00	1.0	0.0	0.0
4	5	01/22/2020	Gansu	Mainland China	1/22/2020 17:00	0.0	0.0	0.0

Figure 4.2 First five rows of the data.

	SNo	Confirmed	Deaths	Recovered
count	12569.000000	12569.000000	12569.000000	12569.000000
mean	6285.000000	1389.236853	63.734903	358.123956
std	3628.502101	8118.966031	594.915053	3317.143032
min	1.000000	0.000000	0.000000	0.000000
25%	3143.000000	4.000000	0.000000	0.000000
50%	6285.000000	46.000000	0.000000	1.000000
75%	9427.000000	318.000000	3.000000	20.000000
max	12569.000000	136675.000000	16523.000000	64014.000000

Figure 4.3 Filling missing values and summarizing statistics for numerical columns.

Date	Confirmed	Deaths	Recovered
01/22/2020	555.0	17.0	28.0
01/23/2020	653.0	18.0	30.0
01/24/2020	941.0	26.0	36.0
01/25/2020	1438.0	42.0	39.0
01/26/2020	2118.0	56.0	52.0
...	...	...	...
04/02/2020	1013157.0	52983.0	210263.0
04/03/2020	1095917.0	58787.0	225796.0
04/04/2020	1197405.0	64606.0	246152.0
04/05/2020	1272115.0	69374.0	260012.0
04/06/2020	1345048.0	74565.0	276515.0

76 rows × 3 columns

Figure 4.4 Number of cases per day.

		Confirmed	Deaths	Recovered
Province_State	Country_Region			
Montreal, QC	Canada	4.0	0.0	0.0
Norfolk County, MA	US	2.0	0.0	0.0
Alabama	US	1952.0	49.0	0.0
Alameda County, CA	US	2.0	0.0	0.0
Alaska	US	185.0	6.0	0.0
...	...	...	...	...
Xinjiang	Mainland China	76.0	3.0	73.0
Yolo County, CA	US	1.0	0.0	0.0
Yukon	Canada	6.0	0.0	0.0
Yunnan	Mainland China	184.0	2.0	172.0
Zhejiang	Mainland China	1264.0	1.0	1230.0

Figure 4.5 Cases per country.

Next, we import the data from the three time series to forecast the total number of cases worldwide in the next 7 days. The diagram in Fig. 4.6 shows the workflow of the prediction model.

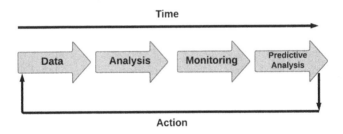

Figure 4.6 Flowchart of predictive analytics.

Then we import the fbprophet library. Prophet is open source software and we use it as a procedure for forecasting time series data, where non-linear trends are fit with yearly, weekly, and daily seasonality. Prophet is robust to missing data and shifts in the trend and it can also handle outliers.

Prophet finds applications across Facebook in producing reliable forecasts for planning and goal setting. We can make a reasonable forecast on messy data with no manual effort needed [6].

The input to Prophet is always a data frame with two columns **ds** and **y**. The **ds** column should be of a format **YYYY-MM-DD** for a date or **YYYY-MM-DD HH:MM:SS** for a timestamp. The **y** column must be numeric and represents the measurement we wish to forecast. First, we forecast the confirmed cases in the coming 7 days (as shown in Fig. 4.7)

	ds	y
71	2020-04-02	1013157.0
72	2020-04-03	1095917.0
73	2020-04-04	1197405.0
74	2020-04-05	1272115.0
75	2020-04-06	1345048.0

Figure 4.7 Converting the data into date and number of confirmed cases.

4.5 Results and discussion

The prediction method will assign each row in the future a predicted value which it names Yhat. If the model will pass in historical dates, it will provide an in-sample fit. Now we predict the future with the date, the upper limit, and the lower limit of the y-value and generate a week ahead forecast of confirmed cases using Prophet with 95% of accuracy by creating a base model. Figs. 4.8, 4.9, and 4.10 show a snapshot of the predicted model outcome for different cases. It contains the following parameters:

- S.no. – Serial number
- Observation date – Date of the observation given as MM/DD/YYYY
- Province/state – Province or state of the observation
- Country/region – Country of observation
- Last update – Time in UTC at which the row is updated for the given province or country
- Confirmed – number of confirmed cases until that date
- Deaths – number of deaths until that date
- Recovered – number of recovered cases until that date

	ds	yhat	yhat_lower	yhat_upper
78	2020-04-09	1.468555e+06	1.428641e+06	1.512396e+06
79	2020-04-10	1.536919e+06	1.493327e+06	1.578731e+06
80	2020-04-11	1.606790e+06	1.557354e+06	1.651051e+06
81	2020-04-12	1.668670e+06	1.616425e+06	1.719477e+06
82	2020-04-13	1.731460e+06	1.664374e+06	1.791036e+06

Figure 4.8 Predicting the future.

	ds	yhat	yhat_lower	yhat_upper
78	2020-04-09	78356.250778	74789.897882	81960.622766
79	2020-04-10	82267.066262	78879.197436	85955.639383
80	2020-04-11	86215.972576	82399.399111	89785.537348
81	2020-04-12	89771.991602	85695.714461	93941.829307
82	2020-04-13	93437.192430	89348.359412	97462.425313

Figure 4.9 Predicting death cases.

	ds	yhat	yhat_lower	yhat_upper
78	2020-04-09	280046.591441	266304.063606	293348.320635
79	2020-04-10	290646.454734	276589.351785	305026.351845
80	2020-04-11	302138.590206	288746.024144	315736.905568
81	2020-04-12	312162.065791	297681.015971	326552.430029
82	2020-04-13	322757.450412	308092.647193	336976.415418

Figure 4.10 Predicting recovered cases.

There are three datasets of confirmed, death, and recovered cases which are time series data on the numbers of confirmed cases, death cases, and recovered cases.

Here first we analyze which country has a maximum number of cases by plotting the pie chart shown in Fig. 4.11.

Next, we analyze the maximum number of cases and the minimum number cases worldwide, as shown in Fig. 4.12.

At last, we predict the numbers of confirmed, death, and recovered cases, as shown in Figs. 4.13 and 4.14.

Early diagnosis of coronavirus can be helpful to improve the quality of life of patients and enhance their life expectancy. Statistical modeling has been used to develop different COVID-19 prediction models. The different statistical models were trained on the COVID-19 dataset with optimized tuning parameters. All classification techniques were investigated with the "Prophet" software. For the validation of the proposed model, the dataset was taken from Kaggle (https://www.kaggle.com). The dataset has day-level information on the number of confirmed cases, deaths, and recovered cases from the novel coronavirus. The data are available from 22 January 2020. Table 4.1 shows the accuracy and error for predicting different parameters.

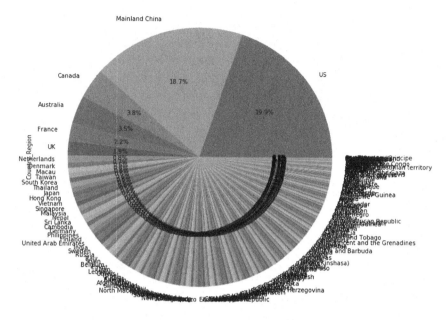

Figure 4.11 Pie chart to analyze which country has the maximum number of cases.

	Confirmed	Deaths	Recovered
count	76.000000	76.000000	76.000000
mean	57149.447368	3803.013158	29688.236842
std	33579.497577	4274.667879	25587.122691
min	444.000000	17.000000	28.000000
25%	31203.750000	948.250000	2115.250000
50%	66125.500000	2704.500000	27698.000000
75%	67800.000000	3192.750000	57115.750000
max	136675.000000	16523.000000	64014.000000

Figure 4.12 Maximum and minimum number of cases.

Table 4.1 Performance of the model for predicting different parameters.

Predicting parameter	Accuracy (%)	Error (%)
Confirmed cases	96	4
Death cases	96	4
Recovered cases	95	5

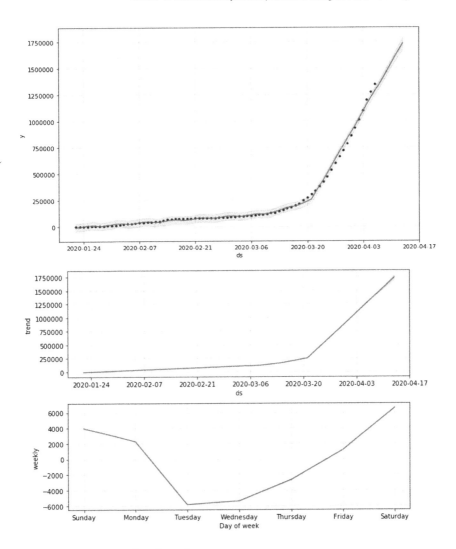

Figure 4.13 Forecast of confirmed cases.

4.6 Conclusion

The presented model helps us in analyzing the global COVID-19 outbreak and also predicts the spread in the coming 7 days. The model predicts the confirmed, death, and recovered cases with 95% accuracy. By analyzing the pie chart we can see that these days the USA has the maximum number of cases and there are 136,675 confirmed cases in the entire world. Now by studying the prediction graphs of confirmed, death, and recovered cases, we

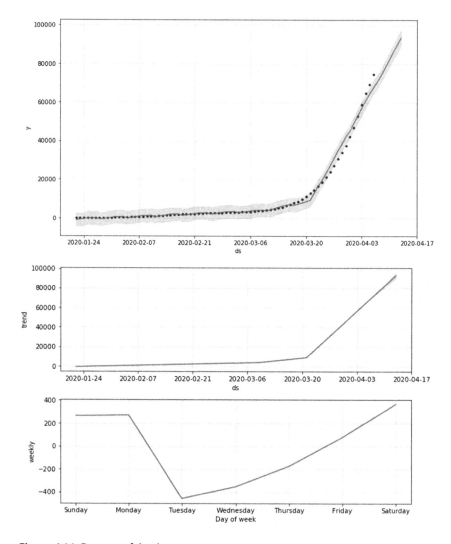

Figure 4.14 Forecast of death cases.

can see that the slope decreases midweek and rises at a rapid pace at the end of the week. These graphs indicate that the number of cases will increase in the coming days but as you can see, the number of recovered cases also increases. Hence we can conclude that if we do not take precautions the spread of this virus will increase rapidly.

References

[1] G. Aneiros-Pérez, P. Vieu, Nonparametric time series prediction: a semi-functional partial linear modeling, Journal of Multivariate Analysis 99 (5) (2008) 834–857.

[2] Y. Bao, T. Xiong, Z. Hu, Multi-step-ahead time series prediction using multiple-output support vector regression, Neurocomputing 129 (2014) 482–493.

[3] C.L. Wu, K.W. Chau, Data-driven models for monthly streamflow time series prediction, Engineering Applications of Artificial Intelligence 23 (8) (2010) 1350–1367.

[4] R.N. Yadav, P.K. Kalra, J. John, Time series prediction with single multiplicative neuron model, Applied Soft Computing 7 (4) (2007) 1157–1163.

[5] Y.A. Le Borgne, S. Santini, G. Bontempi, Adaptive model selection for time series prediction in wireless sensor networks, Signal Processing 87 (12) (2007) 3010–3020.

[6] S. Brahim-Belhouari, A. Bermak, Gaussian process for nonstationary time series prediction, Computational Statistics & Data Analysis 47 (4) (2004) 705–712.

[7] U. Thissen, R. Van Brakel, A.P. De Weijer, W.J. Melssen, L.M.C. Buydens, Using support vector machines for time series prediction, Chemometrics and Intelligent Laboratory Systems 69 (1-2) (2003) 35–49.

[8] M. Zounemat-Kermani, M. Teshnehlab, Using adaptive neuro-fuzzy inference system for hydrological time series prediction, Applied Soft Computing 8 (2) (2008) 928–936.

[9] P. Melin, J. Soto, O. Castillo, J. Soria, A new approach for time series prediction using ensembles of ANFIS models, Expert Systems with Applications 39 (3) (2012) 3494–3506.

[10] E. Kayacan, B. Ulutas, O. Kaynak, Grey system theory-based models in time series prediction, Expert Systems with Applications 37 (2) (2010) 1784–1789.

[11] L. Zhao, Y. Yang, PSO-based single multiplicative neuron model for time series prediction, Expert Systems with Applications 36 (2) (2009) 2805–2812.

[12] D.Ö. Faruk, A hybrid neural network and ARIMA model for water quality time series prediction, Engineering Applications of Artificial Intelligence 23 (4) (2010) 586–594.

[13] R. Zemouri, D. Racoceanu, N. Zerhouni, Recurrent radial basis function network for time series prediction, Engineering Applications of Artificial Intelligence 16 (5–6) (2003) 453–463.

[14] X. Wang, M. Han, Online sequential extreme learning machine with kernels for nonstationary time series prediction, Neurocomputing 145 (2014) 90–97.

[15] L. Zhang, W.D. Zhou, P.C. Chang, J.W. Yang, F.Z. Li, Iterated time series prediction with multiple support vector regression models, Neurocomputing 99 (2013) 411–422.

[16] R. Chandra, M. Zhang, Cooperative coevolution of Elman recurrent neural networks for chaotic time series prediction, Neurocomputing 86 (2012) 116–123.

[17] M. Ardalani-Farsa, S. Zolfaghari, Chaotic time series prediction with residual analysis method using hybrid Elman–NARX neural networks, Neurocomputing 73 (13–15) (2010) 2540–2553.

[18] S.F. Crone, N. Kourentzes, Feature selection for time series prediction–a combined filter and wrapper approach for neural networks, Neurocomputing 73 (10–12) (2010) 1923–1936.

[19] C.M. Lee, C.N. Ko, Time series prediction using RBF neural networks with a nonlinear time-varying evolution PSO algorithm, Neurocomputing 73 (1–3) (2009) 449–460.

[20] H. Yang, K. Huang, I. King, M.R. Lyu, Localized support vector regression for time series prediction, Neurocomputing 72 (10–12) (2009) 2659–2669.

[21] J.M.P. MenezesJr, G.A. Barreto, Long-term time series prediction with the NARX network: an empirical evaluation, Neurocomputing 71 (16–18) (2008) 3335–3343.

[22] I. Rojas, O. Valenzuela, F. Rojas, A. Guillén, L.J. Herrera, H. Pomares, M. Pasadas, Soft-computing techniques and ARMA model for time series prediction, Neurocomputing 71 (4–6) (2008) 519–537.

[23] A. Sorjamaa, J. Hao, N. Reyhani, Y. Ji, A. Lendasse, Methodology for long-term prediction of time series, Neurocomputing 70 (16–18) (2007) 2861–2869.

[24] X. Cai, N. Zhang, G.K. Venayagamoorthy, D.C. Wunsch II, Time series prediction with recurrent neural networks trained by a hybrid PSO–EA algorithm, Neurocomputing 70 (13–15) (2007) 2342–2353.

[25] C. Harpham, C.W. Dawson, The effect of different basis functions on a radial basis function network for time series prediction: a comparative study, Neurocomputing 69 (16–18) (2006) 2161–2170.

[26] Y. Chen, B. Yang, J. Dong, Time-series prediction using a local linear wavelet neural network, Neurocomputing 69 (4–6) (2006) 449–465.

[27] T. Van Gestel, J.A. Suykens, D.E. Baestaens, A. Lambrechts, G. Lanckriet, B. Vandaele, J. Vandewalle, Financial time series prediction using least squares support vector machines within the evidence framework, IEEE Transactions on Neural Networks 12 (4) (2001) 809–821.

[28] C. Richard, J.C.M. Bermudez, P. Honeine, Online prediction of time series data with kernels, IEEE Transactions on Signal Processing 57 (3) (2008) 1058–1067.

[29] Y. Qin, D. Song, H. Chen, W. Cheng, G. Jiang, G. Cottrell, A dual-stage attention-based recurrent neural network for time series prediction, arXiv preprint, arXiv:1704.02971, 2017.

[30] J.T. Connor, R.D. Martin, L.E. Atlas, Recurrent neural networks and robust time series prediction, IEEE Transactions on Neural Networks 5 (2) (1994) 240–254.

[31] E.S. Chng, S. Chen, B. Mulgrew, Gradient radial basis function networks for nonlinear and nonstationary time series prediction, IEEE Transactions on Neural Networks 7 (1) (1996) 190–194.

[32] O. Castillo, P. Melin, Hybrid intelligent systems for time series prediction using neural networks, fuzzy logic, and fractal theory, IEEE Transactions on Neural Networks 13 (6) (2002) 1395–1408.

[33] D. Li, M. Han, J. Wang, Chaotic time series prediction based on a novel robust echo state network, IEEE Transactions on Neural Networks and Learning Systems 23 (5) (2012) 787–799.

[34] Y. Gao, M.J. Er, NARMAX time series model prediction: feedforward and recurrent fuzzy neural network approaches, Fuzzy Sets and Systems 150 (2) (2005) 331–350.

[35] K. Dev, S.A. Khowaja, A. Jaiswal, A.S. Bist, V. Saini, S. Bhatia, Triage of potential COVID-19 patients from chest X-ray images using hierarchical convolutional networks, arXiv preprint, arXiv:2011.00618, 2020.

[36] K. Chakraborty, S. Bhatia, S. Bhattacharyya, J. Platos, R. Bag, A.E. Hassanien, Sentiment analysis of COVID-19 tweets by deep learning classifiers—a study to show how popularity is affecting accuracy in social media, Applied Soft Computing 97 (2020) 106754.

CHAPTER 5

Verbal sentiment analysis and detection using recurrent neural network

Mohan Debarchan Mohanty[a] **and Mihir Narayan Mohanty**[b]

[a]College of Engineering and Technology, Biju Pattnaik University of Technology, Bhubaneswar, India
[b]ITER (FET), Siksha 'O' Anusandhan (Deemed to be University), Bhubaneswar, India

5.1 Introduction

Human sentiment is the expression of one's mental state. Attitude can be expressed and recorded in the form of text, image, video, and speech. The analysis of human attitudes using machines is a difficult task. Currently, the field of human attitude expression analysis is growing exponentially. The area of research results in real-life application. The goal is to establish an automated and machine-based process, but enhancing accuracy is a major challenge. The popularity of this research is also increasing in both the academic and industry sectors. It helps to detect and classify various types of human emotion and attitude by analyzing different aspects. It plays a major role in crime detection. In the current research, the application includes criminal activity detection, lie detection, business and commerce, politics and polling, cyber security, medicine, etc. Detection through effective traces like voice, video and multi-modal sentiment analysis results in a certain accuracy level. Basically text, video, and internet contents are noisy and unstructured [1–5]. However, text-based sentiment analysis with machine learning models is in progress. It is used for customer satisfaction in businesses and is quite developed research that solves some industrial inconveniences. Nevertheless, other aspects of sentiment analysis are to be considered, such as only verbal communication and visualization. There are three major classes in multi-modal-based studies on sentiments: (i) spoken reviews [6–8], (ii) human–machine interactions [9], and (iii) visual sentiment analysis [10].

In [11], sentiment is defined as continuing temperament evoked when persons encounter an exact matter, human being, or thing. Sentiment analysis from text has been applied to some applications including stock

Advanced Data Mining Tools and Methods for Social Computing
https://doi.org/10.1016/B978-0-32-385708-6.00012-6
85

market performance prediction [12], movie box-office performance prediction [13], and election result prediction [14]. Concern, reaction, sensation, and judgment are used interchangeably for qualitative sentiment testing [15]. The authors of [16] tried to define emotions that differ from the mood. According to this study, emotions are a temporary phenomenon that necessitates triggers and involves reactions, psychological changes, actions, expressions, and feelings.

Similarly, in [15] the authors discussed the variation amongst emotion, view, sentiment, and sensation within the perspective of text expression. They differentiated the sentiment from emotion depending on their duration and depicted that sentiment is long-standing whereas emotion is temporary. Additionally, opinion is an expression that does not need to be emotionally charged. Due to this reason sentiment testing is determined based on the detection of the polarity of different opinions (either positive or sometimes negative). According to cognitive theory explained in [17], a synchronized set of analysis of an object, entity, or incident is graded as emotions and counted as sentiment.

However, it is not clear how sentiment is represented in terms of sentimental characters and by isolated emotions. The emotions of a person result from his or her sentiment. As an example, an individual may suffer from sadness due to the bad health condition or demise of a dear one. So, the positive sentiment towards the loved one or the adverse condition due to the sentimental link results in a kind of emotion, in essence, termed sadness. Furthermore, the analysis has progressed so far with the following.

5.2 Sources for sentiment detection

Sentiment can be analyzed from different sources. Several of such sources to detect sentiment from human beings are discussed in this section.

5.2.1 Sentiment in text

In the early 2000s, many works have been performed on sentiment analysis from text. Pang and Lee reviewed this in [18], and some new algorithms are suggested in recent research works.

5.2.2 Sentiment analysis in visionary data

Several works have been developed based on vision-oriented emotion recognition. These works are developed for sentiment analysis by utilizing popular computer vision techniques [19,20] by (i) modeling, (ii) detecting, and (iii) leveraging information about sentiment present in facial expressions and body gestures and from different multimedia resources. In the later stage, the objective is to identify the same type of sentiment through visual multimedia as through human observers. A few authors have worked on sentiment detection from multimedia data sources [21,22].

5.2.3 Sentiment analysis in speech

Detection of sentiment from speech by analyzing the utterance variations is a quite new field for researchers. Focusing on the auditory part of verbal communication, the recognition of variation among the characteristics of sentiment and emotion is difficult [23]. In [24], Mairesseet *et al.* have focused on pitch information related to different features and concluded that pitch contains more information about sentiment than textual cues. Costa Pereira *et al.* [25] developed an algorithm to recover the information from speech for sentiment detection. They considered a query, spoken by a person, and recovered the documents that represent the documents related to the query. Similar work was performed by Perez-Rosas and Mihalcea [26], who focused more on the linguistic data from spoken reviews using a speech processing technique. Kaushik *et al.* [27,28] focused on spontaneous speech signals generated in a natural way for sentiment analysis. A trend has been observed by Metze *et al.* [29] that the recognition of sentiment is increasing more in recent works from natural spontaneous speech signals.

5.3 Literature survey

Sentiment analysis has become an active research area since very little work has been done in this field. There is a wide range of applications and benefits to businesses, organizations, and industry. It is important to know about the people's opinion on a topic, news, product, and brand. These research problems are related to many practical challenges. This provides a strong motivation to conduct research in this field, which has never been studied before. Some of the related works are mentioned in the next section.

Using polarity and its intensity, sentiment evaluation can be described in a single-dimensional space. To represent the sentiment of a person, emotion, arousal, valence, dominance, and predictability are necessary. These can be enhanced by utilizing multi-level sentiment analysis. For this, the intensity of sentiment was analyzed [30,31]. An enhanced random subspace method considering a part of speech analysis was projected for sentiment analysis in terms of classification of different types of sentiments [19]. The content lexicon subspace rate and utility lexicon subspace rate were utilized for the purpose of controlling stability among the diversity and accuracy of support learners. The efficiency of the proposed algorithm is tested by using 10 publicly available datasets on sentiment. Stylistic as well as syntactic features were utilized to classify opinions present in different web forums in different languages. For Arabic speech signals, different feature extraction techniques were considered and integrated with linguistic characters. The entropy-weighted genetic algorithm (EWGA) was also developed, which is a hybridized genetic algorithm that incorporates the information gain heuristic for feature selection. Features were selected by incorporating the data gained by EWGA, which was formed by hybridizing different genetic algorithms. The basic purpose of designing EWGA was to get better performance and a better evaluation of the concerned features. The projected features and algorithms were tested on a standard dataset of movie reviews and the US and Middle Eastern web medium postings. The results obtained by the combined structure of EWGA and support vector machine (SVM) indicate a very high performance in comparison to the state-of-the-art methods[32].

In favor of automatic detection of sentiment from natural audio-based streaming documents, authors have developed a combined method using part of speech tagging as well as maximum entropy (ME) modeling. Furthermore, they proposed another technique based on tuning of signals that sensationally decreases the number of model characteristics in ME while classification competency is maintained [27]. Using the decoded speech for automatic recognition and the ME sentiment model, the projected method was able to approximate the correct sentiment. An approach enabling an interactive dialogue system to recognize user emotion and sentiment in real-time was discussed in [33].

A new methodology for multi-modal sentiment analysis was proposed in [21]. Sentiment analysis was conducted for different videos from the web by introducing a model that uses audio, video, and textual modalities as an information source. These features were extracted using the decision-level fusion method. The sentiment can be classified in utterance-level and visual data streams. To extract the sentiment from video reviews, a multi-modal dataset consisting of sentiment annotated utterances was used. With this, the multi-modal sentiment analysis can be effectively performed [34]. To perform sentiment analysis of short texts, a deep convolutional neural network (CNN) was used. This method exploited sentence-level information from characters. They applied a methodology for two corpora of two unique spaces: the Stanford Sentiment Treebank (SST), which contains sentences from film audits, and the Stanford Twitter Sentiment corpus (STS), which contains Twitter messages [35]. A deep neural network model was used with the parallel combination of CNN and long short-term memory (LSTM)-based network. The audio sentiment vector (ASV) was analyzed as a feature and it reflected the sentiment information in an audio [22]. This model was trained by utterance-level data and ASV was extracted and fused creatively. In the CNN model branch, spectrum graphs produced by signals are fed as inputs while in the LSTM model branch, inputs include spectral centroid (SC), Mel-frequency cepstral coefficient (MFCC), and other recognized traditional acoustic features that were extracted from dependent utterances in an audio.

The deep learning-based framework could identify the top malware/carding sellers [36]. The authors used snowball sampling and thread classification to estimate sellers' product and service quality depending on customer feedback. This framework donates to secretive economy research since it provides the generalizable framework for identifying the key cybercrime architects.

Several attempts were made to build a sentiment analysis classifier for spoken reviews [7]. The goal is to understand the difference in sentiment classification performance while utilizing the manual against automatic transcriptions, as well as the spoken versus written reviews. A new dataset was introduced that consists of videos of cellular phones and fiction books. Similarly, the Twitter data could be analyzed for sentiment analysis purposes [37]. Part of speech (POS) and features were analyzed by using the tree kernel. Different features can be considered for sentiment analysis such as visual forces of perceived feelings, field sizes of members, voicing likelihood, sound din, discourse principal frequencies, and the assumption scores (polarities) from text sentences in the shut inscription [38].

5.4 Machine learning techniques for sentiment analysis

There are two types of machine learning techniques, namely supervised and unsupervised techniques. The supervised approach builds a feature vector of each input in which certain aspects are quantified to train the machine learning tools. It is validated against reference annotated texts. Supervised sentiment analysis was used for the classification of texts as subjective or objective [39], using annotations that tag evaluative content but not its orientation. Naive Bayes classifiers and SVMs were used as machine learning models adopted in many earlier works. These approaches calculated features over bag-of-words models of the reviews [40]. Another improvement over this approach was used as treebanks in [41]. Most supervised approaches to sentiment analysis are trained in a certain domain or communication context, such as social media or news. A combination of ME and stochastic gradient descent optimizations is proposed in [42]. A tool called Swiss Cheese [43] achieved the best results to date by training CNNs with large datasets of Tweets with emoticons. Some of the authors claimed that the bootstrap parametric ensemble framework performs best on average [44].

While unsupervised methodologies permit an estimation dependent on master information without explained information, the master information utilized for the estimation is frequently encoded. One of the most broadly utilized reference lexica for notion examination is the General Inquirer (GI) [45], which takes a rundown of positive and negative terms. The GI is frequently joined with other lexica [46], as an approach to expand the review of solo strategies.

As clarified by Das and Chen [47], solo estimation examination can ascertain more exact sentence-level groupings through theoretical conditions, motivated by the idea of language as a semantic processor that extracts the important information from a sentence [48]. This is actualized through logical valence shifters: decides that distinguish changes in valence by recognizing nullifications, intensifications, and so on [49].

As of late, it is seen that the most encouraging advancement in assumption examination is the use of profound learning. Portrayal learning can use enormous scope datasets to process word embeddings that are important for conclusion examination, creating naturally broadened lexica [50]. While the deduction of word classes dependent on profound learning strategies is accomplishing results near those of human annotators [51], extrapolating word slant persistent factors dependent on word embeddings still requires critical work [52]. Profound recurrent neural networks (RNNs) have been applied to the assignment of subjectivity recognition [41], and word vector portrayals can consolidate directed and unaided realization when applied to slant examination [53]. Regarding Twitter supposition investigation rivalries, so far the most outstanding accomplishments of profound learning are a portion of the top situations in different SemEval rivalries, which have applications to dialects other than English [54,55]. As of now, one of the most generally utilized bundles for profound learning depends on treebank comments and was prepared on film audit datasets, and is remembered for the Stanford CoreNLP suite7. The issue of supposition examination in the text is a long way from illuminated; however, recent advancements have made opinion investigation a reality.

5.5 Proposed method

As mentioned, many ways have been adopted by researchers since some decades. However, some challenges and arguments are still there as the definition could not provide a clear view. In this work, human voices are considered by considering those arguments. One such content regards emotion and sentiment. As we feel and observe, both feelings are inter-dependent. Without sentiment, there is no emotion and vice versa. The environment along with the mental condition creates human sentiments. Therefore, the negative, neutral, and positive sentiments are considered in this work as aggressive, cool, and jolly, respectively. Short-term aggression is considered in case of a traffic jam and the voice is recorded as "Oh shit what a horrible condition," whereas long-term aggression is taken for example when loved ones pass away, with phrases such as "Oh my God, what's happening to me" and "Why such loss?" In case of a cool situation, a monk-like voice is recorded saying phrases like "It is destiny, why worry?" and "Be loyal to your work." For a short-term and long-term jolly mood, the voice is recorded saying phrases like "Wow, it is a beautiful movie" and "Thank God for my success," respectively. Based on these voices the spectral features are extracted and used in deep RNN.

5.5.1 Feature extraction

Pitch, vitality, beat, etc., are responsible for the voice quality and are the most significant acoustic boundaries. To profit acknowledgment, a separa-tion between phoneme classes utilizing a more extravagant arrangement of ghostly highlights stays alive toward this path. These class-level casing-based otherworldly highlights have outflanked the comparing highlights separated at the expression level. This has driven the creators to decide on the ex-traction of casing-level spectral roll-off (SR), SC, and spectral flux (SF) alongside the well-known MFCCs for this errand. An edge length of 256 examples with 128 examples outline move on every expression has been utilized for this reason. Every articulation is pre-handled with a low-pass channel with Hamming window that has been utilized.

5.5.2 Spectral centroid

The spectral tilt and slope of a signal can be found by using this feature extraction technique. The spectrum of every signal frame of an utterance is extracted from the signal by using the following relation;

$$SC_p = \frac{\left(\sum_{k=1}^{\frac{N}{2}} f(k) \times |S_p(k)|\right)}{\left(\sum_{k=1}^{\frac{N}{2}} |S_p(k)|\right)}, \tag{5.1}$$

where $S_p(k)$ is the short-time Fourier transform (STFT) of every frame $p, p = 1, 2, \ldots, P$. For a signal $s(n)$ with some fast Fourier transform (FFT) points N, the frequency at bin k is denoted by $f(k)$. High values of SC_p indicate sharpness (brighter texture) or the presence of high-frequency content in an emotional signal [51]. The value of N is considered as 256 in the proposed approach.

5.5.3 Spectral roll-off

In this approach, the frequency of minimum fractions of energy residues is used. In the case of a right-skewed speech signal, the maximum value is used which can be used for analyzing the different speech emotions. The mathematical representation of this approach is

$$\sum_{k=1}^{K} |S_p(k)| \leq 0.85 \sum_{k=1}^{\frac{N}{2}} |S_p(k)|, \tag{5.2}$$

where K represents the maximum bin, the SR (SR_p) equal to $f(k)$. The spectral component of human hearing is in log scale in nature. A *PSD* value of 0.85 relates to the voiced part of the speech. It is an empirical value. Hence it is considered in *SR* computation, though it can vary between 0.8 and 0.95 based on different signal conditions.

5.5.4 Spectral flux

The SF provides information on the change in the local spectrum. It varies between different emotions and can be expressed as

$$SF_p = \sum_{k=1}^{N/2} \left(|S_p(k)| - |S_{p-1}(k)|\right)^2. \tag{5.3}$$

5.5.5 Mel-frequency cepstral coefficient

The spectrum of the signal having frequency 'f' is scaled into Mel-frequency f' using the relation

$$f' = 2595 \times log_{10}\left(\frac{f}{700}\right). \tag{5.4}$$

Computing the logarithm of Mel-frequency coefficients and then applying discrete Cosine transform (DCT) gives us the desired MFCCs.

Initially, extract $C = 16$ MFCCs from each utterance of an emotion. For P frames per utterance, the size of the MFCC feature matrix becomes $P \times C$. Generate a vector using the first MFCCs ($c = 1$) of all the frames of an utterance where $c = 1, 2, \ldots, C$. It can be represented as $L_1 1, L_2 1, \ldots, L_P 1$. Similarly, other MFCC feature vectors for $c = 2, c = 3, \ldots, c = 16$ are formed and can be represented as

$$L_u = [L_{11}, L_{21}, \ldots, L_{P1}], [L_{12}, L_{22}, \ldots, L_{P2}], \ldots, [L_{1C}, L_{2C}, \ldots, L_{PC}], \tag{5.5}$$

where $u = 1, 2, \ldots, U$ is the number of utterances in an emotional state.

5.5.6 Pitch

Pitch is one of the most important features in emotion recognition. It represents the fundamental frequency. Depending on age and gender, the pitch varies and is dependent on the recognition technique for preventing misclassification. In the proposed approach an auto-correlation function (ACF) is considered for estimating pitch.

5.5.7 Multi-layer perceptron

The multi-layer perceptron (MLP) is another artificial neural network process containing a number of layers. In a single perceptron, distinctly linear problems can be solved but it is not well suitable for non–linear cases. To solve these complex problems, MLP can be considered. From the network architecture presented in Fig. 5.1, it can be observed that MLP is a feedforward neural network combined with multiple layers. Generally, it is used in case of different machine learning purposes.

The weights of the network are set in random order before starting the training. After completing the learning step by using the training data (x_1, x_2, y), the model is validated. In the training set, data x_1 and x_2 are the

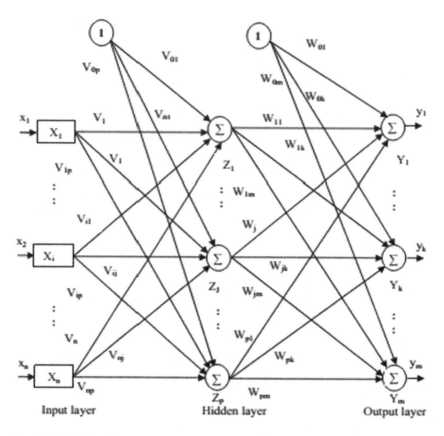

Figure 5.1 MLP architecture.

input and y is the corresponding expected output of the input data. The output is dependent on neurons and the weight of the neural network. It can be represented by

$$y = wx + b, \tag{5.6}$$

where w is the weight and b is the bias.

The weighted vector and inclination vector of the main layer creates the weighted network and is referred as the inclination vector of the subsequent layer for the non-linear component [11,12]. The yield is associated with the contributions of different neurons in the shrouded layer and is not noticeable in the yield [12]. the yield assigns as 0 and. 0 indicates no diabetes and 1 indicates diabetes.

5.5.8 Radial basis function network

A radial basis function network (RBFN) consists of an input layer, a hidden layer, and a linear output layer as presented in Fig. 5.2. In the proposed RBFN, 10 input, 7 hidden, and 4 output neurons are considered. The number of input neurons is the same as the number of features. The classifier classifies each sample into one of four electrocardiogram (ECG) classes. So the output neuron size is 4. In total, 7 hidden neurons are present in the hidden layer because if we use more neurons, then there is a chance of overfitting. Also, using too few neurons in the hidden layer will create an underfitting problem. Overfitting and underfitting affect the performance of the classifier. In the proposed approach, the Gaussian kernel is used as a kernel function. The hidden layer is dependent on a non–linear RBF kernel function. The network output can be obtained by finding the distance aiming the input data vector and center vector of the Gaussian function. The output matrix can be obtained by

$$
\begin{bmatrix} y_l \\ y_2 \\ \vdots \\ y_j \end{bmatrix} = \begin{bmatrix} R\,\|x_1 - c_1\| & R\,\|x_1 - c_2\| & \cdots & R\,\|x_1 - c_j\| \\ R\,\|x_2 - c_1\| & R\,\|x_2 - c_2\| & \cdots & R\,\|x_2 - c_j\| \\ \vdots & \vdots & \vdots & \vdots \\ R\,\|x_j - c_1\| & R\,\|x_j - c_2\| & \cdots & R\,\|x_j - c_j\| \end{bmatrix} \begin{bmatrix} w_1 \\ w_2 \\ \vdots \\ w_j \end{bmatrix},
$$

$$(5.7)$$

where R is the RBF, c_j is the center, $|x - c_j|$ is the distance between input and the center. $x_1, x_2, ..., x_j$ are the input neurons, $y_1, y_2, ..., y_j$ are the output neurons, and $w_1, w_2, ..., w_j$ are the weights of the network. The target output is obtained by updating the corresponding weights. The output to weight and input is given as

$$
y = \sum_{j=1}^{N} R\left(\|x - c_j\|\right) w_j, \tag{5.8}
$$

where w_j is the weight of the jth center and N is the length of the data. The network is operated with the kernel function that is Gaussian and is expressed as

$$
R\left(\|x - c_j\|\right) = \exp\left[-\frac{(x - c_j)^2}{2\sigma^2}\right], \tag{5.9}
$$

where σ is the width of the center.

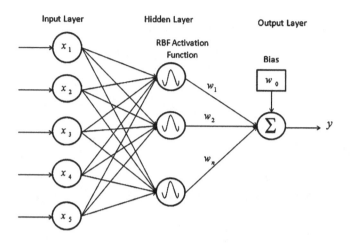

Figure 5.2 Structure of the RBF network.

5.5.9 Probabilistic neural network

The selection of a suitable classifier for emotion recognition is a challenging job. Well-known classifiers for emotion classification are the linear discriminant analysis classifier and k-nearest neighbor (kNN) classifiers that have been utilized in numerous studies [17–20].

Even though probabilistic neural network (PNN) is not the best classifier, it gives great measurable properties. Classification performances of decision trees, for example, RF, artificial neural networks (ANNs), and PNN, are comparable. ANN needs most estimation time, while the preparation and testing for RF generally take longer than for PNN.

Neural networks have numerous weaknesses, for example, complex enhancement, low strength, and much preparation time. Irregular forest interestingly is easy to use, since just a single variable must be set by the client. Be that as it may, its characterization accuracy cannot fulfill the artificial intelligence strategies while its vigor was among the best [27,28]. PNN is a unique class of RBFs utilized for characterization [21,22,24–28]. It is advantageous to numerous applications of emotion recognition. It is one of the non-parametric strategies. This sort of system embraces probabilistic techniques to arrange the information. The PNNs are successful discriminative classifiers with a few extraordinary attributes; specifically, they are a lot quicker and more exact than MLP systems. The systems are generally insensitive to anomalies having a naturally equal structure and behave like an ideal classifier as the size of the preparation set increases. PNN depends on Bayes ideal grouping. PNNs can create exact anticipated objective like-lihood scores with no neighborhood minimum issues. No broad retraining is necessary if preparing tests are included or excluded.

These qualities make PNNs effective. In PNN, the activities are sorted out into a multi-layered feedforward system with four layers: an input layer, a design layer, the summation layer, and a yield layer. On a very basic level, it depends on the Bayesian classifier strategy. The main layer disperses the contribution to the neurons in the example layers. This layer utilizing the given arrangement of information focuses as the focuses structures the Gaussian capacities. It classifies the preparation set with the end goal that each info vector is spoken to by an individual handling layer called the summation layer. The number of handling components is equal to the number of classes to be perceived in the summation layer. Information is transferred from the info testing vectors to the information preparing vectors and processed, and a vector that shows the closeness of the preparation and testing inputs is delivered. For each class of testing inputs the summation layer entireties the commitments of past layer yield by giving a net yield vector of probabilities. Essentially an averaging activity of the yields from the example layer for each class is performed by the summation layer. A PNN utilizes a Parzen window probabilistic thickness work estimator for every one of the classes with a blend of Gaussian premise capacities [26]. Fig. 5.3 shows the essential structure of the PNN.

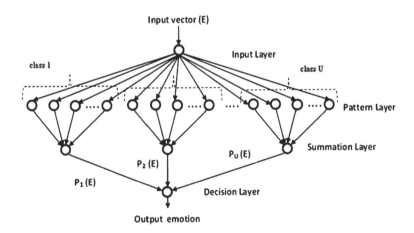

Figure 5.3 PNN architecture.

5.5.10 Recurrent neural network

RNN is a type of supervised learning neural network model. In this model, neurons are connected with one or more feedback loops. These input circles are intermittent cycles after some time or succession. The training of the RNN is conducted in a supervised manner that needs a training set that represents the input and expected output. The aim is to optimize the weights of the neural network for minimizing variations among the output and target. Input, recurrent hidden, and output layers are the three basic layers in a simple RNN. The structure of the RNN model is presented in Fig. 5.4.

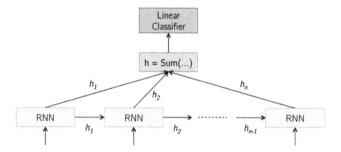

Figure 5.4 RNN architecture.

5.5.11 Deep RNNs with multi-layer perceptron

Deep models of neural systems can speak to a capacity exponentially more productive than shallow designs. While RNNs are innately somewhere deep in the time given each shrouded state is a component of all past concealed states, it has been indicated that the interior calculations are actuality very shallow. The deep mechanism in RNNs with perceptron can be categorized into three approaches such as input to hidden, hidden to hidden, and hidden to output.

5.5.12 Deep input to hidden

One of the fundamental goals is to convey the MLP structure into the progress and output layer, which is known as deep RNNs and deep output RNNs, respectively. For obtaining such a strategy, two parameters can be considered. The first is an additive $\oplus$ operator, that takes two vectors, the input vector x and hidden state h, and whose operation is represented as

$$h' = X \oplus h. \tag{5.10}$$

A more significant portrayal of information implies a simpler portrayal of connections between transient structures of information. This strategy has accomplished better outcomes than when taking care of the system with unique information in discourse acknowledgment and word implanting applications. In Fig. 5.5 the architecture of RNN with MLP is introduced.

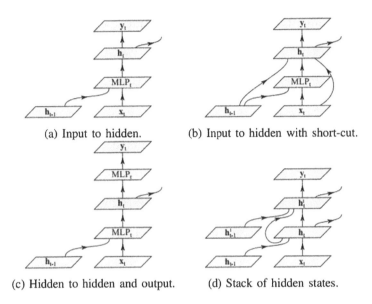

(a) Input to hidden.   (b) Input to hidden with short-cut.

(c) Hidden to hidden and output.   (d) Stack of hidden states.

Figure 5.5 Architecture of DRNN with MLP.

5.5.13 Deep hidden to hidden and output

Most information for deep RNNs is present in the hidden layers. In this step, the method of information deliberation, as well as hidden layer development from past datasets and updated input data, is exceptionally non-linear. An MLP can demonstrate this non-linear capacity, which encourages an RNN to rapidly adjust to quickly changing input data while having a decent memory of past occasions. An RNN can have both an MLP experiencing significant change and an MLP before the output layer (a model is introduced in Fig. 5.4) [44]. A deeply hidden layer up to the output layer can unravel the variables of varieties in the hidden state and encourage achievement of the objective. This function permits a more minimized hidden state of the network, which may bring about a more educational recorded rundown of the past data inputs.

The input layer has N input units. The contributions to this layer is a succession of vectors through time t, for example, $\{..., x_{t-1}, x_t, x_{t+1}, ...\}$, where $xt = (x_1, x_2, ..., x_N)$. The information units in a completely associated RNN are associated with the concealed units in the shrouded layer, where the associations are characterized with a weight lattice W_{IH}. The shrouded layer has M concealed units $h_t = (h_1, h_2, ..., h_M)$, that are associated with one another through time with intermittent associations (Fig. 5.5b). The statement of concealed units utilizing little non-zero components can generally improve execution and strength of the system. The concealed layer characterizes the state space or "memory" of the framework as

$$h_t = f \cdot h(o_t), \tag{5.11}$$

where $o_t = W_{IH}X_t + W_{HH}X_t + b_h$, $fH(\cdot)$ is the hidden layer activation function, and bh is the bias vector of the hidden units. The hidden units are connected to the output layer with weighted connections WHO. The output layer has P units $y_t = (y_1, y_2, ..., y_P)$ that are computed as

$$y_t = f_o(W_{HO}h_t + b_0), \tag{5.12}$$

where $f_o(\cdot)$ is the initiation capacities and b_0 is the predisposition vector in the yield layer. Since the info target sets are consecutive through time, the above advances are rehashed subsequently after some time $t = (1, ..., T)$. Eqs. (5.1) and (5.3) show an RNN is comprised of certain non-direct state conditions, which are inerrable through time. In each time step, the shrouded states give an expectation at the yield layer dependent on the information vector. The concealed condition of an RNN is a lot of qualities, which separated from the impact of any outer elements sums up all the extraordinary fundamental data about the past conditions of the system over many time steps. These coordinated data can characterize the future behavior of the system and make exact expectations at the yield layer. An RNN utilizes a basic non-linear actuation work in each unit. Be that as it may, such a straightforward structure is equipped for displaying rich elements, on the off chance that it is very much prepared through time steps.

5.5.14 Gradient-based learning methods

In the deep learning approach, gradient descent (GD) is one of the popular optimization algorithms for adjusting the weights of the network. The basic principle of this optimization technique is to find the optimized weights by calculating the derivatives of the error function concerning every weight matrix of the model. To minimize the loss, the optimization algorithm changes the value of the weights which is a derivative of the error rate proportional to the weights. It happens by the output of the considered non-linear activation function. This optimizing approach is also known as batch GD, which calculates the gradient value of the entire dataset at every iteration. The proposed approach can be represented by

$$\theta_{t+1} = \theta_t - \frac{\lambda}{x} \sum_{k=1}^{U} \frac{\partial L}{\partial \theta}, \qquad (5.13)$$

where X represents the considered training set data, the learning rate is represented by λ, and θ denotes the set of parameters. The proposed approach is very cost-expansive in case of huge training datasets and does not perform well in online training.

We can process a series of vectors x by concerning a repetition method at each timestamp:

$$h_t = f_w(h_{t-1}, x_t), \qquad (5.14)$$

where h_t is the new state, f_w is the function with parameter w, h_{t-1} is the old state, and x_t is the time stamp.

The state consists of a single "hidden" vector h:

$$h_t = f_w(h(t-1), x_t), \qquad (5.15)$$
$$h_t = tanh(W_{hh}h_{t-1} + W_{xx}x_t), \qquad (5.16)$$
$$y_t = W_{hy}h_t. \qquad (5.17)$$

5.6 Results and discussion

The parameters of the RNN classifier are chosen for obtaining optimized results. In the proposed case, the batch size is considered as 64 and the learning rate is 0.12. The momentum coefficient 0.7 is fixed in the case of the first epoch and it gradually increases subsequently to 0.84 for the other epochs. The dropout rate for the input and hidden layers is 0.4 and 0.9, respectively.

In the proposed work a non-linear activation function is taken with RNN. As the proposed classification approach is designed for a multi-class classification problem, the softmax activation function is used in the output layer. It calculates the posterior probability of each corresponding class. The

RNN is trained with the backpropagation algorithm that derives the cost function. The cost function is used for measuring the cross-entropy among the target probabilities and softmax output value. For designing a generalized neural network classifier, the amount of neurons is kept equal for every hidden layer. As the aim is to classify five different types of emotions, the final output layer is the composition of five types of softmax activation layer. Each activation layer corresponds to each human emotion. It is chosen for obtaining an average output score.

Likewise, the activation function $exp\left[\frac{(W_i-W')^T(W_i-W')}{2\sigma^2}\right]$ has been used for the RNN structure. Here, σ is the smoothing parameter, where W_i and W' are the corresponding weight and the pattern vectors. A complete algorithm on RNN has been well derived in [56]. Table 5.1 is given for the parameters used in deep RNN.

Table 5.1 Deep RNN design parameters.

RNN parameters	Tested values
Learning rate	0.12, 0.24, 0.34, 0.45
Hidden neurons	16, 42, 64, 96, 122, 156

Table 5.2 Accuracy of sentiment prediction using spectral features.

Classifiers	Accuracy					
	Aggression		Cool		Jolly	
	ST	LT	ST	LT	ST	LT
MLP	66.5	61.9	66.4	61.6	67.5	62.0
RBFN	69.2	62.4	69.6	62.0	69.5	62.6
PNN	75.7	70.7	77.3	71.1	74.9	71.3
Deep RNN	93.4	90.2	95.6	91.3	95.5	92.8

From Table 5.2 it can be observed that the DRNN classifier performs better than other neural network-based classifiers. The performance is measured for large dimension features obtained through the frame-level feature extraction approach. The performance of other neural network-based classifiers such as MLP, RBFN, and PNN is not satisfactory in the case of large input data. In over-sensitized training data, the smoothing parameter and dependency variable have a major role.

5.7 Conclusions

In this chapter, we presented our work on the complex task of sentimental analysis from verbal statements. We reviewed the literature and found most of the works have been performed using text, image, video, and multi-modal analysis. Still, we obtained promising results with the verbal statements. However, accuracy may not be sufficient with this method. As the human attitude depends upon the brain function, probably the brain signals for the thought procedure along with expressions like speech, text, image, and video with sufficient data are to be analyzed. This will be done in future work.

References

[1] E. Cambria, B. Schuller, Y. Xia, C. Havasi, New avenues in opinion mining and sentiment analysis, IEEE Intelligent Systems 28 (2013) 15–21.
[2] C. Song, X.K. Wang, P.F. Cheng, J.Q. Wang, L. Li, SACPC: a framework based on probabilistic linguistic terms for short text sentiment analysis, Knowledge-Based Systems (2020) 105572.
[3] J. Guerreiro, P. Rita, How to predict explicit recommendations in online reviews using text mining and sentiment analysis, Journal of Hospitality and Tourism Management 43 (2020) 269–272.
[4] G. Xiao, G. Tu, L. Zheng, T. Zhou, X. Li, S.H. Ahmed, D. Jiang, Multi-modality sentiment analysis in social Internet of things based on hierarchical attentions and CSATTCN with MBM network, IEEE Internet of Things Journal (2020).
[5] Z. Sun, P. Sarma, W. Sethares, Y. Liang, Learning relationships between text, audio, and video via deep canonical correlation for multimodal language analysis, in: Proceedings of the AAAI Conference on Artificial Intelligence, Vol. 34, No. 05, 2020, April, pp. 8992–8999.
[6] L.-P. Morency, R. Mihalcea, P. Doshi, Towards multimodal sentiment analysis: harvesting opinions from the web, in: Proceedings of the 13th International Conference on Multimodal Interfaces, 2011, pp. 169–176.
[7] M. Wöllmer, F. Weninger, T. Knaup, B. Schuller, C. Sun, K. Sagae, et al., Youtube movie reviews: sentiment analysis in an audio-visual context, IEEE Intelligent Systems 28 (2013) 46–53.
[8] V.P. Rosas, R. Mihalcea, L.-P. Morency, Multimodal sentiment analysis of Spanish online videos, IEEE Intelligent Systems 28 (2013) 38–45.
[9] C. Langlet, C. Clavel, Adapting sentiment analysis to face-to-face human-agent interactions: from the detection to the evaluation issues, in: 2015 International Conference on Affective Computing and Intelligent Interaction (ACII), 2015, pp. 14–20.
[10] D. Borth, R. Ji, T. Chen, T. Breuel, S.-F. Chang, Large-scale visual sentiment ontology and detectors using adjective noun pairs, in: Proceedings of the 21st ACM International Conference on Multimedia, 2013, pp. 223–232.
[11] J. Deonna, F. Teroni, The Emotions: A Philosophical Introduction, Routledge, 2012.
[12] J. Bollen, H. Mao, X. Zeng, Twitter mood predicts the stock market, Journal of Computational Science 2 (2011) 1–8.
[13] S. Asur, B.A. Huberman, Predicting the future with social media, in: Proceedings of the 2010 IEEE/WIC/ACM International Conference on Web Intelligence and Intelligent Agent Technology-Volume 01, 2010, pp. 492–499.

[14] A. Tumasjan, T.O. Sprenger, P.G. Sandner, I.M. Welpe, Predicting elections with Twitter: what 140 characters reveal about political sentiment, in: Fourth International AAAI Conference on Weblogs and Social Media, 2010.

[15] M.D. Munezero, C.S. Montero, E. Sutinen, J. Pajunen, Are they different? Affect, feeling, emotion, sentiment, and opinion detection in text, IEEE Transactions on Affective Computing 5 (2014) 101–111.

[16] K.R. Scherer, What are emotions? And how can they be measured?, Social Science Information 44 (2005) 695–729.

[17] K.R. Scherer, A. Schorr, T. Johnstone, Appraisal Processes in Emotion: Theory, Methods, Research, Oxford University Press, 2001.

[18] B. Pang, L. Lee, Opinion mining and sentiment analysis, Foundations and Trends in Information Retrieval 2 (2008) 1–135.

[19] G. Wang, Z. Zhang, J. Sun, S. Yang, C.A. Larson, POS-RS: a random subspace method for sentiment classification based on part-of-speech analysis, Information Processing & Management 51 (2015) 458–479.

[20] S. Poria, E. Cambria, N. Howard, G.-B. Huang, A. Hussain, Fusing audio, visual and textual clues for sentiment analysis from multimodal content, Neurocomputing 174 (2016) 50–59.

[21] Z. Luo, H. Xu, F. Chen, Audio sentiment analysis by heterogeneous signal features learned from utterance-based parallel neural network, in: AffCon@ AAAI, 2019, pp. 80–87.

[22] B. Liu, Sentiment analysis and opinion mining, Synthesis Lectures on Human Language Technologies 5 (2012) 1–167.

[23] S. Crouch, R. Khosla, Sentiment analysis of speech prosody for dialogue adaptation in a diet suggestion program, ACM SIGHIT Record 2 (2012) 8.

[24] F. Mairesse, J. Polifroni, G. Di Fabbrizio, Can prosody inform sentiment analysis? Experiments on short spoken reviews, in: 2012 IEEE International Conference on Acoustics, Speech and Signal Processing (ICASSP), 2012, pp. 5093–5096.

[25] J.C. Pereira, J. Luque, X. Anguera, Sentiment retrieval on web reviews using spontaneous natural speech, in: 2014 IEEE International Conference on Acoustics, Speech and Signal Processing (ICASSP), 2014, pp. 4583–4587.

[26] V. Pérez-Rosas, R. Mihalcea, Sentiment analysis of online spoken reviews, in: INTERSPEECH, 2013, pp. 862–866.

[27] L. Kaushik, A. Sangwan, J.H. Hansen, Sentiment extraction from natural audio streams, in: 2013 IEEE International Conference on Acoustics, Speech and Signal Processing, 2013, pp. 8485–8489.

[28] L. Kaushik, A. Sangwan, J.H. Hansen, Automatic sentiment extraction from YouTube videos, in: 2013 IEEE Workshop on Automatic Speech Recognition and Understanding, 2013, pp. 239–244.

[29] F. Metze, A. Batliner, F. Eyben, T. Polzehl, B. Schuller, S. Steidl, Emotion recognition using imperfect speech recognition, 2010.

[30] A. Zadeh, Micro-opinion sentiment intensity analysis and summarization in online videos, in: Proceedings of the 2015 ACM on International Conference on Multimodal Interaction, 2015, pp. 587–591.

[31] J.R. Fontaine, K.R. Scherer, E.B. Roesch, P.C. Ellsworth, The world of emotions is not two-dimensional, Psychological Science 18 (2007) 1050–1057.

[32] M.N. Mohanty, B. Jena, Analysis of stressed human speech, International Journal of Computational Vision and Robotics 2 (2011) 180–187.

[33] E. Kouloumpis, T. Wilson, J. Moore, Twitter sentiment analysis: the good the bad and the omg!, in: Fifth International AAAI Conference on Weblogs and Social Media, 2011.

[34] M.H.R. Pereira, F.L.C. Pádua, A.C.M. Pereira, F. Benevenuto, D.H. Dalip, Fusing audio, textual, and visual features for sentiment analysis of news videos, in: Tenth International AAAI Conference on Web and Social Media, 2016.

[35] V. Pérez-Rosas, R. Mihalcea, L.-P. Morency, Utterance-level multimodal sentiment analysis, in: Proceedings of the 51st Annual Meeting of the Association for Computational Linguistics (Volume 1: Long Papers), 2013, pp. 973–982.

[36] E. Tromp, M. Pechenizkiy, Senticorr: multilingual sentiment analysis of personal correspondence, in: 2011 IEEE 11th International Conference on Data Mining Workshops, 2011, pp. 1247–1250.

[37] R. Pascanu, C. Gulcehre, K. Cho, Y. Bengio, How to construct deep recurrent neural networks, arXiv preprint, arXiv:1312.6026, 2013.

[38] S.M. Mohammad, S. Kiritchenko, X. Zhu, NRC-Canada: building the state-of-the-art in sentiment analysis of tweets, arXiv preprint, arXiv:1308.6242, 2013.

[39] J.M. Wiebe, R.F. Bruce, T.P. O'Hara, Development and use of a gold-standard data set for subjectivity classifications, in: Proceedings of the 37th Annual Meeting of the Association for Computational Linguistics, 1999, pp. 246–253.

[40] K. Dave, S. Lawrence, D.M. Pennock, Mining the peanut gallery: opinion extraction and semantic classification of product reviews, in: Proceedings of the 12th International Conference on World Wide Web, 2003, pp. 519–528.

[41] R. Socher, A. Perelygin, J. Wu, J. Chuang, C.D. Manning, A. Ng, et al., Recursive deep models for semantic compositionality over a sentiment treebank, in: Proceedings of the 2013 Conference on Empirical Methods in Natural Language Processing, 2013, pp. 1631–1642.

[42] M. Hagen, M. Potthast, M. Büchner, B. Stein, Webis: an ensemble for Twitter sentiment detection, in: Proceedings of the 9th International Workshop on Semantic Evaluation (SemEval 2015), 2015, pp. 582–589.

[43] J. Deriu, M. Gonzenbach, F. Uzdilli, A. Lucchi, V.D. Luca, M. Jaggi, Swisscheese at semeval-2016 task 4: sentiment classification using an ensemble of convolutional neural networks with distant supervision, in: Proceedings of the 10th International Workshop on Semantic Evaluation, 2016, pp. 1124–1128.

[44] A. Hassan, A. Abbasi, D. Zeng, Twitter sentiment analysis: a bootstrap ensemble framework, in: 2013 International Conference on Social Computing, 2013, pp. 357–364.

[45] J. Stone, Thematic text analysis-new agendas for analyzing text content, in: Test Analysis for the Social Sciences: Methods for Drawing Statistical Inferences from Texts and Transcripts, 1997, pp. 35–54.

[46] T. Wilson, J. Wiebe, P. Hoffmann, Recognizing contextual polarity in phrase-level sentiment analysis, in: Proceedings of Human Language Technology Conference and Conference on Empirical Methods in Natural Language Processing, 2005.

[47] R. Das, M. Chen, Yahoo!(2001) for Amazon: sentiment parsing from small talk on the Web, in: EFA 2001 Barcelona Meetings.

[48] R.C. Schank, L. Tesler, A conceptual dependency parser for natural language, in: Proceedings of the 1969 Conference on Computational Linguistics, 1969, pp. 1–3.

[49] L. Polanyi, A. Zaenen, Contextual valence shifters, in: Computing Attitude and Affect in Text: Theory and Applications, Springer, 2006, pp. 1–10.

[50] D. Tang, F. Wei, N. Yang, M. Zhou, T. Liu, B. Qin, Learning sentiment-specific word embedding for Twitter sentiment classification, in: Proceedings of the 52nd Annual Meeting of the Association for Computational Linguistics (Volume 1: Long Papers), 2014, pp. 1555–1565.

[51] E. Fast, B. Chen, M.S. Bernstein, Empath: understanding topic signals in large-scale text, in: Proceedings of the 2016 CHI Conference on Human Factors in Computing Systems, 2016, pp. 4647–4657.

[52] P. Mandera, E. Keuleers, M. Brysbaert, How useful are corpus-based methods for ex-
      trapolating psycholinguistic variables?, Quarterly Journal of Experimental Psychology
      68 (2015) 1623–1642.
[53] A.L. Maas, R.E. Daly, P.T. Pham, D. Huang, A.Y. Ng, C. Potts, Learning word vectors
      for sentiment analysis, in: Proceedings of the 49th Annual Meeting of the Associa-
      tion for Computational Linguistics: Human Language Technologies-Volume 1, 2011,
      pp. 142–150.
[54] J. Deriu, A. Lucchi, V. De Luca, A. Severyn, S. Müller, M. Cieliebak, et al., Leveraging
      large amounts of weakly supervised data for multi-language sentiment classification,
      in: Proceedings of the 26th International Conference on World Wide Web, 2017,
      pp. 1045–1052.
[55] H.K. Palo, M.N. Mohanty, M. Chandra, Emotion analysis from speech of different
      age groups, in: Proceedings of The Second International Conference on Research in
      Intelligent and Computing in Engineering, 2017, pp. 283–287.
[56] H. Salehinejad, S. Sankar, J. Barfett, E. Colak, S. Valaee, Recent advances in recurrent
      neural networks, arXiv preprint, arXiv:1801.01078, 2017.

CHAPTER 6

A machine learning approach to aid paralysis patients using EMG signals

Manisha Choudhary[a], Monika Lokhande[a], Rushikesh Borse[a], and Avinash Bhute[b]

[a]Department of Electronics and Telecommunication, School of Electrical Engineering, MIT Academy of Engineering, Alandi, India
[b]Department of Information Technology Engineering, School of Computer Technology, MIT Academy of Engineering, Alandi, India

6.1 Introduction

Our body uses electric signals to control and communicate with other parts of the body. When we want to move any body part, our brain sends signals via neurons to the muscles of that part of the body and activates those muscles. The contraction of these muscles is brought about by muscle fibers firing action potentials and changing shape. This electrical activity of muscles can be recorded and put to use. The signals that are generated due to responses from the brain, followed by contraction or expansion of muscles, are referred to as electromyography (EMG) signals. The amplitudes of surface EMG signals can be used for controlling hand or arm movement [9]. EMG signals are generated only when a person moves his hand on his/her own, that is, when there is the involvement of the brain as well as muscle movement. If some person moves the hand of another person, there is only contraction and expansion of muscles and no involvement of the brain, and therefore EMG signals are not generated.

EMG is also the way to assess the health of muscles and nerve cells that control them. EMG signals have been used a lot for the diagnosis of neuromuscular disorders, prosthetics, human–machine interface control, and human movement tracking [28]. The electrical activity of the muscles in response to nerve stimulation of muscles is studied and disorders can be identified. Paralysis is one such disorder where patients cannot make the necessary movement of muscles [25]. It happens because the messages between the brain and muscles cannot be passed on properly. Neuromuscular

Advanced Data Mining Tools and Methods for Social Computing
https://doi.org/10.1016/B978-0-32-385708-6.00013-8
107

diseases adversely affect the muscular and nervous system and degrade the working of skeletal muscles.

Many people suffer from spinal cord injury or have muscular deficiencies. They are unable to make necessary movements on their own because the signals from their brain are unable to reach their muscles. Recent advancements in the field of EMG signal processing and analysis are advantageous to assist the disabled and elderly people who can only make limited or no movements. To overcome this problem, we have designed a system that helps in controlling the movements of paralyzed people. This is done by connecting them to a system such that when a normal person makes movements, that in turn can bring about movement in the body of a paralyzed person. The arm of a normal person is connected via electrodes to a device called EMG SpikerShield. This device is used for EMG signal processing (filtering, amplification) after EMG signals are generated by the movement of the muscle of the person.

The EMG signals are recorded via a spike recorder application and features can be extracted from these signals. The specific movement of the body can be identified and classified using some machine learning algorithms. The signal is further transferred via a transcutaneous electrical nerve stimulator (TENS) unit to the body of the paralyzed person and the body movement of this person is brought about. Thus, a combination of EMG and machine learning can help in providing aid to paralysis patients. In this proposed system, we have focused only on hand movements. However, in practice classification of EMG signals is difficult because they have non-linear and time-varying characteristics. The features extracted from the EMG signal thus need to be processed to make them efficient for the classification of movement. The study of EMG signal processing, feature extraction, an classification techniques helps in developing an efficient EMG-based human–machine interface system [19].

The chapter is organized as follows. The associated works related to feature extraction from EMG signals, their classification using machine learning algorithms, human–computer interaction, and human–machine interaction are detailed in Section 6.2. The system model is discussed in Section 6.3, and implementation and results are discussed in Section 6.4. This chapter focuses on bringing about human–human interaction.

6.2 Associated works

Before describing the proposed method, we give a broad survey of associated works on feature extraction and classification of EMG signals and on providing aid to people with disabilities with the usage of EMG signals. There has been a significant amount of work involving the use of EMG signals to carry out experiments on muscles and analyze their health.

EMG and its applications have been attracting researchers from the 1990s. Due to the increasing usage of computers, the human–machine interface has attracted much attention, and EMG signals are a way to achieve that. Around 12 hand gestures have been interpreted by the system set up in [1] while focusing mainly on three arm muscles. The experiment was performed on some healthy people who did not have any neuromuscular diseases. The EMG signals were recorded from the arms of these people and were processed following a procedure of sampling, high-pass filtering, low-pass filtering, and amplification. The different gestures interpreted were based on how many degrees of movement the arms had.

Various hand gestures like hand opening, hand closing, hand relaxation, etc., have been discriminated from EMG signals using neural networks in [13]. Feature extraction methods from EMG, followed by discriminating the movement and comparing the complexity and robustness, have been presented in [27]. When EMG signals have to be used for stimulation of some muscles, the muscle response and stimulation artifacts have to be eliminated [21]. The details of various filter implementations with different filter lengths are portrayed. Adaptive filters have been compared with fixed comb filters for both real and simulated data that have been obtained from a normal person and a paralyzed person. This paper also presents mathematical modeling of muscle responses and filter outputs in the utmost detail. Another study [6] highlights the advantages of isotropic filters over filters with anisotropic transfer function as they can detect the activity of single motor units more efficiently. They not only improve the spatial selectivity of the EMG recording arrangement but also improve the spatial resolution by up to 30%. The filter responses for different depths of motor units (1 mm, 2.5 mm, etc.) are reported in this paper. In [20] EMG is used to control the prosthetic arm by identifying various hand movement commands. This has been done by various parameters obtained from EMG signals. Hence, there has been a significant amount of study involving EMG in the 1990s.

Even after the 1990s, EMG has been considered a reliable technique for muscle movement detection. In [18] motor unit (MU) action potentials have been identified from EMG signals after relevant processing of the signal. These action potentials have been identified using continuous wavelet transform. The pre-processing and post-processing of the EMG signal has been discussed to make it suitable for clinical applications. To the simulated signal, white Gaussian noise is added with the help of the bandpass filter. The single-threshold and double-threshold methods applied on the simulated signal are compared and the corresponding standard deviation (SD), bias, and signal-to-noise ratio (SNR) are obtained for different threshold coefficients. In [23] the muscle unit action potentials (MUAPs) generated when muscles are at rest and for six different contracting positions are presented. The muscles in focus are mainly the vastus lateralis (VL) and the rectus femoris (RF). The EMG signal is modeled mathematically and its equation is obtained and studied. Frequency domain techniques for EMG signal processing which are based on first- and second-order moments and mean correlation and variance (VR) have been analyzed. The variation of the signal in the frequency domain is visualized with the help of graphs. The EMG signals were recorded from four healthy males in the age group of 23 to 33 years old. The procedure of signal acquisition by placing the surface electrodes at different contracting positions for MUAP estimation techniques is discussed in detail.

The research in [24] deals with two developments, one being controlling virtual devices based on gesture recognition while the other is a Bayesian method to decompose EMGs into individual MUAPs. The pattern recognition for identifying gestures is based on Markov models which operate on real-time data, i.e., moving averages of EMG signals. For controlling a virtual device, experiments are done on a joystick and a keyboard. In the Bayesian methodology, a forward model and optimization techniques for parameters of the model are essential. The gesture recognition methodology is a traditional procedure involving gesture selection, electrode application, signal acquisition, feature extraction, training, and testing of the pattern recognition model. Another research [26] involves EMG-based hand motion estimation using support vector machine (SVM). Seven hand motions, including hand opening, hand closing, supination, motionless, etc., have been identified. EMG electrode configuration, control of artificial limbs, and the identification of 16 different movements with an accuracy of 93% are discussed in [10]. The authors also emphasized the electrode selection algorithm for experimentation. The control of a robotic arm using EMG signals from upper limbs using the traditional procedure of signal acquisition, signal processing, and then employing a classifier is presented in various works [2].

A human–machine interface to control exoskeletons that utilizes EMG signals from the muscles of the operator has been presented in [7] along with torque applied and similar parameters. Another feasible EMG-based human–computer interaction [11] for the disabled has been proposed using a RISC-type microprocessor, PIC16F73, and a Bluetooth-based wireless communication system. Another study on detecting the intention of movement of a paralysis patient has been presented in [15] using both electroencephalography signals (from the brain) and EMG signals (from muscles).

In recent years also the analysis of EMG signals has been an interesting topic. There have been many contributions in this regard that can also provide aid to the disabled or people with paralysis. For people having disabilities in upper arms, daily life is tough. The development of an artificial human arm controlled by muscle EMG could help in controlling the prosthetic hand [12]. This would help disabled people to live more comfortably. The EMG measurement method used here involves sensing the EMG using electrodes, followed by a microcontroller (Arduino) where the conversion of the analog signal to a digital signal takes place. Furthermore, signal processing involves the amplification of the signal and suppressing the noise. The movement of the artificial arm then happens by the hardware involving servo motors. The kinematics equations for this movement are listed.

People with physical disabilities that result from diseases such as spinal cord injury, paralysis, and amputation need assistance, which is possible with the use of hand gestures for human–computer interaction [22]. The human–computer interface model for physically disabled people has been successfully implemented with up to 98% accuracy using artificial neural network (ANN). Six gestures, including hand extension, hand grasp, wrist extension, thumb flexion, etc., have been identified in the above paper.

A detailed study of a research platform for controlling prosthetic hands based on EMG pattern recognition is reported in [8]. Hand motion estimation using EMG signals with an SVM algorithm is discussed in [14]. The paper [5] focused on identifying hand gestures from the EMG signal which was acquired by a sensor-based band. Time domain multi-feature extraction and classification of human hand movements by EMG signals have also been presented in [3]. The classification of movement for an EMG-based human–robot interface using machine learning is detailed in [4][17]. Thus, there has been a significant amount of research in this regard for many years, and improvements in technology are leading to more contributions. Many of these systems can now be implemented in real-time and can be applied to aid disabled people with ease.

6.3 System model

Fig. 6.1 shows the proposed system model which includes recording EMGs via electrodes, processing of the EMG signals using EMG SpikerShield, recording and visualizing the EMG signals on the BYB Spike Recorder App, and extracting features from it before using a classifier.

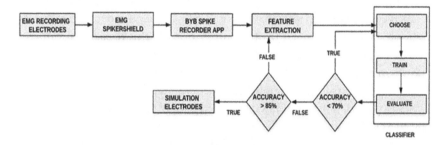

Figure 6.1 System design for the human–human interface.

The EMG signals from healthy males and females have been collected via the EMG recording electrodes. Two electrodes are placed on the arm and one on the back of the wrist of the person. The signal obtained is a very low-level (weak) signal and also noise creates randomness in the recorded EMG signal. This signal is then passed to EMG SpikerShield for processing, where it is amplified and noise is filtered out. The signal obtained from here can be recorded using the BYB Spike Recorder App. Using this application, the signal is converted to .wav format and given to MATLAB®. In MATLAB, the resulting signal can be viewed and visualized. Features are extracted from this signal by applying mathematical functions using the MATLAB script. The features extracted are namely mean absolute value (MAV), root mean square (RMS), SD, VR, wavelength, and zero crossing (ACR). Using these parameters, different movements of the hands can be distinguished and identified. Hand movements like hand up and hand down are the focus of our study.

The processed data contain the six parameters for every recording from a different person, forming the database. This database is used for classification and is given to the classifier. Different machine learning models like k-nearest neighbor (KNN), SVM, and decision trees have been used for the classification of the abovementioned hand movements. The model is trained on some recorded data (EMG) and then tested for new users. Only if the accuracy of the above models is greater than 70%, the signal can be given to the disabled. Such signals have to be further processed (post-processing) and can then be given to those suffering from paralysis via the stimulation electrodes connected to their body. These output signals cause a rise in action potentials of the arm muscles in the body of the patient and due to the instigating voltage, the desired movement is brought about in the body of the paralyzed/physically disabled people. Each block and each processing step is further explained in Sections 6.3.1, 6.3.2, 6.3.3, and 6.3.4.

6.3.1 System architecture

The system set up for controlling a disabled patient using EMG signals consists of EMG recording electrodes, EMG SpikerShield, Arduino, and the TENS unit. The hardware connections and signal flow in the system are shown in Fig. 6.2.

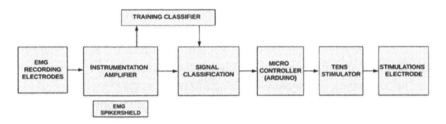

Figure 6.2 Connections of hardware kit for signal flow.

The Controller (Master): The Controller is the person whose muscle activity is recorded to control the person with a disability. The Controller can be any normal (healthy) male or female, child or adult. The EMG recording electrodes are connected to the arm of this person and EMG signals are recorded when this person moves his arm. The strength of the recorded signals depends on how strong this person moves. The recorded EMG signal is a low-level signal and it contains noise.

EMG SpikerShield: EMG SpikerShield allows us to record the electrical activity of muscles and send it to the microcontroller (Arduino). This device is connected to Arduino by placing it on top of Arduino and connecting all the pins to female headers of Arduino. It is used to amplify the weak EMG signal recorded from the Master and also to filter out noise.

For amplification, an instrumentation amplifier (AD623 IC) is used, while TLC2274 IC is used for rejecting noise. Thus, this device is responsible for all the signal processing so that a strong EMG signal will reach the Slave at the end, which can bring about the movement in the Slave with the same intensity as that of the Master.

BYB Spike Recorder App: The recorded EMG signals can be viewed on the screen using this spike recorder application and they can be saved or stored. The signal strength, variations, amplitude, and other parameters of the signal can be visualized using this application. The recorded signal is saved in .wav format and it is imported into MATLAB. Using MATLAB, the desired features are extracted from the signal like ZCR, mean, VR, wavelength, etc. These features help in distinguishing different signals and they further form the dataset. After recording multiple signals from different people (Master), the resulting data are saved in .csv format.

Arduino: Arduino receives the output signal from EMG SpikerShield and it facilitates the control of the disabled (Slave). The signal received is analog and to use the Arduino code it is converted to a digital signal by breaking it into some series of discrete numbers. Arduino interprets these signals using the code and then uses this analysis to command or control the Slave (or other devices) just as any microcontroller would do. Thus, for our system, depending on the signal Arduino commands the movement of the Slave whether it is a hand up or hand down movement. It plays a vital role in controlling the human–machine interface.

Train Classifier: The .csv file generated previously is our dataset and it can be read easily by the machine learning model. This dataset is fed to the classifier and hand movements of the Master are classified. The classifiers used are decision tree, KNN, SVM, and naive Bayes. The classifiers are trained on the dataset (60:40 for training and testing) and their accuracy is checked. The performance of the classifier is evaluated by testing the model on unseen data. Both training and test accuracies help in deciding the reliability of the classifier and comparing the performance of different classifiers.

TENS unit: The TENS unit provides enough current to stimulate the muscles of the Slave. The electric signals are transferred to the Slave by this unit and it activates the muscles of the paralyzed/disabled person, causing movement. The frequencies generated by this unit should fall in the range of acceptable frequencies for the human muscles. If the frequencies exceed or are lower than the allowed frequencies, it may not only cause inappropriate results but also be unsafe for the Slave. The frequency of the TENS unit is set between 10 and 20 Hz. The power of the TENS device is increased slowly until a response is seen in the body of the Controlled, while the Controller is making hand movements.

The Controlled (Slave): The Slave is the paralyzed person whose activity we wish to control when the Master moves. This person is connected via electrodes to the TENS unit that provides electricity to his arm's nerves harmlessly. This disabled or paralyzed person can make the necessary movement when connected to the system. The system designed is thus capable of bringing about a human–human interface and providing aid to paralysis patients.

6.3.2 Connecting surface EMG electrodes

The electrodes for EMG signal acquisition from the Master are placed on the arm of the person and one on the back of the wrist, as shown in Fig. 6.3. The orange (mid gray in print version) muscle electrode cable wire from EMG SpikerShield is then connected to the electrodes on the arm. The measured EMG signals and frequencies vary from 0 to 30 mV peak-to-peak and from 10 Hz to 500 Hz, respectively, depending upon the individual and activeness of their muscles.

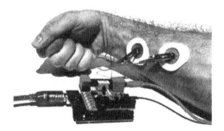

Figure 6.3 EMG signal acquisition from the arm of a person (courtesy of Backyard Brains) [16].

For the Slave, two surface EMG electrodes are placed across the ulnar nerve. It is preferred to place them on the backside of the forearm. The EMG signals recorded from the Master are stored using EMG SpikerShield and they are sent to the Controlled using a TENS unit as mentioned above. The time duration for which the signals are recorded is 4 to 5 seconds. The frequency and pulse duration of these signals has to be adjusted before sending them to the Slave. The frequency range should be from 10 to 20 Hz and the pulse duration has to be between 50 and 80 milliseconds.

6.3.3 Feature extraction

The extraction of features from the signal and then using it for classification is a well-established concept in machine learning. Continuing this tradition, we extracted time domain features of the EMG signal. These extracted features form the database. This feature extraction is used to reduce the overfitting and to increase accuracy.

Time domain features are extracted from the recorded EMG signal and a dataset is prepared using these features. This dataset is fed to the algorithms to predict the hand movements of the person. The amplitude of the EMG signal is random in nature with Gaussian distribution and ranges from 0 to 10 mV peak-to-peak. The RMS value and the mean squared (MA) value are the two parameters that are used to measure the amplitude of the EMG signal.

We describe the features in short.

1. Mean absolute value: The MAV is understood as a time domain variable because it is measured as a time function. The area under the EMG signal is represented by MAV once it has been rectified, which means each one of the negative voltage values is made positive. The RMS provides a more reliable measure of the EMG signal; hence it is usually preferred over the MAV. The MAV is calculated as follows:

$$MAV = \frac{1}{N} \sum_{i=1}^{N} x_i. \tag{6.1}$$

2. Root mean square: The square root of the average power of the EMG signal for a given period of time is represented by the RMS value. The amplitude of the EMG signal is measured as a function of a time, so we can consider it as a time domain variable. The RMS is calculated as follows:

$$RMS = \sqrt{\frac{\sum_{i=1}^{N} x_i^2}{N}}. \tag{6.2}$$

3. Standard deviation: The SD shows how much the EMG signal deviates from the mean value of the signal. It is the square root of the VR and shows the amount of variability in the data. It is calculated as follows:

$$SD = \sqrt{\frac{\sum (x_i - MAV)^2}{N}}. \tag{6.3}$$

4. Variance: VR shows the deflection of the EMG signal from its mean or absolute value. VR of data is a way to measure the spread of each data

point from the average. It also captures the power of the EMG signal as a feature. It is calculated as follows:

$$VR = \frac{\sum (x_i - MAV)^2}{N}. \tag{6.4}$$

5. Waveform length: Waveform length (WL) is the distance over which the wave's shape repeats. It is the cumulative length of the waveform over the segment of time. WL is calculated as follows:

$$WL = \sum_{i=1}^{N} |x_i - x_{i-1}|. \tag{6.5}$$

6. Zero crossing: ZCR counts how frequently the EMG signal passes the zero amplitude axis. To avoid background noise, a threshold condition is used. It provides an approximation estimation of frequency domain properties. ZCR is calculated as follows:

$$ZCR = \frac{1}{T} \sum_{t=1}^{T} |x(t) - x(t-1)|. \tag{6.6}$$

The recorded EMG signals are stored using the BYB Spike Recorder App in .wav format. This .wav file consists of the electric signals generated by the arm movement of the Controller. It is read in MATLAB and the EMG signal is plotted. The above six features (mean, SD, RMS, wavelength, etc.) are obtained using MATLAB code. These features that are extracted from the recorded EMG signals will form the dataset, which is saved in the form of a .csv file. This dataset is fed to the machine learning algorithm for the classification of arm movements. The last (seventh) feature/attribute in the dataset is the class. There are two classes for hand movement, i.e., hand up and hand down. Since the data are labeled, supervised machine learning algorithms are used for the hand movement classification.

6.3.4 Classifiers

After feature extraction, supervised machine learning models are used for performing the classification on the feature dataset obtained as the training data are labeled. Four classification algorithms, namely decision tree, KNN, SVM, and naive Bayes, have been used for our feature set.

1. Decision tree: Decision trees are used for both classification and regression problems. They break down datasets into smaller subsets, and the final output is a tree with leaf nodes and decision nodes. The root node is the topmost decision node, which is the best predictor. Categorical and numerical data can be handled by decision trees. Generally, they give low prediction accuracy compared to other machine learning algorithms because there is a high probability of overfitting. There are two well-known attribute selection measures: (i) the Gini index and (ii) information gain. We have used the Gini index as an attribute selection measure. The Gini index is also referred to as the Gini ratio. It measures the impurity of the node.

2. KNN: The KNN algorithm is a non-parametric method used to determine the nearest neighbors based on Euclidean distance. It takes some labeled points and the labeling of other points is based on these. While labeling a new point, the labeled points closest to the new point (its nearest neighbors) are taken care of. The class of the new point is predicted according to the k-nearest neighbors. It is a strong algorithm for noisy datasets. We must determine the worth of the value of K, which can be challenging.

3. SVM: SVM is a supervised machine learning algorithm used for regression as well as classification tasks. It uses the kernel trick method to transform the data. The optimal boundary between the possible outputs is determined by these transformations. An SVM model is essentially a representation of various classes during a hyperplane in multi-dimensional space. The hyperplane is generated iteratively by SVM so that the error is often minimized. The goal of SVM is to divide the datasets into classes to seek out a maximum marginal hyperplane.

4. Naive Bayes: Naive Bayes is an algorithm which is used for both regression and classification based on the Bayes theorem. It assumes that every feature manifests an independent contribution to the probability. The naive Bayes classifier is easy to build and helpful for very large datasets. It requires a little amount of training data and therefore the results are generally accurate.

6.4 Simulation and results

6.4.1 Simulation of circuits on Proteus software

The EMG signal is given to EMG SpikerShield which will enable to control movements of other persons connected via electrodes. The human–human interface of SpikerShield facilitates controlling the other person. In this circuit, shown in Fig. 6.4, the instrumentation amplifier, designed using Op-Amps, is used to amplify low-level signals by rejecting noise. The output of the amplifier is given to the analog pins of the Arduino board. AD623 IC is used, which is an instrumentation amplifier IC, and TLC2274 is an IC which exhibits high input impedance and low noise.

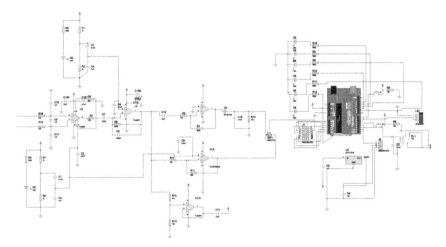

Figure 6.4 Proteus circuit of EMG SpikerShield.

The circuit of TENS, shown in Fig. 6.5, consists of a CMOS 555 timer that produces a brief pulse to feed a 1:10 miniature transformer. A parallel resonant circuit of the transformer is formed with a 4.7-nF capacitor and the resonance brings the required increase in the output voltage. This circuit delivers enough current to cause muscle contraction and can be used to modulate the frequency, intensity, and pulse width of the signal. When the TENS unit is applied at a high frequency (greater than 50 Hz), its intensity is such that it is below the muscle contraction threshold, and when it is applied at a low frequency (less than 10 Hz), the intensity is such that it produces muscle contraction. The circuits were converted to .pdf by Proteus and then the images were obtained and used here.

6.4.2 Implementation and results of machine learning algorithms

The processed signal obtained from EMG SpikerShield is fit for further processes. The feature dataset obtained after extracting features from the Spike recorder and mathematical conversions of Eqs. (6.1)–(6.6) using MATLAB

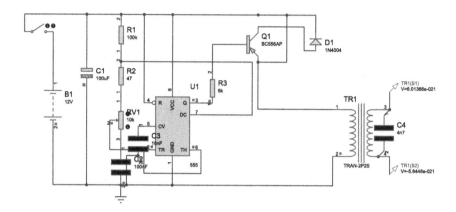

Figure 6.5 Proteus circuit of TENS unit.

is fed to the classification algorithms. Accuracies of 90% for decision tree, 60% for KNN, 95% for SVM, and 95% for naive Bayes were obtained. For KNN, the values of k were varied and accuracies for those were checked. For k = 2, the test accuracy was 35% which was much lower compared to the accuracy for k = 3. After increasing k until 20, at k = 20 a test accuracy of 60% was obtained. Table 6.1 shows the training and test accuracies for all four algorithms and Table 6.2 shows the training and test accuracies for various values of K.

Table 6.1 Comparative analysis of various machine learning algorithms.

Classifier	Training accuracy	Test accuracy
Decision tree	90%	90%
KNN (k = 20)	60%	60%
SVM	96%	95%
Naive Bayes	93.3%	95%

Table 6.2 Comparative analysis for different values of K in KNN.

K	Training accuracy	Test accuracy
2	70%	35%
5	66%	50%
10	56%	55%
20	60%	60%

Comparative analysis of Training Accuracies for various Machine Learning Classifiers

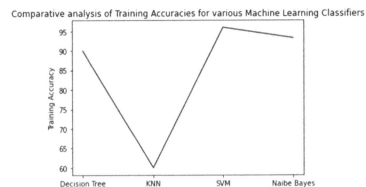

6(a) Training Accuracies of the four classifiers

Comparative analysis of Testing Accuracies for various Machine Learning Classifiers

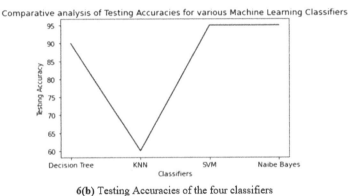

6(b) Testing Accuracies of the four classifiers

Figure 6.6 Comparative analysis of training and testing of the four classifiers used.

Fig. 6.6 shows the comparative analysis of both training and test accuracies of the classifiers we have used, i.e., decision tree, KNN, SVM, and naive Bayes. The graph shows that the training and test accuracies for the decision tree are both 90%, the training and test accuracies for KNN are 60%, the training accuracy for SVM is 96% while the test accuracy is 95%, and for naive Bayes the training and test accuracies are 93% and 95%, respectively. It is visible that all the algorithms perform better than KNN. The KNN classifier is not able to learn the data with good accuracy and the result is that it can also not predict with good accuracy. SVM classifies the hand movements better than the other three classifier models. Thus, the SVM classifier can be most reliable for interpreting hand movements in real-time.

The two hand movements, up and down, were classified using the machine learning algorithms. A confusion matrix is also referred to as an error matrix. It allows the visualization of the performance of an algorithm. Confusion matrices were obtained for all four classifiers. Normalized confusion matrices are represented as each of the class has 1.00 samples. Fig. 6.7 shows the normalized confusion matrices for decision tree, KNN, SVM, and naive Bayes. The diagonal elements in the confusion matrix represent the number of true predicted classes and the off-diagonal elements are those corresponding to the misclassified class. The dataset had data of 50 normal people and after splitting using a 60:40 ratio for training and testing, a total of 20 records of people are used in testing, and thus a total of 20 predicted classes are there in the confusion matrix where normalized values are displayed.

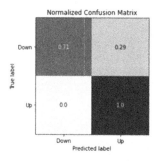

7(a) Normalized confusion matrix for Decision Tree

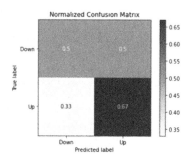

7(b). Normalized confusion matrix for KNN

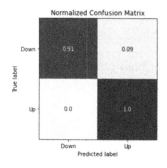

7(c). Normalized confusion matrix for SVM

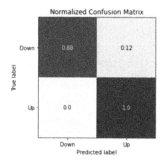

7(d). Normalized confusion matrix for Naïve Bayes

Figure 6.7 Confusion matrices obtained after applying various machine learning approaches to the dataset.

In our model, the target variable "down" is considered as "positive" and "up" is considered as "negative." The accuracy of the machine learning model depends on the amount of training data, the algorithm used, and the number of features. We need to maximize the accuracy of the model so that it will classify the data accurately.

6.5 Conclusion

In this chapter, we presented one of the applications of EMG signals for the human–human interface using feature extraction from EMG signals and then the classification of hand movements using machine learning. We classified an EMG dataset using decision tree, KNN, SVM, and naive Bayes algorithms and a comparative study has been conducted. All algorithms gave an accuracy of around 90% except KNN, whose accuracy was 60%. This application could be very helpful in providing aid to people with disabilities like paralysis whose body parts are not damaged, but their nervous system is not capable of communicating with the muscles. After obtaining data from a normal person, features extracted from the EMG signal will help to control the movements of the disabled person using EMG Spiker-Shield and a machine learning classifier. Apart from paralysis patients, this procedure could be applied to people suffering from many neuromuscular diseases and unable to move their body parts, especially limbs.

The classification of hand movements was performed using different algorithms and the comparative analysis of the algorithms shows that KNN cannot be a reliable classifier. It was observed that the training and test accuracies were best for the SVM algorithm. Thus, SVM can best classify the hand movements from EMG signals. In real-time, if considering the hand movements, the SVM classifier is proven to bring about the most efficient human–human interface between a normal person and a disabled person.

References

[1] O.A. Alsayegh, EMG-based human-machine interface system, in: 2000 IEEE International Conference on Multimedia and Expo. ICME2000, Proceedings. Latest Advances in the Fast Changing World of Multimedia (Cat. No.00TH8532), volume 2, 2000, pp. 925–928.
[2] P.K. Artemiadis, K.J. Kyriakopoulos, An EMG-based robot control scheme robust to time-varying EMG signal features, IEEE Transactions on Information Technology in Biomedicine 14 (3) (2010) 582–588.
[3] A. Bhattacharya, A. Sarkar, P. Basak, Time domain multi-feature extraction and classification of human hand movements using surface EMG, in: 2017 4th International Conference on Advanced Computing and Communication Systems (ICACCS), 2017, pp. 1–5.

[4] N. Bu, M. Okamoto, T. Tsuji, A hybrid motion classification approach for EMG-based human–robot interfaces using Bayesian and neural networks, IEEE Transactions on Robotics 25 (3) (2009) 502–511.

[5] A. Devaraj, A.K. Nair, Hand gesture signal classification using machine learning, in: 2020 International Conference on Communication and Signal Processing (ICCSP), 2020, pp. 0390–0394.

[6] C. Disselhorst-Klug, J. Silny, G. Rau, Improvement of spatial resolution in surface-EMG: a theoretical and experimental comparison of different spatial filters, IEEE Transactions on Biomedical Engineering 44 (7) (1997) 567–574.

[7] C. Fleischer, G. Hommel, A human–exoskeleton interface utilizing electromyography, IEEE Transactions on Robotics 24 (4) (2008) 872–882.

[8] P. Geethanjali, K.K. Ray, A low-cost real-time research platform for EMG pattern recognition-based prosthetic hand, IEEE/ASME Transactions on Mechatronics 20 (4) (2015) 1948–1955.

[9] Y. Geng, L. Yu, M. You, G. Li, A pilot study of EMG pattern based classification of arm functional movements, in: 2010 Second WRI Global Congress on Intelligent Systems (GCIS 2010), volume 3, Los Alamitos, CA, USA, IEEE Computer Society, Dec 2010, pp. 317–320.

[10] H. Huang, P. Zhou, G. Li, T.A. Kuiken, An analysis of EMG electrode configuration for targeted muscle reinnervation based neural machine interface, IEEE Transactions on Neural Systems and Rehabilitation Engineering 16 (1) (2008) 37–45.

[11] Inhyuk Moon, Myoungjoon Lee, Museong Mun, A novel EMG-based human-computer interface for persons with disability, in: Proceedings of the IEEE International Conference on Mechatronics, 2004, ICM '04, 2004, pp. 519–524.

[12] C. Joochim, N. Siriwatcharakul, Artificial human arm controlled by muscle electromyography (EMG), in: 2018 Third International Conference on Engineering Science and Innovative Technology (ESIT), 2018, pp. 1–5.

[13] K. Kuribayashi, S. Shimizu, K. Okimura, T. Taniguchi, A discrimination system using neural network for EMG-controlled prostheses-integral type of EMG signal processing, in: Proceedings of 1993 IEEE/RSJ International Conference on Intelligent Robots and Systems (IROS '93), volume 3, 1993, pp. 1750–1755.

[14] L. Liao, Y. Tseng, H. Chiang, W. Wang, EMG-based control scheme with SVM classifier for assistive robot arm, in: 2018 International Automatic Control Conference (CACS), 2018, pp. 1–5.

[15] E. Lóopez-Larraz, N. Birbaumer, A. Ramos-Murguialday, A hybrid EEG-EMG BMI improves the detection of movement intention in cortical stroke patients with complete hand paralysis, in: 2018 40th Annual International Conference of the IEEE Engineering in Medicine and Biology Society (EMBC), 2018, pp. 2000–2003.

[16] Tim Marzullo, Backyard brains (neuroscience for everyone!), https://backyardbrains.com/experiments/humanhumaninterface.

[17] R. Meattini, S. Benatti, U. Scarcia, D. De Gregorio, L. Benini, C. Melchiorri, An sEMG-based human–robot interface for robotic hands using machine learning and synergies, IEEE Transactions on Components, Packaging and Manufacturing Technology 8 (7) (2018) 1149–1158.

[18] A. Merlo, D. Farina, R. Merletti, A fast and reliable technique for muscle activity detection from surface EMG signals, IEEE Transactions on Biomedical Engineering 50 (3) (2003) 316–323.

[19] A. Patel, J. Ramsay, M. Imtiaz, Y. Lu, EMG-based human machine interface control, in: 2019 12th International Conference on Human System Interaction (HSI), 2019, pp. 127–131.

[20] Sang-Hui Park, Seok-Pil Lee, EMG pattern recognition based on artificial intelligence techniques, IEEE Transactions on Rehabilitation Engineering 6 (4) (1998) 400–405.

[21] S. Sennels, F. Biering-Sorensen, O.T. Andersen, S.D. Hansen, Functional neuromuscular stimulation controlled by surface electromyographic signals produced by volitional activation of the same muscle: adaptive removal of the muscle response from the recorded EMG-signal, IEEE Transactions on Rehabilitation Engineering 5 (2) (1997) 195–206.

[22] M. Shafivulla, SEMG based human computer interface for physically challenged patients, in: 2016 International Conference on Advances in Human Machine Interaction (HMI), 2016, pp. 1–4.

[23] S. Shahid, J. Walker, G.M. Lyons, C.A. Byrne, A.V. Nene, Application of higher order statistics techniques to EMG signals to characterize the motor unit action potential, IEEE Transactions on Biomedical Engineering 52 (7) (2005) 1195–1209.

[24] K.R. Wheeler, M.H. Chang, K.H. Knuth, Gesture-based control and EMG decomposition, IEEE Transactions on Systems, Man and Cybernetics. Part C, Applications and Reviews 36 (4) (2006) 503–514.

[25] Y.H. Yin, Y.J. Fan, L.D. Xu, EMG and EPP-integrated human–machine interface between the paralyzed and rehabilitation exoskeleton, IEEE Transactions on Information Technology in Biomedicine 16 (4) (2012) 542–549.

[26] M. Yoshikawa, M. Mikawa, K. Tanaka, Real-time hand motion estimation using EMG signals with support vector machines, in: 2006 SICE-ICASE International Joint Conference, 2006, pp. 593–598.

[27] M. Zardoshti-Kermani, B.C. Wheeler, K. Badie, R.M. Hashemi, EMG feature evaluation for movement control of upper extremity prostheses, IEEE Transactions on Rehabilitation Engineering 3 (4) (1995) 324–333.

[28] J. Zhang, C. Ling, S. Li, Human movements classification using multi-channel surface EMG signals and deep learning technique, in: 2019 International Conference on Cyberworlds (CW), 2019, pp. 267–273.

CHAPTER 7

Influence of traveling on social behavior

Ajanta Das and Mousumi Halder
Amity Institute of Information Technology, Amity University, Kolkata, West Bengal, India

7.1 Introduction

With the exponential growth and popularity of networking sites, human beings are mostly busy with interacting or sharing their thoughts and views socially. Networking of human beings or simply a virtual human chain can do wonder. At the current outset, a virtual human chain can improve society through a common message or can abruptly change depression into an enjoyable world. People can talk to their friend or meet virtually to refresh their monotonous life schedule at home. On the other hand, social networking can be used to do some investigation on the person's nature [1]. Social networking sites include many factors that are contextual which helps us to evaluate trust, faith, liking, and preferences. People use different social sites based on their interest, preferences, and friends' influences. The preferences and usage of social media is directly dependent on personal interest and preferences [3]. Persons who do not like to share much activity through social media seem to use simple messaging applications to interact and communicate. Often these comments become public due to a lack of protection methodology. Sometimes, analysis also involves suspicious traits of human nature, like social networking users giving fake reviews and opening fake accounts to perform some louche activities. However, preferences of the users depend on their views and opinions, which they achieved through life experiences. Hence, the analysis of behavior that is carried out through social networking sites is mostly based on their traveling habits or patterns. It may depend on factors like interacting comments, emojis, and reactions on social networks among their core group of friends [7].

There are no such enchanting and extraordinary feelings such as traveling or looking around new places. For the first time ever, it has become unimaginable to travel to the most wanted and favorite places. It is not possible to mention all benefits obtained from traveling in this chapter, so the most important ones are presented in the following.

Advanced Data Mining Tools and Methods for Social Computing
https://doi.org/10.1016/B978-0-32-385708-6.00014-X
127

By nature, traveling regulates imagination by reality. People from all ages willingly take part in journeys. Traveling gives us a great feeling of achieving new things in new regions. Traveling helps to experience and explore existing cultures throughout the world. When we discover new things traveling, this is an exciting and thrilling experience. In addition, it helps to have creative thoughts and broadens the horizon of our mental state. In our day-to-day life and busy work schedules, we all always need some sort of relaxation. Thus, vacation can be the stress-free part of our life. Let us also consider the health status of people who do not take vacation [9].

- In [6], it is reported that men who did not take vacations had a 32% higher chance of dying from a heart attack than those who did take vacations.

- According to heart research centers, people who took much less vacation in life or in a year have an increased chance of heart disease. Women who are always occupied in the household and do not visit new places have an increased risk to have heart attacks and stroke.

The objective of this chapter is the following:

1. To become aware of general comments and interactions on specific travel sites and social networking sites.
2. To read and analyze the comments and reactions that people make on social networking sites.
3. To judge whether their topics are relevant or not.
4. To develop a traveling pattern analysis methodology of human beings using a machine learning technique.
5. To identify the positive and negative human behavior based on the available information on social networking sites.

The latest research is presented in Section 7.2. Social networking has become inevitable in our life; hence its importance is presented in Section 7.3. Necessary parameters for traveling are mentioned in Section 7.4. Section 7.5 presents a categorical analysis and a comparison of behavioral analyses based on traveling. Recognition of human social behavior is presented using machine learning techniques, specifically classification and clustering methods, in Section 7.6. Finally, Section 7.7 concludes the chapter.

7.2 Related work

This section presents the research related to prediction of the time to reach a destination while traveling, choice of destination, choice of travel mode, human behavior, travel patterns, etc. All these aspects are studied mostly based on social networking sites and using machine learning or deep learning techniques. In [10], the author presents a mechanism to predict the time to reach a destination from a particular point through a particular vehicle driven by a specific driver. This estimated time prediction is based on a continuous learning process. This prediction process uses the historical data about the particular vehicle and the driver to consider a set of semantic variables and conditions to be correctly estimated. In [8], the objective of the research is to identify tourism destinations based on social media. Actually, the destination communication strategy is studied based on social media. Moreover, the tourism destination becomes competitive through various social media strategies. In [21], the authors present behavioral analysis of travel mode based on a comparison between machine learning and logit models. Travel mode can be an integrated transit system comprised of buses, shuttles, cars, etc. So, they present an empirical evaluation of these approaches based on stated preference (SP) survey data. In this paper, behavioral interpretation is facilitated based on the predictive performance and capabilities of these approaches. The authors also presented a comparison of performances of well-known machine learning classifiers to predict individual choices of four travel modes. In [1], the authors utilize human activity schedules in travel behavior research to propose a feasible and operational conceptual framework. So, basically, major thrust is given on social networking sites, and the individuals who are interacting with their contacts in different layers and can decide on a travel schedule are identified. The authors claim that this computational model can aid in decision making of firms or governments. In [18], the researchers establish the relationship between travel behavior patterns and daily traffic congestion from the perspective of trip chains. Prediction of traffic congestion depends on a causal effect of holiday travels or pre-defined trip chain. They discussed characteristics of trip chain, which is mostly dependent on the tour-based approach and revealed preference (RP)-SP fusion data. In [19], a model is proposed using variational Bayesian inference methods for multiple discrete-continuous travel behavior data. The proposed research is based on a bipartite generative model for handling large datasets. Next, the dataset is used to train in the machine learning framework. Finally, an analytical method is used for interpretation and economic analysis. In [4], traveler classification is performed and similar travel behavior is detected and classified into five different clusters using a deep learning algorithm. Using social networks, similar behavioral patterns of travelers are detected. Authors have proposed a community detection algorithm based on the Jacard similarity concept. Finally, the activity map for each traveler is built and image classification is performed using a deep learning algorithm. The findings of the abovementioned survey are that the time to destination, travel mode, choice of destination, economic situation, traffic congestion based on travel patterns, and community detection for similar types of travel are analyzed and predicted. However, the novelty of the present research is to analyze or recognize human behavior based on the comments or reactions posted on social networking sites using classification and clustering techniques. Therefore, the scope of this research is to collect pictures or posts available from Twitter and categorize human behavior based on the comments or reactions available from Twitter. Last but not least, this chapter also presents clusters of comments based on innovation, attractiveness, energy, and passion.

7.3 Importance of social networking in real life

These days, people are becoming more and more addicted to social networking sites. Some of the people or social site users also write unclear reviews that are not understandable, highlighting that users themselves are confused and unable to express themselves properly. The emotions, human reactions, feelings, and thoughts are more expressed in social media than in real life or face to face. People show their anger in the form of comments on various social sites. Thus, it is becoming much more complicated to deal with actual behavior of people. Behavior disorders are very common on social media. The social media themselves are responsible for this. The social media comments and reviews are highly effective for some users. Not all people have the same mindset and they may have a tendency to get hurt whenever they are the victim of silly comments and trolling. Thus, there are many potential factors affecting the usage of social media that can cause depression and hypertension. It may also cause negative effects on the children and teenagers who are inclined towards bad things. Because of different way of use of the social networking sites, now social media platforms are ready to compete among themselves [5].

Some commonly used social networking sites are **Facebook, Instagram, Snapchat, LinkedIn,** and **WhatsApp**.

- **Facebook**: This is the most common social networking platform. It connects people all over the world. It gives us the opportunity to not only share our views but also to share our opinions through various online stickers available on the site of Facebook.
- **Instagram**: This is mainly a photo and video sharing social media platform. Instagram profiles can be private or public.
- **Snap chat**: This is the most popular messaging application that allows us take snaps (photos or videos). Once they are seen they automatically disappear.
- **LinkedIn**: This is mainly a professional social networking site. LinkedIn can help people grow their business or career. On this website, users connect with people who are already part of some organizations and working in some fields. So, it helps us to find jobs and build once's career as per the qualifications.
- **WhatsApp**: This is a very trending application for smart phone users. It provides us with the possibility to use less data and also allows us to make video calls and voice calls.

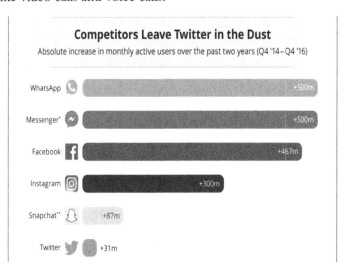

Figure 7.1 Number of users of different social networking sites [15].

As shown in Fig. 7.1, users are more inclined to use other social networking sites compared to Twitter. Users are actively interested in using Twitter because they can easily connect with stars and celebrities. Famous people and public icons use this platform to stay connected with their following fans. Although Twitter is a microblogging social media service, the spamming problem on Twitter is emerging day by day as this platform is also used to promote blogs, brands, products, and other articles. Moreover, the risk of fraud is very high on Twitter [15].

People are involved in all the abovementioned sites or on other networking sites, but our main goal is to analyze how many of them are registered on these social networking platforms and actively use them in regular activities. The task is to categorize the audience visiting these sites and sharing their updates on traveling. This chapter categorically divides people into five different sets, i.e., unknown people, relatives, known people, friends, and friends of friends (mutual friends), for example, A, B, C, D, and E. The mentioned sets may vary in factors like gender, demography, culture, and friends who are involved. This also helps to find user interactions and their participation with the topic of traveling. Now we have

i {A} = {unknown people, relatives, known people, friends, friends of friends (mutual friends)}.

The elements of this set involved in a common group of travel blogs share pictures and their experiences and add comments. Moreover,

ii {B} = {relatives, known people, friends, friends of friends (mutual friends)}

In Set B, elements, known to each other through some link, are not in unknown groups of traveling but reacting and sharing views on others' pictures. Also,

iii {C} = {known people, friends, friends of friends (mutual friends)}.

The elements in Set C belongs to common groups, often traveling together and sharing their status and views and uploading their pictures of traveling details. These types of people are usually very active on social networking sites. Moreover,

iv {D} = {friends, friends of friends (mutual friends)}.

In Set D, the group of people knows each other, often participating in meetings, visiting various places with each other, and sharing or uploading their pictures in social networking sites. Finally,

v {E} = {friends}.

In this set only friends are involved, so they are often directly connected with each other and seem to be active on social sites, and they may or may not always share their blogs socially rather they simply send links, pictures, and their opinions in the form of messages.

From the above sets, we can determine that involvements of people on social networking sites are not the same. Considering their stories, blogs, and uploaded history, we can start the analysis of traveling depending on the mood and types of people. Various social and online platforms are responsible for making traveling easy for people and every day more people are involved.

7.4 Dynamics of traveling

Traveling is something very important that one must experience in order to have an inner mental balance. People are busy and get wrapped up in themselves in this competitive world. The burden of relentless working increases fatigue and causes tremendous stress levels, followed by depression and various health issues. Traveling to known or unknown places refreshes the mind and acts as an energy tonic, even to most workaholic persons. Fresh air and sunshine in a new place or a new environment is a mood enhancer that elevates the mental health state and can help people to get rid of depression. Human beings at any age or with any occupation, student or working or maintaining a household, returning from long vacations can do their corresponding tasks or jobs effectively with a fresh mindset and a refreshed health state [20].

In order to make a tour plan a few things need to be decided firmly. So, the decisive factors of traveling depend on answers to four specific questions:

i   Where to go?
ii When to go?
iii How to go?
iv With whom go?

The answers of the above questions directly prompt choice of location (hilly regions or the sea side or forests or plateaus), choice of season (summer vacation or winter or puja vacation, long weekend or short break), choice of transport (journey by train or flight or bus or bike), and finally choice of companionship (friends or family or tour group or office colleagues or solo). Hence, the very first decision for a tour plan is the location to be identified and next the other factors will be decided on, as the location is the primary factor during travel.

The remaining factors are *choice of season, choice of transport, and choice of companionship.* Analysis of all the possible choices is presented in the following:

- (a) **Choice of season**: Travel and tourism is mainly weather- and climate-dependent. The climatic changes in mountainous regions are strongest. It is always preferable not to visit hill stations on rainy days.

Car driving becomes dangerous when taking narrow paths through the mountain during rainy seasons [11].

The extreme change of climate causes various effects on the environments. The coastal areas get affected because of flood and huge rainfall. The upper surface of the earth gets influenced by the heat, rainfall, and snowfall. Rainfall can cause the removal of the upper layer of the soil. The huge amounts of heat and sun light in the summer season cause drying of the soil and soil fertility is also reduced. Snowfall on the other hand is not suitable for any harvesting and farming. The low humidity and moisture in the atmosphere cause drying of leaves and trees. Thus, the beauty of nature is hampered by climatic changes.

Forests also get affected because of the changing weather conditions. Warm summer and extreme heat reduce water availability in forests. Thus, wildlife is affected, resulting in a decrease in wildlife diversity. Low amounts of rainfall cause drying of leaves and green plants. The incidence of forest fires is also increasing because the atmospheric carbon dioxide levels are higher. The effects of climate and weather on traveling are presented in Fig. 7.2. Climate changes due to fluctuation of temperature, and temperature fluctuates due to carbon dioxide emission. So, in Fig. 7.2 the red line (mid gray in print version) reflects the temperature and the black line represents traveling in those years. It is also observed that in the 21st century, people traveled more frequently compared to the 1980s and 1990s [16].

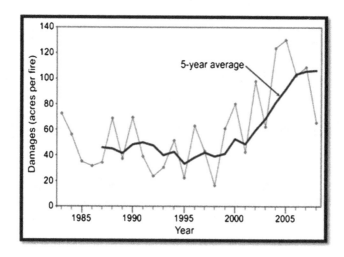

Figure 7.2 Effects of climate on traveling [13].

- (b) **Transport modes** are the major factors by which passengers and freight achieve mobility and travel from one place to another. It depends on people how they like to travel. Nowadays, people are more inclined towards traveling by bike rather than by train, airplane, bus, and other modes of transportation. Bike travelers are also said to "bike cruising" [16]. This type of travel is coming in fashion, and most bike travelers are choosing bike rides to travel long distances without facing any kind of problems. When traveling by bike, we often do not have to think much. Pre-planning processes are not applicable in the case of bike cruising. Currently, due to the COVID-19 pandemic, people can only travel by bike, as social distancing is also maintained. Moreover, bike traveling is also affordable and the availability of bikes is increasing day by day. The transit survey shows that bike cruising is increasing every year (Fig. 7.3) [11].

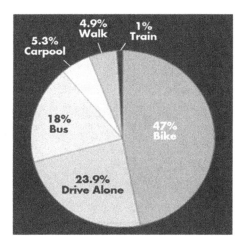

Figure 7.3 Rapid increase in bike cruising [12].

- (c) **Choice of companion**: The choice of companion is completely dependent on the factor of interest. Age, a friendly nature, and understanding between two people underlie the decision to travel together. In [14], the choices of human beings with whom they will travel are analyzed. Social networking sites often help us to find travel companions among friends, family members, colleagues, or other group members [16].

7.5 Dynamics-based social behavior analysis

The continuous popularity and usage of social networking sites are also providing us the ability to mathematically observe the human population. Travelers often prefer to use public transport which are available through social networking rather than any other modes of transport because they are cheaper. But decision making processes of people are also involved in this. Social networks provide us not only with the platforms to communicate with each other but also with the opportunity to join social groups, and users can protect their privacy by leaving any group when desired.

We analyze people's behavior by looking at their activities on social media. We can observe their traces of views and friendships in which they mostly participate. They make friends, and they join a preferential group on the basis of their interest. The behavior may vary with the change in behavior of others. The supervised learning ability helps us to find correlations of behaviors among them (see Fig. 7.4).

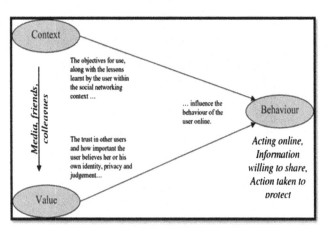

Figure 7.4 Combination of behavior [7].

7.5.1 Categorical behavioral analysis

Behavioral analysis can be divided in three different categories:

- (a) *Behavior among two users*: In this type of behavior two users are directly connected with each other and have friendly communication on online platforms. They may come from the same place or from different regions. For example, two users may know each other personally or they may virtually meet each other online and become friends. Due to social media, a hotel's customer service is no longer limited to what happens around. Rather, customer behavior includes in-person interactions and the interactions between customers and consumers on social platforms. When a consumer tweets a complaint, this helps to remedy the situation immediately, which is a large task for the tourist guides, considering there are tens of thousands of customers on social media.

- (b) *User to entity behavior*: Understanding behavior of an individual or a group is difficult because of two main factors: the travel behavior's wide of range coverage and the fact that different people have different views on traveling. This makes it difficult to collect information from the various data available on social platforms.

Some people who actively share posts on social media and comment on others' posts. A user link may be established between two users who show friendly behavior or similar buying pattern or who join the same group. Community joiners are those who like to join social media or any online groups. This type of behavior often gives rise to link prediction problems. This type of behavior is exhibited and such connections occur on social media with respect to entities on social media (for example, user–generated content). For instance, liking a post on Facebook or posting a tweet on Twitter are examples of user-entity behavior.

- (c) *End user to community group behavior*: Many online travel communities are available in social media. Online communities include real travelers who regularly post journal entries, articles, and photographs, sharing their personal traveling experiences. The forums, particularly the chit and chat forums, are where the real conversation takes place. Community members also plan city meet-ups, which offer a great opportunity to connect with fellow travel enthusiasts [2].

We analyze people's behavior by looking at their activities on social media. We can observe their traces of views and friendships in which they mostly participate. They make friends, and they join a preferential group on the basis of their interest. The behavior may vary with the change in behavior of others. The supervised learning ability helps us to find correlations of behaviors among them. People can also block their friends if they are not willing to continue their friendship [11].

7.5.2 Online behavior recognition

Online behavior can be used to identify the perceived benefits of the internet for travel planning such as relationships between the perceived mentality and the changes of travel planning behavior. However, it appears logical that the extent of the perceived benefits of internet use may be directly associated with the extent to which the travel planning behavior changes. For example, one might expect that travelers using the internet to share their travel experiences with different people will perceive that the internet is highly beneficial. Based upon this logic, a second objective of this online behavior analysis is to investigate the relationship between the perceived benefits of online travel planning and changes in travel planning behavior caused by the use of the internet. Online social media influence people in various ways and help them to judge any kind of post. Suppose any traveling page contains 80% of negative comments. Then our human psychology will determine that something is negative in the specific post that has been shared. When negative perception is blinked in our mind we derive our stimuli towards negativity. Internet effectiveness has been proved during the lockdown period due to COVID-19. Most of the people join traveling groups and watch the videos of different blogs.

7.5.3 Age group-based comparative analysis

The young age group is separately distinguished on the basis of studies and expeditions because most of their trips are related to their study purposes. Certain social groups are effectively made for children also. During the COVID-19 pandemic, online studies captured the major part of the social field. Polls are raised on certain topics and opinions are taken from different people. For example, on Instagram and Youtube, various opinions are analyzed as people can just press/click on the different options to share their opinion. Children also actively take part in this in the form of quizzes. Individuals in their early twenties tend to go out and socialize more. Most of the younger groups tend to go and travel for amusement purposes. Certain vacations are needed for refreshment. They are often expected to work either full- or part-time. However, due to the socioeconomic conditions currently prevailing in Serbia, the unemployment rate is high [20], especially in the age group below 35 years. On the other hand, older age groups and those approaching retirement are more likely to be employed and go to work regularly. While shopping as a trip purpose is reported in most age groups, its part of the daily travel distribution increases with age, while traveling for recreation and entertainment declines. However, the oldest respondents were found to be much more active in this respect than their middle-aged counterparts, as they regularly took walks and socialized with other pensioners and visited shops, markets, parks, etc.

As those in their late twenties to early sixties are considered to be of working age, they are expected to arrange their vacation mostly based on family requirements. Some of them frequently take official tours, but it is not possible for their family members to accompany them on the tour. So, the number of solo travelers is increasing, as people also try to make official trips on 1-day vacations, considering official tours as vacation trip. In this case, people are traveling with their colleagues. This survey excludes regular evening walks, morning walks, window shopping on markets to get rid of a monotonous life, relaxing, or playing in park, as these are not mind relaxing, such as taking time off to spend some quality time and explore new places for a total change and refreshment.

7.5.4 Influence of traveling on human behavior

When we travel we interact with new people who are carrying different opinions and thoughts. We are always trying to immerse ourselves in other cultures that directly affect our openness and personality traits, and, depending on our overall traveling experience, the change of our behavior can affect the others as well. These are lasting effects that cannot be erased from our minds easily. When we are out of our comfort zone we have to change our personality and behavior. In addition, the psychological concepts of different people clash, and there is a psychological concept called the "Big Five Factors" [11], including openness, extroversion (being friendly with others and sharing things with other people easily), neurotics, conscientiousness, and agreeableness. Interacting with new people and immersing oneself in a new culture directly affect our friendliness personality trait and, depending on our overall experiences that we have gained from the real world and from day-to-day life, may cause a permanent change in others.

7.6 Recognition of human social behavior using machine learning techniques

In this section, our proposed methodology is used to analyze the human social behavior recognition based on the availability of social networking site data. Social networking sites include Facebook, LinkedIn, Twitter, and Instagram. The proposed methodology uses a machine learning technique considering the data volume. Information about the history, background, and reviews of tourist spots (temple, museum, Taj Mahal, shopping mall, and Fuji Mountain), restaurants (vegetarian cuisine and Italian gourmet pizza), routes (from the hotel to tourist spots and restaurants), and transportation (bus, train, rental car, etc.) was gathered carefully, which helped many people to decide about their tours. Even fares of taxi, buses, and other transport modes are also indicated by the social media users [20].

Here, we mainly focus on the identification and description of considerations and self-disclosures of a specific behavior change relevant to traveling. In this chapter, the proposed approach provides an additional source of data for traveling behavior of an individual with the help of reviews and comments identified in Twitter. Hence, demographic analysis from Twitter is presented in the following using well-known classification and clustering techniques.

Clustering using machine learning technique is a method used to divide the dataset into clusters based on similarities that have been determined. The core target of this research is counting the number of likes of posts per Twitter or LinkedIn account related to tourist destinations in various traveling places that can be within India or outside. The experiences are collected through the above pictures to categorize the object of the researcher and presented in Figs. 7.5–7.9. Then from each picture or post, the number of reactions, number of comments, and number of retweets is classified to recognize positive or negative behavior. An explanation of positive and negative classifiers is presented in Eq. (7.1), Eq. (7.2), and Eq. (7.3). Collected data and categorized data are presented in Table 7.1 and Table 7.2, respectively. We have

$$\text{collected data} = \text{comments} + \text{reactions} + \text{retweets}, \quad (7.1)$$

$$\text{positive classifier} = \text{positive comments} + \text{positive reactions} + \text{retweets}, \quad (7.2)$$

$$\text{negative classifier} = \text{total comments} - \text{positive comments}. \quad (7.3)$$

Furthermore, positive comments are clustered based on innovation, energy, attraction, and passion characteristics of human beings. Some of the detailed comments are presented in Fig. 7.9.

A bar diagram for each post presenting the ratio between the percentage of positive classifications and the percentage of negative classifications is shown in Fig. 7.10. It is observed that for each post minimum 90% of data are recognized as positive. Moreover, for some posts it is found that 100% is classified as positive (Fig. 7.5). These inferences establish that social media affect people positively.

Figure 7.5 #Beachvibes [17].

Figure 7.6 #London [17].

Figure 7.7 #Travel & #Tourism [17].

Figure 7.8 #Slovenia [17].

Figure 7.9 Chichen Itza, Yucatan, Mexico [17].

Table 7.1 Data collection from Twitter.

Posts	Number of comments	Number of reactions	Number of retweets	Total collected data
Fig. 7.5	12	12	0	24
Fig. 7.6	61	185	3	249
Fig. 7.7	14	41	0	55
Fig. 7.8	36	211	2	249
Fig. 7.9	5800	16000	968	22768

Table 7.2 Classification of data.

Posts	Total collected data	Positive classifications	Negative classifications
Fig. 7.5	24	24	0
Fig. 7.6	249	230	19
Fig. 7.7	55	51	4
Fig. 7.8	249	241	8
Fig. 7.9	22768	21100	1668

Table 7.3 Clustering of positive comments.

Posts	Total	Energetic	Innovative	Attractive	Passionate	Undefined
Fig. 7.5	12	0	6	1	0	5
Fig. 7.6	61	52	4	2	2	1
Fig. 7.7	14	4	0	10	0	0
Fig. 7.8	36	15	6	14	1	0
Fig. 7.9	5800	1000	3000	1500	3000	0

Clustering of positive comments is presented in Eq. (7.4) and categorical data for each post are presented in Table 7.3. We have

$$\text{positive comments} = (\text{energetic} + \text{innovative} + \text{attractive} + \text{passionate} + \text{undefined}) \text{ comments.} \quad (7.4)$$

7.7 Conclusion

Traveling analysis is very useful to understand the changing behavior of people according to their traveling preferences. Traveling research is important as it helps to increase the traveling education factors. When we travel, we spread across the world to see different cultures and heritages.

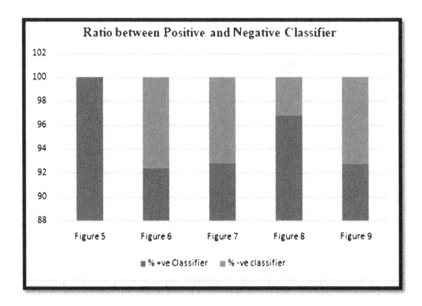

Figure 7.10 Ratio between positive and negative classifications.

Analysis is mainly focused on the travelers who travel across the world and share their feelings, opinions, and views based on traveling. Even though social media keep us connected to family while on vacation and offer us a huge virtual platform to share our instant reviews, these online platforms have had negative consequences as well like overtourism. This chapter has shown how complicated the impact of social media is. To gather more insight, we spoke with leaders in the travel industry to get their take on how social media platforms affect the way we travel today.

Traveling greatly influences growth in life. It allows us to do things and partake in activities that are different from day-to-day life. Traveling also provides practical education as it allows us to learn new things about the social life, economy, geography, and history of different cultures around the world. Thus, analysis of traveling helps us to make knowledgeable decisions on traveling. Traveling research is important as it helps to expand our knowledge and cultural heritage as we travel to various places to explore new things along with new people. Analysis is mainly focused on the travelers who travel across the world and share their feelings, opinions, and views based on traveling [20].

The present study reveals that human nature and behavior can be determined through social media sites. The likes, comments, and posts people share on social media can often seem immaterial, but the impact of these reactions is proof of human addictions, desires, anxieties, and happiness [15]. The most positive aspect is that self-study through social media may improve our behavior if necessary, and often the impact is valuable for creating better relationships.

References

[1] K. Axhausen, E. Zürich, Concepts of Travel Behavior Research, Chapter 11, Jan. 2007.

[2] B. Borges, Marketing 2.0. Wheat Mark, 2009, pp. 45–63. D. Brinlee, Does Internet Advertising Work?, 2007, http://www.askdeb.com/internet/advertising.

[3] D. Chaffey, Internet Marketing, Strategy, Implementation and Practice, 2nd edition, Pearson Education Limited, 2003, pp. 115–186.

[4] Y. Chi, Q. He, A. Khanj, Travel behavior classification: an approach with social network and deep learning, https://doi.org/10.1177/0361198118772723, June 2018.

[5] Competition among social media, https://www.smartinsights.com/ecommerce/social-commerce/social-commerce-trends-for-2020-you-need-to-look-out-for/. (Accessed 14 April 2020).

[6] J. Donath, D. Boyd, Public displays of connection, BT Technology Journal (2004) 71–82, E. Eric, 2008 Growth Puts Face book in Better Position to Make Money, 2008, http://venturebeat.com/2008/12/18/2008-growth-putsfacebook-in-better-position-to-make-money.

[7] Environment problem on travelling, https://www.bbc.com/news/science-environment-49349566. (Accessed 15 April 2020).

[8] A. Királová, A. Pavlíčeka, Development of social media strategies in tourism destination, Procedia – Social and Behavioral Sciences 175 (2015) 358–366.

[9] K. Lacy, M. Hernandez, Twitter Marketing for Dummies, 2009, pp. 14–20, K. Nicole, Building a Brand through Social Networks, 2007, http://mashable.com/2007/05/08/brand-social-networks/RicadelaA, 2007.

[10] L.P. Masiero, M.A. Casanova, M. Carvalho, Travel time prediction using machine learning, https://doi.org/10.1145/2068984.2068991, November 2011.

[11] Problem in social media, https://link.springer.com/referenceworkentry/10.1007.

[12] Rate of bicycle, https://www.explainthatstuff.com/bicycles.html. (Accessed 15 April 2020).

[13] Social Media and Tourism Domain within the Context of Using a Search Engine (Adapted from Xiang et al., 2008), https://www.researchgate.net/figure/Cruise-Tourist-Segmentation-Based-on-Cluster-Analysis-Travel-Motivations. (Accessed 15 April 2020).

[14] Solo traveler and companion, https://www.onetravel.com/going-places/the-secrets-of-successful-solo-travelers. (Accessed 14 April 2020).

[15] Table of travelling factors, https://www.researchgate.net/figure/Cruise-Tourist-Segmentation-Based-on-Cluster-Analysis-Travel-Motivations. (Accessed 15 April 2020).

[16] Transit Survey Reports, https://www.ucdavis.edu/news/transit-survey-47-percent-ride-bikes-campus/.

[17] Travel, https://twitter.com/travel.

[18] B. Wang, C. Shao, J. Li, J. Weng, X. Ji, Holiday travel behavior analysis and empirical study under integrated multimodal travel information service, Transport Policy (April 2015), https://doi.org/10.1016/j.tranpol.2014.12.005.

[19] M. Wong, B. Farooq, A bi-partite generative model framework for analyzing and simulating large scale multiple discrete-continuous travel behaviour data, pre-print submitted to Elsevier, May 11 2020.

[20] D.W. Wyatt, H. Li, J. Tate, Examining the Influence of Road Grade on Vehicle Specific Power (VSP) and Carbon Dioxide (CO2) Emission over a Real-World Driving Cycle, SAE Technical Paper 2013-01-1518 Society of Automotive Engineers, Warrendale, Pennsylvania, 2013.

[21] X. Zhao, X. Yan, A. Yu, P.V. Hentenryck, Prediction and behavioral analysis of travel mode choice: a comparison of machine learning and logit models, Travel Behaviour and Society (ISSN 2214-367X) 20 (2020) 22–35, https://doi.org/10.1016/j.tbs.2020.02.003.

CHAPTER 8

A study on behavior analysis in social network

Poulomi Samanta[a], Dhrubasish Sarkar[a], Premananda Jana[b], and Dipak K. Kole[c]

[a]Amity Institute of Information Technology, Amity University, Kolkata, India
[b]Netaji Subhas Open University, Kalyani, India
[c]Dept of CSE, Jalpaiguri Government Engineering College, Jalpaiguri, India

8.1 Introduction

A comprehensive list of data mining techniques allows for the detection of useful data from massive databases. By using some of the algorithms we can find out the thought patterns of users and the trends they are following. It also reduces the time to discover content or data which come from the network. These data are used to obtain knowledge and facilitate decision making processes. The data mining methods are designed to understand and measure the activity, and this is helpful to analyze different behaviors of nodes on an online social network. Data mining is also important to survey the history and the application of web-based network systems. By those techniques, the underlying rules can be found and our data can be analyzed using these, which is helpful to understand the properties of different areas. It is also useful to gain more information for further knowledge expansion in the virtual social environment. Then, the network system can be improved in terms of building behavior and other improvements.

By this type of platform, we create a behavioral image in various domains. By analyzing the data, we can gain a better understanding of the behavior of modern virtual worlds, which makes it a useful and significant platform for our work. It is a powerful platform that can be developed for use in e-commerce, education, communication, information science, economy, politics, etc. Nowadays, it can be easily accessed and it is available to serve the customer [3].

Social network analysis (SNA) is the process which is used to investigate the behavior of different social structures, with the use of graph theory and network relationships. This is characterized by the edges and nodes of network structures. As we know from graph theory, links or relations are

Advanced Data Mining Tools and Methods for Social Computing
https://doi.org/10.1016/B978-0-32-385708-6.00015-1

147

termed edges and individual persons or things in the network are called nodes; the main domain is the social media site and relations or links are working between individuals and groups.

If the behavior of individuals is analyzed, we can understand what inspires a person to join a group on social sites and what is the reason to abandon social sites and groups. For instance, from the posts of individuals on different sites the impact of a product or a movie can be predicted before launching it. These types of analyses are needed to comprehend the behavior of individuals on social media. On social media platforms, individuals are observed to demonstrate different behaviors. It can be the individual's behavior, which is focused on one individual person, or it can be a collective behavior, focused on the similar behavior of a group of individuals. There may be planning, or it can be unplanned action.

Different methods are discussed to analyze behavior in this study. These are used to build games and also used to understand the behavior of individuals [10].

The goal of this chapter is to understand the basic concepts of individual and collective behavior to highlight the concepts, structures, graphical representations, and network users. We will briefly discuss basic concepts of behavior analysis, the use of behavior analysis in social networks, social influence in SNA education, the future scope, and the outcomes.

8.2 Basic concepts of behavior analysis in social networks

The software architecture has different components. That architecture may have one single type or group types. The software components have interred relations and visibility. The visibie (external) factor is service, features, error processing, etc. The data and information flow are in a pattern, where the structure is shown as individual nodes of collection. The behavior of the people and groups and their interaction with each other within the network zone have been studied and analyzed. To sort out the pattern (as a tool to analyze the data) of communication, graph theory was used here [3].

Different techniques or methods are used to analyze user preferences and give choice to or influence the user, according to their needs. Therefore, it can be understood that the user's behavior analysis plays an important role in the analysis of data from online social networks [9].

In social media, nodes are referred to as actors, where the individual is a node within a network zone. A connection or link with others is known as a line or edge. Nodes represent individual persons or users, and links or edges presented the interactions among them. By SNA we can analyze a person, i.e., the types of connection that a person has and likes and dislikes by the person on the platform. Moreover, the kind of information and thoughts he/she likes to share with others or exchanged ideas can also be analyzed. As part of SNA in education, the locations of the nodes are compared, as well as the positive and negative effects on the educational curriculum, achievements in the educational field, and the volume of each participant in the education field. If the behavior of a student is focused on, then the individual who has better links to connect with others, has better resources, and has good educational support can be found. This means that he/she is helped, and the node can grow further [2][4].

The online structure of a society is made up of a large number of people making a virtual community. Data on a group's behavior can be mined and analyzed. For example, if a small group or an organization is analyzed, the behavior of an individual or a group may be understood globally based on a social platform [11].

On the other hand, we may obtain some pattern of individuals and groups or communities by this type of analysis. It is calculated by some methodology and modeled with some equations. To conduct social media analysis of a particular node or a group of nodes, it is necessary to understand the activity or behavior on the platforms. So, for the purpose of simplification we need to follow some steps. At first, the types of behavior must be understood. The behavior can be divided into different types for more simplification. These are as follows.

8.2.1 Individual behavior

Daily activities on social media, such as writing reviews, writing tweets, recommending or sharing posts, liking and commenting on videos, reading blogs, watching online news, writing comments, listening to music, liking posts, reviewing any product, watching educational videos, etc., are individual behavior. If those behaviors are examined, individual patterns may be obtained.

Generally, individuals are categorized into three categories based on their behavior. Those are the *user to user* type, the *user to group* type, and the *user to entity* type. Different types of behavior and what they actually do in real-world scenarios are presented in Table 8.1.

Table 8.1 Different types of individual behavior.

Type of individuals' behavior in social media (shows in Fig. 8.1)	Description
User to user	These types of behavior affect two different individuals or independent nodes in the virtual network.
	Messaging, making friends, inviting, suggesting, following, blocking and unfollowing someone, and subscribing to any page or channel are user–user behavioral examples.
User to group/community	These types of behavior are executed between a person and a group of people. Community joining behavioral theory was developed by Backstrometal [11].
	The relation between a teacher and a group of students of a class, joining and leaving groups on social media, sharing one's thoughts in a group, and participating in a discussion are typical behaviors of the user to group/community type.
User to entity	The goal is to upload or share some entity on social media by an individual.
	Uploading a photo, posting a video, and writing blog are typical examples.

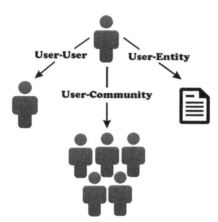

Figure 8.1 Individual behavior [3].

8.2.1.1 Methodology

Complicated data must be divided into different groups to analyze them by different methodologies and understand them. The methodology of behavior analysis is comprised of four steps that helps to link individuals with another individuals and communities or groups. Generally, to conduct behavioral analysis on data from social media, one need to go through the four components. Table 8.2 shows different steps and where they can be used.

Table 8.2 Four steps of behavior methodology.

Component	Description
Observable behavior	The first aspect of analysis is the observation of behavior of an individual to understand their preferences. Sometimes the time they joined is considered as an important weapon, when their behavior is analyzed.
Features	Another important thing to understand about an individual's behavior is whether the properties of data are relevant or not. The role of the feature in analyzing data holds lot of value to get the proper result. Sociological theories can help in this topic. For instance, the number of people in a group is counted as a feature.
Feature–behavior association	This association says something about the link between features within an individual's behavior, i.e., how it will affect behavior when the features are changed.
Evaluation strategy	Lastly, calculation is necessary to understand the result. Different techniques are used to find the results. Various types of evaluations, such as causality detection, classification accuracy determination, and randomization tests, are used to understand community or group joining behavior that we can use for calculation.

8.2.1.2 Modeling

Model of behavior can be very important in some cases. By modeling the behavior of an individual on social media, we can deduce whether the specific behavior needs to be observed and how much importance it has when analyzing and predicting the nature.

Table 8.3 Different models and the duties.

Types of modeling that we can use to understand a person's behavior	Details of the modeling type
Threshold models	If some product or advertisement is liked, the link is shared with others, and that product is bought by others, then this type of behavior falls under the threshold model. This only applicable if a person buys the product and his or her friends also buy the same product by the reference of the person. If the case is a bit different, for example, the person's friend ABC (name) bought a similar type of product before the person bought it, then this calculation is done by a collaborative filtering process to find out the average number of the same type of product or how much it is similar. The parameters are node activation and influence probabilities.
Cascade models	The threshold model of the receiver focal is already known, which means the receiver is inspired by the sender's choice. Unlike the threshold model, in the cascade model, it is the sender focal and the sender has the power to influence the receiver. Except these factors, everything is the same as in the threshold model. Cascade models enhance various information that is scattered in media networks.

Here, we discuss some of the models that one can use to analyze individual behavior (Table 8.3).

8.2.2 Collective behavior

Behavior is collective if individuals behave in the same way in a population. These same types of behavior can be designed and coordinated. For instance, individuals are waiting to buy a ticket to a new movie, post their thoughts, and like the trailer online to support the movie or show favor. These cases are formed by individuals and there is no influence by other individuals. We could also say no reference is passed to support the cause. The decision is taken by an individual independently. Then it can be said, it is a collective behavior.

8.2.2.1 Collective behavior analysis

The online structure of a community can be made up of a large number of people. The basic step is to understand the behavior of a group that is analyzed by the preference of users. By investigating organizational activity, we may get to understand the movement of a node or a node community on the social platform [11][18].

The first step of collective behavior analysis is performed by dividing the behavior of the individual. As discussed previously, the same four steps can be done in individual behavior analysis. Then it will be easier to group the individuals by their behavior. In other words, we can say, if collective behavior is divided, we can find individual behaviors separately.

8.2.2.2 Modeling

Collaborative behavior modeling helps us to divide individuals into groups. It is helpful when the nature or activity of a huge number of people must be divided into some parts. For instance, see Table 8.4.

Table 8.4 Collaborative model and their uses.

Collaborative model	Use in real life
Hypothetical model	This type of modeling can be used to predict election results.
Network modeling	This model can also be helpful to find similar things like the characteristics of a population for collaborative behavior modeling purposes. In the network model the property does not create that much value as in collaborative behavior.

8.3 Uses of behavior analysis in social networks

In group or community behavior on social media, different groups or communities are joined by individual users, but there must be some reason behind such activity. There must be some factor that attracts the user to do so.

If we analyze further, we may see that the factors underlying the joining by the user are almost the same in a particular group among independent individuals.

Let us consider the population is P and the community or group is G. Information of group membership is denoted p_i. Now we have

$$P = \{p_1, p_2, \ldots, p_n\}, \text{ where } p_i \in P \text{ and } p_i \text{ is the member of group G.}$$

This means that if one individual thinks about purchasing a product and other people also independently think about the same thing, then all individuals are classified into the same group. If we categorize two types of people over here, then one category will include those who have already joined the community (the community members) and the other category includes those who are not yet member of the community.

Let the community member be an individual under U, denoted s_2, where $s_2 > s_1$; s_2 is a member of the community or group and s_1 is not a member yet. Now the behavior of s1 (the chance that he/she will join the community) must be analyzed.

To understand the group or community joining behavior, at first we need to create hypothesis of the factors affecting joining behavior. In simple words, why would the joining behavior take place? This can be verified based on data from the internet. If we consider these factors among the persons who have already joined the community, then it may be easier for us to simplify the factors to identify future new members.

It may be possible that one individual is attracted by a specific movement while another person was already doing the same thing before and the person may know that other person. Then it can be a valid factor to join that group or community. Also, the group may have a lot of individuals that can attract an individual to join that community.

In [24], the authors have shown that an individual whose friend has already joined that particular group has a higher probability to join. There are also some who have left the group. This type of user behavior is also an important factor.

Now, different types of essential features to analyze community joining behavior will be presented in the next part.

8.3.1 User behavior in community joining and its features [7]

Let CO be the features of group members. So, members of the community between edges (EG) are $EG_{CO} \subseteq EG$. Then the properties of the feature set can be:

- the number of members: $|CO|$,
- the number of nodes with other nodes in CO (in the bank of CO),
- the number of edges with one end in the community and the other in the bank,
- the number of edges with both community ends: $|EG_{CO}|$,
- the number of open triads: $|\{(a, b, c) | (a, b) \in EG_{CO} \wedge (b, c) \in EG_{CO} \wedge (a, c) \in EG_{CO} \wedge a \neq c\}|$,

- the amount of closed triads: $|\{(a, b, c) \mid (a, b) \in EG_{CO} \wedge (b, c) \in EG_{CO} \wedge (a, c) \in EG_{CO}\}|$,
- the ratio of closed to open triads,
- the fraction of individuals in the bank with at least u friends in the group where $2 \leq u \leq 19$,
- the number of activities by individual of the group,
- the number of individuals of the group with least activity (reacts or posts),
- the number of reactions on any post.

Let us consider features with respect to a single individual, I, and her set F of friends in community CO. Then, we need to focus on the following properties of the feature set:

- the number of friends in the group: $(|F|)$,
- the number of adjacent pairs in F: $|\{(a, b) \mid a, b \in F \wedge (a, b) \in EG_{CO}\}|$,
- the number of pairs in M which are connected via a link in EG_{CO},
- the distance (average calculation) between nodes connected via a link in EG_{CO},
- the number of groups of individuals reachable from M using links in EG_{CO},
- the average distance to the reachable group members from M using a path in EG_{CO},
- the number of nodes in M with at least one activity,
- the number of activities made by nodes in M.

There are some methods which are based on the neighborhoods of nodes. They are as follows [3].

By Table 8.5, it can be understood that there are different methods to simplify the problem of behavior analysis. Also, it is shown that there are different formulas that we can use for specific results.

For example, in Fig. 8.2 we see the similarity between node v5 and node v7, v6 and v7, v3 and v1, and v5 and v7, as calculated based on various neighborhood techniques [3].

The *common neighbor* is calculated as follows according to the diagram:

- $\sigma(5,7) = |\{4,6\} \cap \{4\}| = 1$,
- $\sigma(6,7) = 1$,
- $\sigma(1,3) = 1$,
- $\sigma(5,8) = 0$.

The *Jaccard similarity* is calculated as follows according to the diagram:

- $\sigma(5,7) = |\{4,6\} \cap \{4\}| \ / \ |\{4,6\} \cup \{4\}| = 1/2$,
- $\sigma(1,3) = 1$,

Table 8.5 Different methods and formulas.

Name of method	Description	Formulas
Common neighbors	This method describes that the nodes are very similar if they have a lot of common neighbors. The process to connect with other nodes is made easier by common neighbors which indicates more information can be obtained.	$\sigma(x,y) = \|N(x) \cap N(y)\|$, where $N(x)$ = set of neighbors of node x
Jaccard similarity	If there is a neighbor of either x or y to be common, then this method is used to calculate the probability of a node.	$\sigma(x,y) = \|N(x) \cap N(y)\| / \|N(x) \cup N(y)\|$, where the numbers of common neighbors is divided by the total number of either x's or y's friends
Adamic and Adar measure	It says a lower degree of a node makes it a higher rear node, i.e., lower degree = less value or less chances to get influence and make the choice.	$\sigma(x,y) = \sum_{z \in N(x) \cap N(y)} 1 / \log\|N(z)\|$
Preferential attachment	It says that some nodes think that the higher degree one node has, the more chance there is to link up with more new nodes and carry more value.	$\sigma(x,y) = \|N(x)\| \cdot \|N(y)\|$

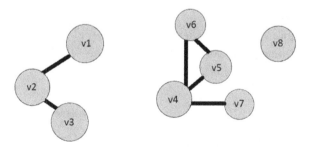

Figure 8.2 Link prediction [3].

- $\sigma(6,7) = 1/2,$
- $\sigma(5,8) = 0.$

    The *Adamic and Adar* measure is calculated as follows:

- $\sigma(5,7) = 1/\log|\{5,6,7\}| = 1 / \log 3,$
- $\sigma(1,3) = 1/\log 2,$
- $\sigma(6,7) = 1/\log 3.$

    Preferential attachment is calculated as follows:

- $\sigma(5,7) = |\{4\}| \cdot |\{4,6\}| = 1 \times 2 = 2,$
- $\sigma(2,4) = 6,$
- $\sigma(2,5) = 4,$
- $\sigma(2,6) = 4.$

By these examples, it is very clear how different methods work using different data or nodes and edges. Also, it seems that there is a possibility that individual nodes have some relation with other nodes, or they may not have any single relation with others.

8.3.2 Collaborative study prediction

Collaboration can be viewed from two perspectives. It can be seen as collaboration among a group of individuals or as collaboration between two different groups. In collaborative behavioral analysis, it is commonly considered among a group of people. When a large group of people undergoes this type of analysis, the complication is reduced and challenges get much simplified [3].

The box-office income of a movie is an interesting example of collaborative analysis behavior. Surely, nowadays it is possible to guess whether the movie will do good business. Different social media sites like Twitter, Facebook, and YouTube have made it possible. A huge number of people review the poster or trailer of the movie on social media. This can be analyzed by collaborative behavior analysis. The following steps are taken.

First, the target variable needs to be set. The target variable is income by the person who is watching that movie. In the next step the features will be analyzed and collected. This is the most important step. The result of our target can be affected by those features. Then, it is necessary to determine the features using different approaches for further prediction and lastly the volume of the effect of the target variable must be measured. By this example, now we understand the stepwise method of collaborative behavior analysis based on social media and how it creates importance on our life.

8.3.3 Related works

J. Xu and H. Chen have described different data mining techniques in the field of crime in 2005 [7]. A vector machine mechanism, clustering, a neural network, and decision trees are described. By Poeczeetal's discovery, we know how posts on social media affect the analysis of public behavior. Stieglitzetal showed different critical challenges regarding data analysis and provided some solutions in 2017.

Using different mining techniques, the user's activity can be analyzed and the result can be used for more convenient and user-friendly features in virtual networks [8]. Data mining is a recent topic that can be used in behavior analysis and in other different ways regarding virtual media [12,13]. Kossinets and Watts gave a lecture on the experimental analysis of the growth is massive on the virtual network platform [14].

Wang and McCallum presented some revolutionary model which is very essential to understand virtual environments [15]. Boorman and Levitt showed different and mathematical models for community analysis and behavior change techniques in the social sciences [16]. Nowadays, the bidirectional encoder representations from transformers (BEAT) model concept to understand search behavior and language processing is getting very famous. It provides results according to the user's expectations by analyzing the type of input [19]. The online food business is making footsteps in the virtual world by online orders, reviews, etc. From there, huge amounts of data are generated. If these are properly analyzed, business growth can be possible in an easier way [20]. Using the BERT model, we also can analyze positive and negative posts on social media and find the behavioral status of individuals or groups and public concerns about health during the pandemic [21]. Segment analysis is one of the ways to collect the opinions or feedback from users and analyze them to collect information for the users' betterment [22]. The BERT model is mainly used to analyze language and from there we can deduce the mindset of the user, how the model works, how it can be used, the underlying mechanism, etc. [23].

8.4 Future direction

All over the world, in the field of social network platforms, the use of up-to-date technology has gained high priority, so automatically huge amounts of data are produced, increasing our interest in experimental work in different areas. The data must be analyzed to serve individuals according to their preferences.

Nowadays, the education and teaching field is growing rapidly. The only reason for that is the emergence of data mining and processing techniques. Various new algorithms exist. The analysis techniques positively affect development all over the world. Various related areas can be improved (education as well as machine learning fields) by using individual behavioral data. The information which comes from different networking sites is helping us to analyze behavior of data and also in the development of new strategies, and that can be useful to get more information on individual in an independent way. These types of data are interpretable, and the formations are high in demand and a direction can be given to understand the individual further and closely. Behavioral data analysis will continue to develop, aiming to reduce complexity [17].

By behavioral analysis we have come to know that the social media field offers lots of opportunities for everyone in the fields of education, business, e-commerce, entertainment, etc. It is a very effective way to build a community to share information.

Online movement has very much increased since the 21st century due to the virtualization of society. Ways to digitally gather or share information have become much more popular than the traditional way by physical means. SNA methods are very useful tools, and by using these, the actual effects according to the change of difficulties at different levels of analysis can be seen. In organizations and online schools, we can see examples of behavioral relationships and new initiatives [5][6]. Contact is boosted, which also helps to identify and understand the critical as well as behavioral sources of users. SNA is not an end result, but a mechanism to evaluate the process further.

As the number of individuals in the online networking world is increasing, now is the time to think differently, develop more convenient types of algorithms and tools, build contacts within rural areas, and understand human behavior. This type of analysis in the virtual world is about making an impact to elucidate the path to connect and make communication for different users easier. In this way we can get involved in a big field, help each other, and interact. Sharing of information is made easy.

Based on this chapter we can easily understand the importance of behavior analysis of social media in different areas (from an individual or an organizational point of view), making an impact on communication and collaboration in different ways in the virtual network.

8.5 Conclusion

In the social media network, individuals exhibit different behavior, which can be divided into collaborative behavior and individual behavior. Individuals' behavior is further divided into three types, i.e., one individual with another individual (one to one), one individual with some entity on the internet, and one individual with a community or group (which happens when individuals join a community under the influence of some particular feature). To analyze behavior, different methods are followed.

Here, the behavior of users on social media is observed and then analyzed to (i) find the essential features for analysis, the relationships among features, and the behavior and (ii) verify the relationships based on new data [17]. Collaborative relationships also help us to understand bigger complicated scenarios; if certain independent individual persons have some similarity in their behavior, then the behavior falls under this category. For example, someone can post something, and a huge number of subscribers like that post. From this particular behavior we can gain some knowledge about the individual subscribers (what they prefer) [1].

Different sites can be used by people according to their needs. Many services are available, and every day it becomes easier to search anything. If something is liked by an individual, more similar options appear on the screen. This kind of behavior is only possible if the person's acts on social media are analyzed.

Time is very important nowadays. By all these analysis processes we can understand users more specifically. If a person is analyzed correctly, we can influence him or her with more new and important content according to their preferences. Hence, it is easier to find important objects quickly. Moreover, the networking sites can be made less complicated and more user-friendly. That is why data mining and behavior analysis on social media platforms are so important.

References

[1] M. Brown, Why social network analysis, https://bookdown.org/chen/snaEd/why-social-network-analysis.html. (Accessed 14 December 2019).
[2] D. Easley, J.M. Kleinberg, Networks, Crowds, and Markets, Cambridge University Press, 2010.
[3] R. Zafarani, M. Ali, A. Huan, Social Media Mining 10 (2014) 319–338.
[4] D. Sarkar, P. Jana, Analyzing user activities using vector space model in online social networks, in: Proceedings of the National Conference on Recent Trends in Information Technology & Management (RTITM 2017), India, 2017, pp. 155–158.

[5] Daniel Z. Grunspan, Benjamin L. Wiggins, Steven M. Goodreau, Understanding classrooms through social network analysis, CBE Life Sciences Education 13 (2) (2014) 167–178, https://www.ncbi.nlm.nih.gov/pmc/articles/PMC4041496/.

[6] Dexway Team, 5 reasons why online learning is more effective, https://www.dexway.com/5-reasons-why-online-learning-is-more-effective/. (Accessed 8 December 2019).

[7] X. Lan, D. Huttenlocher, J.M. Kleinberg, L. Backstrom, Group formation in large social networks: membership, growth, and evolution, in: Proceedings of the 12th ACM SIGKDD International Conference on Knowledge Discovery and Data Mining, ACM, 2006, pp. 41–56.

[8] D. Sarkar, D.K. Kole, P. Jana, A. Chakraborty, Users activity measure in online social networks using association rule mining, in: Proceedings of the IEMCON 2014: 5th International 294 Conference on Electronics Engineering and Computer Science, Elsevier Science & Technology, Kolkata, India, 2014, pp. 172–178.

[9] D. Sarkar, S. Roy, C. Giri, D.K. Kole, A statistical model to deter-mine the behavior adoption in different timestamps on online social network, International Journal of Knowledge and Systems Science (IJKSS) 10 (4) (2019) 1–17, https://doi.org/10.4018/IJKSS.2019100101.

[10] J. Xu, H. Chen, Criminal network analysis and visualization, Communications of the ACM 48 (6) (2005) 100–107, https://doi.org/10.1145/1064830.1064834.

[11] Lada A. Adamic, O. Buyukkokten, E. Adar, A social network caught in the web, First Monday (2003).

[12] P. Domingos, M. Richardson, Mining the network value of customers, in: Proc. 7th Intl. Conf. Knowledge Discovery and Data Mining.

[13] G. Kossinets, D. Watts, Empirical analysis of an evolving social network, Science (2006) 88–90.

[14] X. Wang, McCallum, Topics over Time: a Non-Markov Continuous-Time Model of Topical Trends, 2006.

[15] S. Boorman, P. Levitt, The Genetics of Altruism, 1980.

[16] L. Backstrom, D. Huttenlocher, J.M. Kleinberg, X. Lan, Group formation in large social networks: membership, growth, and evolution, in: Proceedings of the 12th ACM SIGKDD International Conference on Knowledge Discovery and Data Mining, ACM, 2006, pp. 44–54.

[17] D. Morrison, Can Social Network Analysis Help Teachers Change? (Book review: Social Networking Theory and Educational Change. Harvard Education Press, 2010), 2016, https://onlinelearninginsights.wordpress.com/2016/01/26/can-social-network-analysis-help-teachers-change/. (Accessed 8 December 2019).

[18] D. Sarkar, S. Debnath, D.K. Kole, P. Jana, Influential nodes identification based on activity behaviors and network structure with personality analysis in egocentric online social networks, International Journal of Ambient Computing and Intelligence 10 (4) (2019) 1–24.

[19] R. Horev, BERT explained: state of the art language model for NLP, 2018.

[20] N. Hossain, Md.R. Bhuiyan, N.Z. Tumpa, Sentiment Analysis of Restaurant Reviews Using Combined CNN-LSTM, July 2020.

[21] T. Wang, K. Lu, K.P. Chow, Q. Zhu, COVID-19 sensing: negative sentiment analysis on social media in China via BERT model, IEEE Access 8 (2020).

[22] J. Serrano-Guerrero, J.A. Olivas, F.P. Romero, E. Herrera-Viedma, Sentiment analysis: a review and comparative analysis of web services, 2015.

[23] M.S.Z. Rizvi, Demystifying BERT: a Comprehensive Guide to the Groundbreaking NLP Framework, 2019.

[24] L. Backstrom, D. Huttenlocher, M.J. Kleinberg, X. Lan, Group formation in large social networks: membership, growth, and evolution, 2006.

CHAPTER 9

Recent trends in recommendation systems and sentiment analysis

Sutapa Bhattacharya[a], **Dhrubasish Sarkar**[b], **Dipak K. Kole**[c], and **Premananda Jana**[d]

[a]Siliguri Institute of Technology, Siliguri, India
[b]Amity Institute of Information Technology, Amity University, Kolkata, India
[c]Dept of CSE, Jalpaiguri Government Engineering College, Jalpaiguri, India
[d]Netaji Subhas Open University, Kalyani, India

9.1 Introduction

Some famous websites, like Netflix, Amazon, and Yelp, contain a lot of reviews and ratings on a five-point scale. Ratings vary day by day. Recommender systems (also known as recommendation systems) are helpful to provide users with content that is similar to objects they liked in the past. For example, it is possible to generate recommendations about whether a user will consider a movie good/bad/average on the basis of the user's written reviews or opinions. The opinions/reviews/ratings of any person will be very helpful for recommending not only movies, but also new products, restaurants, guest houses, and tourist spots and e-learning [1] applications to them.

The term "recommendation/recommender system" refers to an extensive class of web applications (e.g., learning) capable of predicting the future opinion of a user about a set of items for a user and recommending the top items. Nowadays people have many choices due to the versatility of the internet. Friend recommendations, product recommendations, and video recommendations can be seen on social media. Individual-based choices are the main theme of recommendation systems. According to customers' choices, a recommendation engine discovers data patterns among whole datasets and gives results that are correlated with their wishes and interests. Amazon is a real-world example. Amazon uses a recommendation engine to suggest the goods or products as per customers' requirements. Netflix also uses a recommendation engine for suggestions. Ultimately the target is similar for all giants: to recommend their items to customers. The recommender systems are divided into three categories [2]: (A) content-based

Advanced Data Mining Tools and Methods for Social Computing
https://doi.org/10.1016/B978-0-32-385708-6.00016-3
163

filtering, (B) collaborative filtering, and (C) hybrid systems (a mix of two approaches).

(A) Content-based filtering recommendation: These recommender systems recommend a set of items that are comparable to the ones which the user liked in the past. For a recommendation of any movie to the user, first all similarities of content between the movie's attributes such as title and storyline previously discussed by the users and those which have not been discussed are checked. Content-based recommender systems are based on the reviews generated by users and the items' descriptions. When similarity is high, the item is recommended.

(B) Collaborative filtering recommendation: These recommender systems recommend the preferences of other users with comparable experiences to those of the target user (these users are called "neighboring users") and suggest items that the target user has not rated. The collaborative filtering algorithms are divided into two subcategories: memory-based and model-based approaches. Memory-based approaches directly work with values of recorded interactions, assuming no model, and are essentially based on nearest neighbors search (for example, find the closest users from a user of interest and suggest the most popular items among these neighbors). Model-based approaches assume an underlying "generative" model that explains the user–item interactions and try to discover it in order to make new predictions.

(C) Hybrid recommendation: These recommender systems combine content-based and collaborative-based filtering. Hybrid systems can be implemented by making content-based and collaborative-based predictions separately and then combining them.

Recommendations are made based on the social context in friendship networks. These friendships can improve recommendation systems based on product reviews, movie reviews, e-learning [1], and many other things. Accuracy, precision, recall, and similarity of recommendation systems based on evaluation have been analyzed.

Sentiment analysis can be conducted based on users' own choices in different areas where users give numerical scores rather than making binary choices. The scores may be positive, negative, or neutral. It determines the writer's attitude towards a particular topic or product, i.e., positive, negative, or neutral. Sentiment analysis is also called opinion mining because the process for examining, detecting and extracting opinions from text. Another goal of sentiment analysis is to find the depression level of a person by observing and extracting emotions from texts. In a nutshell, sentiment analysis is the procedure of calculating the emotional tone behind a series of words in order to understand the attitudes, opinions, and emotions of humans expressed in a text.

Another important goal of sentiment analysis is to discover the impact of influence in propagation of opinion of a person about a certain product [3]. Sentiment analysis can be performed in three different ways: (i) at the document level, (ii) at the sentence level, and (iii) at the feature (or aspect) level [4].

(i) Document level: The main objective of document-level analysis is to obtain the general opinion of the entire document, classified as positive or negative. It works only for single documents.

(ii) Sentence level: In sentence-level analysis, first the subjective sentences are identified and then it is determined whether the sentiment indicates positive, negative, or neutral opinions.

(iii) Feature or aspect level: A common approach for aspect-level or feature-level analysis is to concern the study of emotions, opinions and facts that are articulated by people. Among all different types of sentiments these features should be recognized [4].

In a nutshell, sentiment analysis is the most basic [5] method to identify users' preferences.

9.2 Basic terms and concepts of sentiment analysis and recommendation systems

(i) Post: Content which is published on social media by any user to which likes, reviews, comments, etc., can be attached.

(ii) Sentiment: A thought of any person expressing some feelings regarding any matter.

(iii) Opinion: A view of any subject.

(iv) Global sentiment: The opinion expressed in a tweet, post or review as a whole within a certain time frame.

(v) Ratings: In memory-based models, recommendations are made according to similarity values. Ratings are used to estimate the similarity between users and items. The most popular memory-based collaborative filtering methods are neighbor-based methods. All methods are evaluating ratings on the basis of users and similar items.

(vi) Polarity: Polarity helps in opinion mining. It gives positive, negative, and neutral scores. The sum of polarity can be calculated as follows [2]:

Sum of polarity = Σpositive polarity + Σ negative polarity

$$+ \ \Sigma \ \text{neutral polarity.} \qquad (9.1)$$

(vii) Subjectivity: An individual user's attitude or views.

(viii) Objectivity: Objective expressions about entities, procedures, and their properties.

(ix) Precision: Precision measures the accuracy of a classifier. A higher precision means fewer false positives, while a lower precision means more false positives.

(x) Recall: Recall measures the entirety or sensitivity of a classifier. Higher recall means fewer false negatives, while lower recall means more false negatives.

(xi) Mean absolute error: The mean absolute error (MAE) is mainly used for measurement in recommendation systems. It estimates the mean of the absolute difference between the estimates and the predictions. When the MAE value is low, then the collaborative recommendation system is considered to achieve good performance.

(xii) F1 score: The F1 score can be calculated as follows: F1 score = 2 × ((precision × recall) / (precision + recall)). It is also called the F score or the F measure. The F1 score conveys the balance between the precision and the recall.

9.3 Overview of sentiment analysis approaches in recommendation systems

The objective of sentiment analysis is to accurately extract people's opinions from a large number of unstructured review texts and classifying them into sentiment classes, i.e., positive, negative, or neutral. Sometimes "highly positive" and "highly negative" are also considered. Sentiment analysis is also called opinion mining, which refers to the use of natural language processing and text mining to identify the emotional information from text materials.

Sometimes, social media behavior analysis [2] also plays an important role in sentiment analysis and recommendation systems. Through social media, users can read online news, comment, like and share posts, blogs, and videos, and write reviews or opinions about products. There are certain types of online behavior. They can be categorized as follows:

(i) User–user behavior: This includes behavior between two users, for example, sending friend requests or messages from one user to another, playing games, blocking, chatting, etc.

(ii) User–community behavior: This includes behavior between a user and a community, for example, joining or leaving a community, being a fan, or participating in any community event.

(iii) User–entity behavior: This category includes writing a blog, post, or review or uploading a photo to social media.

Different types of approaches of sentiment analysis are (A) lexicon-based approaches and (B) machine learning-based approaches.

A. Lexicon-based approaches: These approaches involve dictionaries of words annotated with semantic polarity and sentiment strength. They produce good outcome with high accuracy but low recall. They require a large dictionary, which is not always possible. A dictionary which contains both positive and negative terms used by lexicon-based approaches is applied to evaluate the polarity of views. The optimistic and pessimistic words in the text are counted. If a text contains more positive words, a positive score will be assigned to the text. If a text contains more negative or pessimistic words, it is given a negative score. If the text contains equal numbers of positive and negative terms, a neutral score is given.

B. Machine learning-based approaches: Sentiment analysis is a well-known machine learning technique that receives words from a text and analyzes them. After analyzing, it measures sentiment intensity. It trains a few exact inputs with known outputs using supervised and unsupervised algorithms. Supervised algorithms discard the output values of the samples, whereas unsupervised algorithms collect all natural structure present within data groups. In supervised learning, linear classifiers and probabilistic classifiers have been used. Support vector machine (SVM) is a well-known linear classification technique. The naive Bayes classifier is actually a probabilistic classifier used for sentiment analysis. Semi-supervised classification using SVM (S3VM) is also used in machine learning-based approaches. Semi-supervised learning occurs when both training and working sets are non–empty. Common examples of unsupervised machine learning algorithms are K-means and Apriori algorithms.

We provide a brief overview of several approaches which are used for sentiment analysis (see Table 9.1) [5].

9.4 Recent developments (related work)

In social networks, a high degree of connectivity can be seen which actually affects recommendation systems [7][8] and also sentiment analysis.

Table 9.1 Several approaches on sentiment analysis.

Name of the approach	Methodology	Outcome
Support vector machine	Supervised algorithm where a large training set is required	A non-probabilistic classifier gives a decision plane
Naive Bayes classifier	This one is also called a supervised algorithm where a subset of Bayesian decision theory is actually used	The value of a definite feature is self-sufficient for the value of any other feature, given the class
Linear regression	The most commonly used type of predictive analysis	The function of a line/hyperplane which is described by the given data is defined, which explains the association between the variables
Semi-supervised learning [6]	Clustering with some labeled data and model selection with unlabeled data	The quality of labeled and unlabeled data
S3VM classifier [6]	S3VM constructs a support vector machine using all the available data from both the training and working sets. It maximizes the margin of both the lower and the upper plane	Decision surface placed in non-dense spaces. It gives a mixture of labeled data (the training set) and unlabeled data (the working set)
Rule-based approach	Created by tokenizing each sentence in every document	It shows positive or negative scores according to a polarity-based approach

Social networks have their own characteristics, and these have affected ratings as well. In the case of recommendation algorithms [3][7], for a set of users U and a set of items I and learns a function f such that

$$f : UXI - - > R. \tag{9.2}$$

This algorithm learns a function that assigns a real value to each user–item pair (u, i), where this value indicates how interested user u is in item i. This value denotes the rating given by user u to item i.

Table 9.2 shows some recommendation system frameworks used in sentiment analysis for measuring prediction, ratings, accuracy, similarity, etc.

Table 9.2 State-of-the-art of sentiment analysis with recommendations.

Paper	Dataset	Approach	Outcome
[9]	Merlot repository	Affective term frequency algorithm	Measures the precision which shows the instances of events
[10]	Twitter API	Gaussian process and ZeroR algorithm	Predicting personality of a user
[11]	DBPedia-2014.	Graph-based word embedding method	Word similarity prediction
[12]	Amazon and Yelp	Opinion-based content modeling and social network structure modeling	Personalized sentiment classification results
[13]	Amazon and API	Amazon recognition algorithm	A facial confidence score is calculated
[14]	IMDB and YELP-2013 and YELP-2014	Bidirectional LSTM with hierarchical structure to obtain a deeper document semantics representation	RMSE and accuracy
[15]	Training dataset	Support vector machine, naive Bayes, maximum entropy	Accuracy, precision, recall
[16]	Amazon camera review dataset	CISER model	Candidate feature extraction and similarity score
[17]	MovieLens 100k dataset	Rating inference approach with collaborative recommendation	Movie ID, user ID, review date, summary (natural language text) written by the user, rating of movies

Actually, sentiment analysis, or opinion mining, is a subfield of natural language processing (NLP) [17] that tries to recognize and extract opinions within a given text. Consider the sentence "The price of the laptop is so high, but it is amazing." This sentence consists of two polarities, i.e., positive as well as negative. The sentence "The best I can say about the laptop is that its speed is very high" gives only positive polarity.

Valence Aware Dictionary and sEntiment Reasoning (VADER) is a lexicon- and rule-based sentiment analysis tool [18][19] that is particularly accustomed to sentiments spoken in social media. VADER not only tells about the positivity and negativity scores, but also tells us about how positive or negative a sentiment is. VADER [16] analyzes sentiments primarily based on certain prominent fields such as punctuation, capitalization, degree modifiers, and conjunctions.

Sentiment analysis has also progressed with deep learning models such as convolutional neural networks (CNNs), recursive neural networks (RvNNs), and recurrent neural networks (RNNs) [20]. Texts can be converted into numbers by word embeddings [21]. The deep learning platform is used in the word2vec model representation. The meaning is used as an input to a classifier (see Table 9.3).

Table 9.3 Some deep learning approaches.

Name of the network	Characteristics	Functions
Recurrent neural network (RNN) [20]	The input measured here is the following words, and the output is the calculation under each category	A higher regularization technique may come through over 40% of accuracy
Recursive neural network (RvNNs) [20]	Graphical representation of structured format of input is considered recursively	Computational model is used for machine learning problems
Convolutional neural network (CNN) [20]	Fully connected 2D structure of one or more feedforward networks	Produces higher accuracy
Long short-term memory (LSTM) [22]	Artificial recurrent neural network architecture consisting of feedback connections	Higher representation of words which are specially applied for a classification task

Now, an unsupervised bidirectional encoder representations from transformers (BERT) model [23] (Fig. 9.1) is adopted to classify sentiment categories (positive, neutral, and negative). It is pre-trained on generic datasets. Using the BERT model, several NLP tasks can be executed.

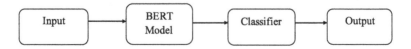

Figure 9.1 BERT model [23] used for sentiment analysis.

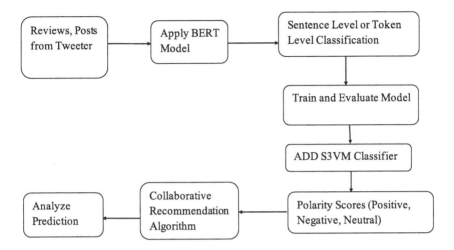

Figure 9.2 Architecture of the proposed sentiment analysis system.

Here, a new architecture (Fig. 9.2) has been proposed where a combination of the BERT model and an S3VM classifier using collaborative filtering recommendation is used. To obtain a user's choices, reviews, and posts from Twitter, some dataset can be taken. These data may be labeled or unlabeled. Through the BERT model we can perform sentence-level classification or token-level classification (e.g., part of speech tagging). By cleaning all special characters and removing stop words, the sentences have been split into tokens, which is known as tokenization.

As a result, some filtered datasets can be obtained. After training and evaluating, the sentiment classification model achieves good accuracy and F1 scores [24]. Then we can apply the well-known S3VM classifier [7]. In the proposed model, the S3VM classifier is used because it gives a dense decision plane. As a result, this method can be verified in more datasets. First of all, the data (labeled and unlabeled) have been collected from online reviews and then frequent candidate features were extracted for grouping.

After that, sentiment identification has been performed according to the polarity score (positive, negative, or neutral). At last, a collaborative filtering recommendation model is evaluated using the MAE (Mean Absolute Error) , precision, and recall values. A context-sensitive word embedding collaborative model is used for final analysis and prediction [25].

Table 9.4 shows the accuracies and F1 scores for different model types for comparison.

Table 9.4 Comparison of all models [26].

Models	Accuracy	F1 score
BERT	0.94	0.94
Logistic regression	0.91	0.91
CNN	0.72	0.72

9.5 Challenges

Sentiments can be extracted from texts and analyzed by either a dictionary of words or by machine learning techniques, but the drawback of the latter method is that the training model must have a high number of examples to obtain good classification without noise. Shifting huge volumes of text data is not easy and time consuming. Moreover, it requires a great deal of expertise. Thus, it is possible to extract essential insights from enormous unstructured datasets. Several challenges [2][8] remain in the field of recommendation system:

(i) Sparsity: A variable with sparse data is one in which a comparatively high percentage of the variable's cells do not contain actual data. The sparsity problem happens when transactional or response data are sparse and inadequate to recognize neighbors and it is a foremost matter restraining the quality of recommendation systems and the applicability of collaborative filtering in general. When a system has a very high item-to-user ratio, then this problem occurs.

(ii) Cold-start problem: In recommendation systems, the cold-start problem means the circumstances are not optimized. It can be seen in collaborative filtering. When new users or new items appear on e-commerce platforms, then collaborative filtering assumes that individual users or items have some ratings for similar users/items even if those ratings are not present. The new-item problem (also known as the first-rater problem) is concerned with obscure items which are basically detrimental to the users.

(iii) Fraud: Every online business wants to boost its transaction volume. More numbers of money transactions and customer data can be hampered by fraud mechanism. It puts more pressure on the rules library to expand. At that time fraud cases are enhanced. Many attacks such as profile injection attacks (using dummy profiles) and average attacks (assigning some fake random value on items) have been observed. Item-based collaborative filtering tends to be more prone to these attacks.

Sometimes, sentiment classification algorithms face problems due to enormous amounts of data because there is a high pressure for subjectivity detection, sentiment prediction, text summary, product feature extraction, opinion spam detection, etc.

9.6 Future direction

Polarity shows how a person's emotional state can be reflected and people's sentiments can change over a period of time. The VADER approach (lexicon-based) and the BERT model with S3VM (machine learning-based) both follow. Collaborative recommendation systems have as input the actual evaluation of the user or the result from sentiment analysis. In the future, hybrid recommendation systems can be used for prediction combined with aspect-level sentiment analysis [27]. Egocentric analysis of online social networks incorporate an efficient influence measured Recommendation System for a list of top most influenceable target users [28]. So, some shortcomings of collaborative recommendation systems can be solved. The paper [29] elaborates other strategy also. Here a personalized recommender system has applied for measuring subjectivity and polarity by analyzing user behavior.

9.7 Conclusion

In this chapter, techniques for constructing recommender systems and sentiment analysis, recent works, and challenges have been highlighted. The proposed method can be enhanced in several aspects. First, different data (labeled and unlabeled) can be used for different sentiment analyses, so the model can be tuned to accommodate more situations. Second, in the sentiment analysis process, different kinds of subjective ideas are involved, causing undesirable effects. The SVM and BERT model can achieve better performance than other techniques in terms of processing speed, accuracy, precision, and recall. Recommendation systems (using both content-based and collaborative filtering) have been used in the healthcare sector as well [30].

It can be concluded that the development of hybrid recommendation systems combined with aspect-level sentiment analysis in the near future is promising.

References

[1] S.S. Kundu, D. Sarkar, P. Jana, D.K. Kole, Personalization in education using recommendation system: an overview, in: A. Deyasi, S. Mukherjee, A. Mukherjee,

A.K. Bhattacharjee, A. Mondal (Eds.), Computational Intelligence in Digital Pedagogy, in: Intelligent Systems Reference Library, vol. 197, Springer, Singapore, 2021, pp. 85–111.

[2] R. Zafarani, Md.A. Abbasi, H. Liu, Social Media Mining: An Introduction, Cambridge University Press, 2014.

[3] R.N. Silvaa, M. Gamitoa, P. Pinaa, A.R. Camposa, Modelling Influence and Reach in Sentiment Analysis, Elsevier, 2016, pp. 48–53.

[4] B. Liu, Sentiment Analysis and Opinion Mining, vol. 5, Morgan & Claypool Publishers, 2012, pp. 1–167.

[5] R.G. Khedkar, S.R. Tandle, Rating prediction based on social sentiment from textual reviews, International Journal of Computer Applications (2019).

[6] S. Ding, Z. Zhu, X. Zhang, An overview on semi-supervised support vector machine, Neural Computing & Applications 28 (2017) 969–978, Springer.

[7] S. Nabil, J. Elbouhdidi, Y. Chkouri, Recommendation System Based on Data Analysis – Application on Tweets Sentiment Analysis, IEEE, 2018, pp. 155–160.

[8] J. Ming, I.K.T. Tan, C.Y. Ting, Recent Developments in Recommender Systems, Springer, MIWAI, 2019, pp. 38–51.

[9] A. Koukourikos, G. Stoitsis, P. Karampiperis, Sentiment analysis: a tool for rating attribution to content in recommender rystems, in: RecSysTEL, 2012, pp. 61–70.

[10] J. Golbeck, C. Robles, M. Edmondson, K. Turner, Predicting personality from Twitter, in: 2011 IEEE International Conference on Privacy, Security, Risk, and Trust, and IEEE International Conference on Social Computing, pp. 149–156.

[11] P. Sen, D. Ganguly, J.F. Jones, Word-Node2Vec: improving word embedding with document-level non-local word co-occurrences, in: Proceedings of NAACL-HLT, 2019, pp. 1041–1051.

[12] L. Gong, H. Wang, When sentiment analysis meets social network: a holistic user behavior modeling in opinionated data, in: Proceedings of the 24th ACM SIGKDD International Conference on Knowledge Discovery Data Mining (KDD '18), ACM, New York, NY, USA, 2018, 10 pp.

[13] R. Suguna, M.S. Devi, A. Kushwaha, P. Gupta, An Efficient Real Time Product Recommendation Using Facial Sentiment Analysis, IEEE, 2019.

[14] Y. Shen, Y. Ma, M. Gu, S. Li, Y. Jin, C. Zhang, Y. Shen, Z. Qi, User and product attention model based on recommendation algorithm for sentiment classification, in: IEEE 4th International Conference on Computer and Communications, 2018.

[15] A.U. Hassan, J. Hussain, M. Hussain, M. Sadiq, S. Lee, Sentiment Analysis of Social Networking Sites (SNS) Data Using Machine Learning Approach for the Measurement of Depression, IEEE, 2017.

[16] S. Hu, A. Kumar, F. Turjman, S. Gupta, S. Seth, Shubham, Reviewer credibility and sentiment analysis based user profile modeling for online product recommendation, Special Section On Cloud - Fog - Edge Computing in Cyber-Physical-Social Systems (CPSS), in: IEEE Access, volume 8, 2020.

[17] C.W. Leung, S.C. Chan, F. Chung, Integrating collaborative filtering and sentiment analysis: a rating inference approach, Hong Kong, pp. 1–5.

[18] C.J. Hutto, E. Gilbert, VADER: a parsimonious rule-based model for sentiment analysis of social media text, in: Proceedings of the Eighth International AAAI Conference on Weblogs and Social Media, 2015.

[19] https://medium.com/analytics-vidhya/simplifying-social-media-sentiment-analysis-using-vader-in-python-f9e6ec6fc52f. (Accessed 14 September 2020).

[20] K. Devipriya, D. Prabha, V. Pirya, S. Sudhakar, Deep learning sentiment analysis for recommendations in social applications, International Journal of Scientific & Technology Research 9 (01) (January 2020).

[21] M. Tomas, et al., Distributed representations of words and phrases and their compositionality, in: Advances, in: Neural Information Processing Systems, 2013.

[22] N. Hossain, R. Bhuiyan, Z.N. Tumpa, Sentiment analysis of restaurant reviews using combined CNN-LSTM, in: IEEE Explore, 11th ICCCNT, 2020.

[23] https://www.analyticsvidhya.com/blog/2019/09/demystifying-bert-groundbreaking-nlp-framework/. (Accessed 18 January 2021).

[24] A. Ziani, N. Azizi, D. Schwab, M. Aldwairi, N. Chekkai, D. Zenakhra, S. Cheriguene, Recommender system through sentiment analysis, https://hal.archives-ouvertes.fr/hal-01683511, 2018.

[25] Suchinda Dutta, Dhrubasish Sarkar, Design of recommendation system using sentiment analysis in online social network, in: E-Proceedings of the International E-Conference on Emerging Technologies (IECET-2020) Organized by Surendra Institute of Engineering & Management, Siliguri, 2020, pp. 317–319.

[26] T. Wang, K. Lu, K.P. Chow, Q. Zhu, COVID-19 sensing: negative sentiment analysis on social media in China via BERT model, in: IEEE Access, volume 8, 2020.

[27] Y. Zhang, R. Liu, A. Li, A novel approach to recommender system based on aspect-level sentiment analysis, in: 4th National Conference on Electrical, Electronics and Computer, Engineering (NCEECE), 2015.

[28] Debnath, D. Sarkar, D. Das, Influenceable targets recommendation analyzing social activities in egocentric online social networks, in: S.N. Mohanty, J.M. Chatterjee, S. Jain, A.A. Elngar, P. Gupta (Eds.), Recommender System with Machine Learning and Artificial Intelligence: Practical Tools and Applications in Medical, Agricultural and Other Industries, Wiley, 2020, pp. 401–416.

[29] S.S. Kundu, K. Desai, S. Ghosh, D. Sarkar, Personalized word recommendation system using sentiment analysis, in: D. Bhattacharjee, D.K. Kole, N. Dey, S. Basu, D. Plewczynski (Eds.), Proceedings of International Conference on Frontiers in Computing and Systems, in: Advances in Intelligent Systems and Computing, vol. 1255, Springer, Singapore, 2021.

[30] D. Sarkar, M. Gupta, P. Jana, D.K. Kole, Recommender system in healthcare: an overview, in: Computational Intelligence for Machine Learning and Healthcare Informatics, 2020, pp. 199–215.

CHAPTER 10

Data visualization: existing tools and techniques

Tej Bahadur Chandra[a] **and Anuj Kumar Dwivedi**[b]
[a]National Institute of Technology, Raipur, Chhattisgarh, India
[b]Govt. Vijay Bhushan Singh Deo Girls PG College, Jashpur Nagar, Chhattisgarh, India

10.1 Introduction

Data visualization has a strong footprint on today's scientific exploration, reasoning, hypothesis formation, and business data analysis. As an analytical tool for scientific or business forecasting it has been accepted worldwide. Data visualization has an important role in making the massively accumulated data over the internet (shopping malls, data centers, etc.) usable for future prediction, strategic development, risk analysis, etc.

The aim of visualization is provide insight into often complex data [1]. Data visualization is a generalized term referring to the presentation of information in the form of a picture, diagram, chart, etc. These visual/pictorial representations are useful to extract information. Data visualization is basically an art, as well as a science. Images have more cognitive impact than pure text-based content, thus now it becomes more science than art. Sometimes these terms can also be used as reporting tools. Data visualization is a general/broad term that describes/defines any form of effort to help people to recognize the significance of data by placing them in a visual context. Innumerable patterns, trends, and correlations that might be obscured in any text-based data can be wide open and recognized very easily with the help/use of data visualization tools/software.

Visualizing data/information is a vital part of statistical practices [2]. Plots are very useful for illuminating structures in the data, examining model assumptions, identifying outliers, and finding unforeseen patterns/designs. Post-analysis visualization is commonly used to communicate the results of statistical analyses. The availability of good statistical visualization software is key in effectively performing data analysis and in exploring and developing new methods for data visualization. Compared static visualization, interactive visualization adds additional natural and powerful ways to explore the data. With interactive visualization an

Advanced Data Mining Tools and Methods for Social Computing
https://doi.org/10.1016/B978-0-32-385708-6.00017-5

analyst can dive into the data and quickly react to visual clues by, for example, refocusing and creating interactive queries of the data.

Popular methods that still dominate, such as line, bar, and pie charts, originate from the 18th century. Current data visualization tools have reached a maturity level that goes beyond that of traditional standard charts and graphs used in spreadsheets, displaying data in more knowledgeable ways such as more detailed pie, bar, and fever charts, scatter plots, histograms, 3D scatter plots, streamgraphs, networks, treemaps, heat maps, Gantt charts, geographic maps, sparklines, dials and gauges, infographics, etc. Also, images may include interactive/communicating capabilities, which empowers users to manipulate them or drill into the data/information for any type of query and analysis. Indicators are designed and used to alert users when pre-defined conditions occur or when an update in data occurs.

The main objective of visualization is to obtain a detailed understanding because a single picture is worth not only many thousands of words, but possibly tera/petabytes of data [3]. Much bigger datasets demand not just visualization, but also advanced visualization techniques and resources.

The objective of any data visualization tool/platform is to reduce business intelligence (BI) complexity, but definitely at a cost. Over time, datasets grow in terms of size/volume and complexity [1], and the demand for data visualization tools is escalating increasingly. At present, BI software developers/vendors implant data visualization techniques/tools into their products, either using self-developed visualization technologies or sourcing them from other vendors/developers that are specialized in visualization.

Exploratory information design/data analysis, descriptive statistics, interactive data visualization, statistical graphics, inferential statistics, infographics, plots, data analysis, and data science are some major dimensions of this emerging field. With the enormous development in the field of computer graphics and data handling techniques, data visualization tools provide more than hundreds of different standard charts and graphs displaying data in more sophisticated ways making patterns, series, trends, and relationships that might remain unnoticed in textual data easily recognizable. This chapter presents a brief overview of several proprietary, open source, and licensed data visualization tools and a comparison between them.

10.2 Prior research works on data visualization issues

Data visualization is not a new area of interest/research. Visual forms of communication of data have been available/found for thousands of years. Data visualization and computer graphics are interrelated terms; in both applications, some form of data is inputted and ultimately an image/picture that reflects various aspects of the inputted data is produced. Currently, with the invent of high-end monitors, computer graphics/vision is the foundation of data visualization. Various research activities support the rise of data visualization as a novel noticeable field within the arena of computer graphics. The objective of this section is to present some selected works related to data visualization.

Visualization can be used to formulate/frame models for the collected data, to confirm models for the data, to visually assess cluster structures, and to identify outliers [4].

There exist a large number of studies on data visualization. The author of [5] presents a good survey on graphical display methods of multi-variant data. Various well-designed ideas for demonstrating high-dimensional data are presented in this survey, and few of them are employed in commercial statistical packages.

The author of [6] determines several shape measures and resolves specific technical issues associated with the graphical presentation and statistical analysis of heuristic shape distributions.

The author of [7] presents an algorithm named "Grand Tour (GT)" in the field of computer graphics systems, for assigning a sequence of projections on 2D subspaces to any specified dimension of a Euclidean space. This algorithm/technique is used to explore multi-variant statistical data by means of an animation. Each view/frame is nothing but an orthogonal projection of the dataset (points) on a 2D subspace.

The original GT [7] algorithm does not recall the path of the projections, but shows only the recent state during a tour process. The author of [8] proposes a modification of GT called Tracking GT (TGT), which shows the trace during the touring process of the projected points.

In the book [9], the ways to represent a rich visual world (which is very dynamic, complex, and multi-dimensional) of experiences and measurements on a static, flat paper (flatland) is explored. Several hundreds of terrific displays of complex data on flatland are solidified. Various design strategies that increase/sharpen the information resolution, resolving the power of VDU screen, are outlined. The goal is to increase the total number of dimensions which can be represented on a plane surface as well as to increase the amount of information per unit area (data density).

The authors of [10] show the powers and limitations of particular linking, focusing, and arranging tools and present a specific system for multi-variant data visualization, called "XGobi." XGobi is presented with examples of linking, focusing, and arranging views, specifically linked scatterplot brushing, high-dimensional projections, and matrices of conditional plots. The authors also propose a basic taxonomy/classification of interactive data visualization, grounded on a triad of data analytic tasks (finding Gestalt, posing queries, and making comparisons). These three tasks are reinforced by three classes of interactive view manipulations: linking, focusing, and arranging views.

In the book [11], visualization pipelines are discussed in a dedicated chapter. The author of this chapter focuses on various perspectives, like the conceptual perspective and the implementation perspective, as well as on algorithm classification. The author of another dedicated chapter focuses on different types of visualization for complex data types: scalar, vector, domain modeling, tensor, image, volume, and non-spatial information data. Finally, the author focuses on visualization software as well. The author presents a taxonomy of visualization software and states that four types of visualization software exist: scientific visualization software, imaging software, grid processing software, and information visualization software.

According to the editors/authors of the book [12], with the increase of electronics/computing capabilities more complex/multi-faceted numerical methods are developed with time, which results in the generation of gigantic numerical/statistical datasets. Also, huge datasets are produced/generated by various data sensing/acquisition devices. The collected data contain text (plain/formatted/hypertext) and numerical information, as well as multimedia information.

Today, data visualization is an active and vital area/domain of research. Recently, with the emergence of heterogeneous and very large data collections used by different business/finance/administration/digital media houses/companies, data visualization is often considered to include both the information and scientific visualization fields. Advanced techniques in terms of computer graphics/visualization were needed to process as well as to visualize these massive datasets.

Data visualization is a vital and crucial part of good statistical practices. Plots are useful for revealing structure in the data, detecting outliers, checking model assumptions, and finding unimagined patterns/ways. Post-analysis visualization is commonly used to communicate the results of statistical analyses. The availability of good statistical visualization software is key in effectively performing data analysis and in exploring and developing new methods for data visualization.

Compared to static visualization, interactive visualization adds natural and powerful ways to explore data. With interactive visualization an analyst can dive into the data and quickly react to visual clues by, for example, refocusing and creating interactive queries of the data.

Furthermore, linking visual attributes of the data points such as color and size allows the analyst to compare different visual representations/illustrations of the data such as histograms and scatterplots.

In a thesis, one researcher explored and developed new interactive data visualization and exploration tools for high-dimensional data. The objective is the implementation of a navigation graph software. Navigation graphs are basically navigational infrastructures for well-ordered exploration of high-dimensional data. The author implemented the first interactive navigation graph software, named RnavGraph [2].

10.3 Challenges during visualization of innumerable data

The selection of a particular visualization tool totally depends on analytical dimensions, key data stories, and the questions we are trying to answer with our visualization [13].

The authors of [14] present a good taxonomy for the systems involved in visualization software. Also, the authors focused on the importance of taxonomy, stating a well-founded taxonomy is an important factor in any research field. Taxonomy is a terminology or common language that facilitates communication about, identification of, and cataloguing of new ideas and discoveries.

The author of the book [13] presents the best available approaches to design data visualization techniques, with some real examples. The author stars with theoretical and practical concepts of data visualization. The author discusses how to overcome any data visualization challenge effectively as well as efficiently. The author also discusses the digital age, the importance of visualization as a discovery tool, various existing visualization skills for the masses, data visualization methodologies, visualization design objectives, and many more valuable issues. According to the author, there are lots of ways to classify the variety of methods for visualizing data. The author of this book presents a good taxonomy of data visualization methods (see Fig. 10.1).

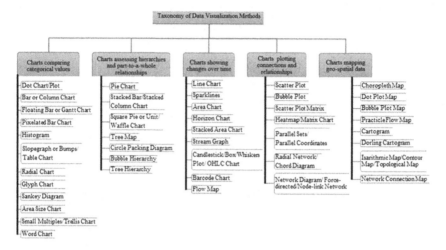

Figure 10.1 Taxonomy of data visualization methods [13].

The authors/editors of the book [15] discuss some specific issues such as volume visualization in the medical field, fluid flow visualization, data structures in scientific visualization, applications of visualization in environment protection, surface-on-surface data, modeling and visualizing volumetrics, and many more specific issues.

The authors/editors of the book [16] on visualization present various valuable ideas and contents on the following subjects: meshes for visualization, volume visualization and medical visualization, vector field visualization, and visualization systems.

The author of the book [17] on scientific visualization presents a roadmap on this topic. The book focuses on potential and pitfalls, models and software, color in scientific visualization, visualization technique selection, scalar visualization, vector visualization, and many more topics in scientific visualization.

The authors/experts of the blog post [18] present three common challenges related to visualizing data. The first is how to collect the data; there are various types of data sources, each having a different access interface, and it requires skilled persons (programmers) to decode and maintain them. The second challenge is called "operationalization," which means how to visualize products with minimal effort. The third one is data discrepancies, which means how to combine similar data coming from diverse sources.

Choosing a particular visualization tool/technique for a particular case needs much carefulness and awareness. This is not just a matter of good/bad, but the optimal choice depends on many factors and conditions.

10.4 Existing data visualization tools and techniques with key characteristics

10.4.1 Amcharts [19]

Amcharts is a programming library and tool that provides extensive JavaScript charts and maps for complex data. It facilitates programming of extensive chart functionalities to generate extended and multi-dimensional data visualizations. The Amchart editor allows easy configuration of selected image/graph parameters using drop-down lists and checkboxes to create browser-based presentations. Except traditional diagrams, it allows data demonstration in spatial diagrams. Visualizations generated using this tool are not only attractive but also have clarity. It uses a data array, which is a part of the JavaScript code placed directly inside the hypertext document to generate graphs. Furthermore, it also other data sources for advanced users.

10.4.2 Arbor.Js [20]

Arbor.Js is a jQuery- and web worker-based graph visualization library. It caters an effective, force-directed layout algorithm and abstraction for screen-refresh and graph organization handles. It allows users to create screen-drawings using canvas, SVG, or even positioned HTML elements, whatever approach is suitable for the project's and performance's needs. The Arbor code is written to make the user's project unique by generating extensive graph data based on the user's visual style, rather than paying attention to the physics and math that make the layouts possible.

10.4.3 Better World Flux [21]

In the core Flux is a glorified histogram. It uses a log scale to compute the width of the Flux that makes variations more clearly perceptible. The colors are assigned based on the geometric mean of the user-selected indicator's index. The indices are the raw data obtained by assigning lowest and highest values for each indicator. To maintain the even spread of the values, some values are converted to a log scale and others are truncated. Moreover, the missing values are approximated using linear regression.

10.4.4 CartoDB [22]

CartoDB is one of the most powerful and intuitive open source choices for predicting and discovering the key components of location data. It enables users to update the geospatial data (Shapefiles, GeoJSON, etc.) to make them publicly/privately available for visualization of a map or dataset. Moreover, it facilitates SQL-based search operations and CartoCSS-based styling in the map. The uploaded map can be visualized/exported using CARTO APIs. CartoDB can be used to build powerful geospatial applications. It works in any modern web browser.

10.4.5 Chart.js [23]

Chart.js is a community-maintained project, which comes with two different variations. It enables us to create awesome charts by instantiating the Chart class. This class provides several different member functions for controlling the behavior of the created charts, which can be used by passing appropriate parameters. Alternatively, the global configuration file can also be modified, which will be used to auto-format the subsequent charts created after that point.

10.4.6 Chroma.js [24,25]

Chroma.js is a small JavaScript library released under the BSD license. It is used for converting different colors and color scales. It can takes input colors from a wide range of formats and perform different operations like converting colors to wide range of formats, analyzing and manipulating colors, linear and Bezier interpolation in different color spaces, etc.

10.4.7 Circos [26]

Circos is a free software package licensed under GPL for visualizing data and information. It was originally written in Perl and can be installed on any operating system. It projects data in a circular layout, which makes it ideal for establishing relationships between objects/positions or multilayered annotations of one or more scales. It provides a suitable method to create publication-quality infographics and examples with high data-to-ink ratio, richly layered data, and pleasant symmetries. It was originally designed for projecting genomic data like structural variations and alignments. However, its flexibility allows one to visualize data in any field – from genomics and migration to mathematical art. The recent versions of Circos provide support for 2D data tracks such as scatter, line, histogram, and heat map plots. The generated extensive graphical projections can be saved in bitmap (PNG) and vector (SVG) images.

10.4.8 Cola.Js [27,28]

Cola.js/WebCoLa is an open standard JavaScript library that uses constraint-based optimization techniques for organizing HTML5 documents. It provides good support for different libraries like Cytoscape.js, D3.js, and svg.js. It is suitable for creating graphs with not more than 100 nodes and supported well in average machines.

10.4.9 Colorbrewer [29,30]

Colorbrewer is a web-based tool released under Apache License 2.0. It is used for assigning color schemes for maps or for handy command-line plotting programs like gnuplot. Each color scheme comes with eight discrete colors and a color palette gradient. In order to use any of the color schemes, one needs to call plot or splot in the gnuplot script or an interactive session.

10.4.10 Creately [31]

Creately is a software tool that provides templates and features for online plotting. It can be easily configured with properties. It also provides real-time collaboration. It provides features like PDF export, easy import of existing Visio files, publishing or embedding privately, seeing the history of all changes, inline comments, real-time collaboration, editable SVG exports, etc. It comes in three variations: a set of libraries, a full featured desktop application, and a mobile application. It is multi-lingual.

10.4.11 Crossfilter [32]

Crossfilter is a JavaScript library that can be used in hypertext documents for investigating large multi-variate datasets. It provides very fast operations on the datasets containing many millions of records. Most of the search commands involve 1D operations. Furthermore, to optimize the search algorithmic complexities, it makes small adjustments to the filter values (incremental filtering), which is significantly compared to beginning from scratch. Currently this library is not under active development, maintenance, and support. Everything in it is scoped under the crossfilter namespace, which is also a constructor. It uses semantic versioning.

10.4.12 CSV [33]

CSV ("comma-separated values") is one of the standard file formats for data exchange between a wide range of applications. This format is widely supported by business, scientific, and consumer applications. It is pervasively used to move/exchange tabular data among programs that basically operate on different or incompatible formats.

10.4.13 JSON [34]

JSON is a subset of JavaScript, which is used as a lightweight universal data-interchange/text format. It is completely language-independent. However, it follows the programming paradigm of C-families. Basically, JSON is created on two structures and all the modern programming languages include support for it in one form or another. In modern browsers, it exhibits hundred times faster parsing compared to the open XML format. Furthermore, it uses a set of keys, which are independent of all other objects, even exclusive of nesting. In addition, it uses context to avoid ambiguity.

10.4.14 Cubism.js [35,36]

Cubism is a D3 plugin released under the Apache License. It is used for projecting time series data and has a better real-time dashboard. It incrementally fetches and renders time series data from a variety of sources. Moreover, it facilitates rapid comparison by scaling data in terms of perception and small multiples aligned by time. It allows optimal utilization of vertical spaces in horizon charts projecting a higher number of metrics in one view, which increases the likelihood of discovery and its usability. It is also provided with in-built support for Graphite and Cube. Moreover, the client-side metric arithmetic allows integration of metrics from various sources leading to greater flexibility. The seamless extensibility using modular components, new chart types, different modes of interactions, and high customizability (using CSS and JavaScript) are its key features.

10.4.15 Cytoscape [37]

Cytoscape is an open source desktop java application for visualizing biological pathways and molecular interaction networks and integrating these networks with annotations, gene expression profiles, and other state data. It is released under the Library GNU Public License (LGPL). It was originally developed for biological research. However, it can be used as a comprehensive standard for complex network analysis and visualization. It comes with a basic set of features for data analysis, integration, and visualization. Moreover, it also includes plugins for additional file format support, network and molecular profiling analyses, scripting, new layouts, and connection with databases.

10.4.16 Cytoscape.js [38,39]

Cytoscape.js is an open source JavaScript library, which is a successor of Cytoscape Web. Although it is not a complete web application, it is widely used for graph analysis and visualization. The interactive graphs, easiness of use, rich display, support for directed and undirected graphs, compound graphs, mixed graphs, multi-graphs, and loops, and support for event-driven models with a core API make it highly useable in different applications. The library is available under a permissive open source license (MIT).

10.4.17 D3.Js [40]

D3.js is a JavaScript library used for manipulating documents. It provides complete support for modern browsers by combining a data-driven approach for DOM manipulation and extensive visualization components. The features like speed, dynamic interaction and animation, support for large datasets, and the huge set of plugins and component collections have made it very popular and useful. In general, D3.js does not have any specific data format for visualization. It uses generic CSV/TSV tables for all types of visualizations, and its core provides data loaders for those files.

10.4.18 Dance.Js [41]

Dance.Js is a simple data-driven visualization framework which includes some components from D3.js and Backbone.js. It has its own data manipulation library, Data.js, which acts as a replacement for the backbone model. Analogous to D3.js, here also we can specify transformations based on data changes. Moreover, for application developers three different cases are considered: (i) the updating nodes to modify, (ii) the entering nodes to add, and (iii) the exiting nodes to remove.

10.4.19 Dapresy [42]

Dapresy Pro offers a comprehensive, infographics-rich visualization platform that is intuitive and engaging. The software provides an extensive set of functionalities to manage and process both data and meta-data (index calculations, weighting, computing of variables, etc.). It also supports a wide variety of file formats like Triple-S and SPSS and comes with APIs for the most commonly used data collection platforms. The agile drag and drop environment provides a template-driven program that can be used by anyone in the organization. It can also be specifically configured for particular user needs.

10.4.20 Data.js [43]

Data.js is a small, fast, and easy-to-use cross-browser-based JavaScript library that allows data-centric web applications by leveraging modern protocols such as JSON and OData and HTML5-enabled browser features. Currently, the library offers a huge set of functionalities to communicate with OData services and leverage storage mechanisms in the browsers such as IndexedDB, and provides a convenient API for efficiently caching lists of data by combining remote services with local storage. The OData support includes receiving data and submitting changes or invoking service operations. The meta-data can be integrated with the API in cases where it is required, and batch operations can be used to minimize round-trips.

10.4.21 Databoard [44]

Google's Databoard is a new platform that enables brands to capture and publish key data-led content and deliver it to their audiences in a build-your-own, ready-to-curate fashion. Google's Databoard had to be much more than an interactive infographic – it had to be a full-blown application for desktop, tablet, and mobile use that puts the user in total control. It catered to this human desire by letting users cherry-pick and share the information that is most important to them and their social and professional circles. Each data point can be shared individually via email or social channels or stored in a shopping cart until they are ready to publish something bigger as a complete infographic-style visual.

10.4.22 Wrangler [45,46]

Wrangler provides an interactive interface for data transformations. It provides an interface for desired transformations and manipulation of visual data in an easy-to-use environment for analysts to iteratively explore the scope of applicable actions and preview their effects. Wrangler uses semantic data types (e.g., classification codes, geographic locations, dates) to assist validation and type conversion. Although it is still in beta phase, it shows promising performance. It can be interactively used for data cleaning, transformation (of messy, real-world data), and export of data in various formats (like Excel, R, Tableau, Protovis, etc.) with minimum overhead of formatting and more focus on analyzing data.

10.4.23 Degrafa [47]

Degrafa is an MXML markup-based declarative graphics framework used to create skins and complex graphics, draw shapes, and also support advanced CSS. Some of the algorithms and functionalities in Degrafa were inspired from various sources. It works with Flex2.0.1 and Flex3 (beta). It comes with a graphics class which enables pre-defined shapes, fills, stokes, code repurposing, advanced CSS, etc., to be used with Flex.

10.4.24 DhtmlxChart [48,49]

DhtmlxChart is an interactive tool for developing a wide variety of charts to be used in web applications. It comes with four chart options, which include various subtypes, different data sources, both 2D and 3D presentations, interactive actions and tooltips, synchronous representation of data properties on the same chart, etc. The complete tool is developed in JavaScript and can be easily integrated with hypertext documents. It can also be used for generating cross-browser HTML5 charts using a JavaScript charting library. It provides support for various common chart types such as complex charts and chart series (plotted separately side by side or stacked).

10.4.25 Dipity [50,51]

By using Dipity, anyone can create its own timeline. It can import data from Picasa, Twitter, Pandora, WordPress, Last.fm, Flickr, Yelp, Blogger, YouTube, and any RSS channel. Timelines look visually attractive and provide easy and smooth scrolling and zooming. There is also a Dipity API available so it is possible to programmatically create, modify, and delete timelines as well as to retrieve data for use in other applications or web services.

10.4.26 Dygraphs [52]

Dygraphs is a flexible, interactive, open source, and fast JavaScript charting library, which enables the user to explore and interpret dense datasets. It works in all recent browsers by including the dygraph.js JavaScript file and the dygraph.css CSS file and instantiating the Dygraph object. This tool can help in visualizing data without any further configuration and also has a rich set of options for configuring its behavior and display. It is available under the MIT License.

10.4.27 BIRT [53,54]

Eclipse's Business Intelligence and Reporting Tool (BIRT) is an open standard software tool for creating extensive visualizations and reports that can be embedded into rich client and web applications that provide the BIRT technology platform, especially those based on Java and Java EE. Today, the BIRT technology platform is one of the most widely adopted data visualization and reporting technologies. BIRT has two main components: a visual report designer for creating BIRT designs and a runtime component for generating those designs that can be deployed to any Java environment. It also includes a charting engine that is both fully integrated into the BIRT designer and can be used in a standalone manner to integrate charts into an application. Its designs are persisted as XML and can access a number of different data sources including JDO datastores, JFire Scripting Objects, POJOs, SQL databases, Web services, and XML. It uses the Data Tools Open Data Access (ODA) framework for adding custom data access methods. It provides output in HTML, paginated HTML, PDF, XLS, DOC, PPT, ODS, ODP, ODT, and Postscript. Many other types of output are possible: ERich Text Format (RTF), Scalable Vector Graphic (SVG), images, and more.

10.4.28 Envision.Js [55,56]

Envision.Js is a JavaScript visualization library for creating fast, dynamic, and interactive HTML5 visualizations. It utilizes touch gestures, providing a smooth interaction for tablet users. It is written to a particular interface. Other graphing libraries can be adapted to it or written specifically for it. It is open source.

10.4.29 Eurostat [57]

Eurostat offers a whole range of important and interesting data that governments, businesses, the education sector, journalists, and the public can use for their work and daily life. Eurostat has built several data visualization tools for its web service.

10.4.30 Excel [58]

Excel is one of the most widely used data analysis, manipulation, and visualization applications in the world, and it is commonly used as a tool for interactive data analysis and reporting. It supports comprehensive data import and connectivity options that include built-in data connectivity to a wide range of data sources, and the availability of add-ins such as Power Query, Power View, PowerPivot, and Power Map. These data models make it easier to "slice and dice" data in PivotTables and PivotCharts and to create Power View visualizations. All editions of Excel support data visualization through charts, data bars, sparklines, and conditional formatting. These can be used to great effect when creating graphical representations of data in a worksheet.

10.4.31 Excel Map/Power Map [59]

Microsoft Power Map for Excel is a 3D data visualization tool that lets us look at information in new ways. With Power Map, anyone can plot geographic and temporal data on a 3D globe or custom map, show it over time, create visual tours, and share with other people. It uses Bing to geocode data based on its geographic properties.

10.4.32 Exhibit [60]

Exhibit is a powerful easy-to-use open source publishing framework for publishing large-scale, data-rich interactive Web pages. Using it, anyone can easily create web pages to publish and visualize data collections ranging from small personal collections in Scripted mode up to large datasets in the server-based Staged mode. It can visualize data in a Web browser with a simple HTML-based configuration. No programming or server-side setup is required.

10.4.33 Factmint [61]

Factmint provides tools for every stage of data management workflow, including ingesting, storing, and analyzing data and visualizing findings. It allows to create interactive data visualizations, which can be rendered from an HTML table or directly from JSON. It is used to progressively enhance HTML tables into interactive SVG data visualizations.

10.4.34 FF Chartwell [62]

It is a typeface for creating simple graphs. It uses OpenType ligatures to transform strings of numbers automatically into charts. All the chart drawing functions of this are provided as small JavaScript libraries. The visualized data remain editable, allowing for hassle-free updates and styling.

10.4.35 Flare [63,64]

Flare is an ActionScript library for creating visualizations that run in the Adobe Flash Player. From basic charts and graphs to complex interactive graphics, the toolkit supports data management, visual encoding, animation, and interaction techniques. It is open source software released under a BSD license. It also provides some utilities for loading external datasets.

10.4.36 Flare [65]

This is a JavaScript plotting library for jQuery. Generally, all browsers that support the HTML5 canvas tag are supported. Flot diagrams or graphs are generated in the SVG format, and in older browsers in the VML format. In the basic version of a diagram or chart, source data are downloaded from the array which constitutes a part of the JavaScript code. It produces graphical plots of arbitrary client-side datasets on-the-fly. It is lightweight.

10.4.37 Flowingdata [66]

Flowingdata explores how statisticians, designers, data scientists, and others use analysis, visualization, and exploration tools to understand data and ourselves.

10.4.38 Fusioncharts Suite Xt [67]

Fusioncharts Suite Xt is a most comprehensive charting solution, which is all about easing the whole process of data visualization through charts. It has the best looking JavaScript charts in the industry, exciting animation, smart designs, and rich interactivity. It works with all web and mobile applications. It is an extensive JavaScript API and brings events and methods for deep integration with other libraries and web frameworks. It gives complete control over each step of the charting process and it is equipped to build the most advanced dashboards for enterprise applications. The only client-side requirement is a modern JavaScript-enabled Web browser with SVG or VML support.

10.4.39 GeoCommons [68]

GeoCommons is an open repository for geographic data, with thematic mapping tools. It includes a large number of features that empower the user to easily access, visualize, and analyze data. It finds images from a spatial R-tree database and returns a compressed response to Google Earth. It is an online free application that allows to use some functionalities of the traditional GIS desktop software.

10.4.40 Gephi [69]

Gephi is the leading open source and free visualization and exploration software for all kinds of graph and network analysis. It uses a 3D render engine to display large networks in real-time and to speed up the exploration. A flexible and multi-task architecture brings new possibilities to work with complex datasets and produce valuable visual results. It provides easy and broad access to network data and allows for spatializing, filtering, navigating, manipulating, and clustering. It provides state-of-the-art layout algorithms for both efficiency and quality. It can read the majority of graph file formats but also supports CSV and relational database import.

10.4.41 Google Chart [70]

Google Chart is a very powerful, simple-to-use, and free service. It provides a perfect way to visualize data on websites. From simple line charts to complex hierarchical tree maps, the chart gallery provides a large number of ready-to-use chart types. Charts are highly interactive and expose events that allow to connect them to create complex dashboards or other experiences integrated with web pages. Charts are rendered using HTML5/SVG technology to provide cross-browser compatibility and cross-platform portability. It provides an interactive dashboard and Dynamic Data-Connect to handle data in real-time using a variety of data connection tools and protocols.

10.4.42 Google Fusion Tables [71]

Fusion Tables is an experimental data visualization web application to gather, visualize, share, and publish data tables. CSV, KML, ODS, XLS, or Google Spreadsheet data can be uploaded to a Fusion Tables table. Table structure, meta-data, and visualization settings are represented as JSON data structures accessible through RESTful HTTP requests. It visualizes bigger table data online and filters and summarizes across hundreds of thousands of rows.

10.4.43 Google Maps [72]

Millions of websites and apps use Google Maps APIs to power location experiences for their users. Google Maps APIs are available for both mobile devices and traditional desktop browser applications and via HTTP web services. It allows for the embedding of Google Maps onto web pages of outside developers, using a simple JavaScript interface or a Flash interface. The API includes language localization for over 50 languages, region localization, and geocoding, and has mechanisms for enterprise developers who want to utilize the Google Maps API within an intranet.

10.4.44 Google Public Data [73]

Google's Public Data Explorer provides public data and forecasts from a range of international organizations and academic institutions. These can be displayed as line graphs, bar graphs, or cross-sectional plots or on maps. It was made available for anyone to upload, share, and visualize datasets. To facilitate this, Google created a new data format, the Dataset Publishing Language (DSPL). Once the data are imported, a dataset can be visualized, embedded in external websites, and shared with others like in a Google Doc. It makes Big Data easy to explore, visualize, understand, compare, and share. All the data charts and maps are updated automatically.

10.4.45 Google Sheets [74]

Google Sheets presents data with colorful charts and graphs in web browsers, and no dedicated software is needed. Built-in formulas, pivot tables, and conditional formatting options save time and simplify common spreadsheet tasks. Google Sheets is free. Existing spreadsheets, including Microsoft Excel files, can be imported and converted to make them instantly editable. Sheets can be exported in .xlsx, .csv, .html, .ods, .pdf, or .txt format.

10.4.46 Highcharts [75]

Highcharts is a JavaScript charting library based on SVG, offering an easy way of adding interactive charts to websites/web applications. It currently supports almost all chart types. It is solely based on native browser technologies and does not require client-side plugins like Flash or Java. Furthermore, there is no need to install anything on a server, such as PHP or ASP.NET. It needs only the highcharts.js core to run. It works in all modern browsers. It runs on any server that supports HTML. It can even run locally from a file system, since all the rendering is done locally in a browser. It is free for non-commercial use.

10.4.47 Highmaps [76]

Highmaps is an HTML5 mapping component optimized for creating schematic maps in web-based projects. It extends the user-friendly Highcharts JavaScript API and allows web developers to build interactive maps to display any information linked to geography. It is perfect for standalone use or in dashboards in combination with Highcharts. It is designed from the ground up with mobile browsers in mind. It is solely based on native browser technologies and does not require client-side plugins like Flash or Java. Furthermore, there is no need to install anything on the server, such as PHP or ASP.NET. It needs only one JavaScript file to run. It is free for non-commercial use. Besides the common Series/Point concept, it accepts the standardized GeoJSON format for map input. With the exporting module enabled, users can export the chart to PNG, JPG, PDF, or SVG format at the click of a button or print the chart directly from the web page.

10.4.48 iWantHue [77,78]

iWantHue allows to generate palettes of colors. The idea behind iWantHue is to distribute colors evenly, in a perceptively coherent space, constrained by user-friendly settings, to generate high-quality custom palettes. The tool itself is available online. Its source code is available on GitHub.

10.4.49 iCharts [79]

iCharts is the leading visual reporting application for NetSuite. It automates reporting tasks and give everyone access to visual, interactive dashboards. It creates and shares interactive visualizations without the user ever leaving the dashboard. It uses a simple drag and drop interface to create mashups, trending reports, pivot tables, and more.

10.4.50 InetSoft [80]

InetSoft's data intelligence platform meshes on-the-fly data modeling with data visualization to enable rapid, iterative development of data views such as interactive dashboards and pixel-perfect reports. The dynamic data models not only serve crafted data views but also empower "citizen developers" to compose self-service data views. The Apache Hadoop/Spark deployable data analytic engine ensures limitless growth for advanced data intelligence. Transforming raw data into visually intelligible information is naturally an iterative, incremental process of data manipulation and visualization. It allows development data models and data views to automatically become such a foundation. It is based on open standards technology that incorporates XML, SOAP, Java language, and JavaScript.

10.4.51 Infoactive [81]

Infoactive is an open source, collaborative project. The source code is available on GitHub.

10.4.52 Infocaptor [82]

Infocaptor is an extremely competent product, capable of addressing many BI, data visualization, and analytics needs at a very modest price. Deployment can either be in-house or on the web, and in either case the interface is browser-based. It is free for startups, Non-profits, and students. It is the cheapest dashboard software. It works with CSV, Excel, or any .txt datasets. The drag and drop interface does not limit thinking in terms of the x- and y-axes. The user can rapidly change visualizations to see data from different angles. It supports a variety of JDBC and ODBC sources including Microsoft Excel, Microsoft Access, Oracle, SQL Server, MySql, DB2, Progress, Sqlite, PostgreSQL, Hadoop Hive, Cloudera Impala, and HTTP API for web services. It is simply a web-based application that works on every platform. Advanced visualization is D3.js-based.

10.4.53 Inkscape [83]

Inkscape is an open source vector graphics editor similar to Adobe Illustrator, Corel Draw, Freehand, or Xara X. It uses SVG, an open XML-based W3C standard, as the native format. It is cross-platform and perfectly compliant with SVG format file generation and editing. Live watching and editing of the document tree in the XML editor is possible. It supports PNG, OpenDocument Drawing, DXF, sk1, PDF, EPS, and PostScript export formats and many more.

10.4.54 InstantAtlas [84]

InstantAtlas is a data visualization and reporting tool used for communicating location-based statistical data held in spreadsheets and desktop Geographic Information System software. It provides tools to load data into pre-built templates, tailor and brand the outputs, and write dynamic reports to meet an almost infinite range of styles and audience capabilities.

10.4.55 JavaScript InfoVis Toolkit [85]

The JavaScript InfoVis Toolkit (JIT) provides tools for creating interactive data visualizations for the Web. It is a lightweight open source toolkit. Particularly of interest to us is the fact that The JIT does not have the capacity to filter data at the visualization level. The toolkit implements advanced features of information visualization like TreeMaps, RGraph, and others.

10.4.56 JfreeChart [86,87]

JFreeChart is an open source, free Java chart library that makes it easy for developers to display professional-quality charts in their applications. It supports many output types, including Swing and JavaFX components, image files (including PNG and JPEG), and vector graphics file formats (including PDF, EPS, and SVG). It is distributed under the terms of the GNU Lesser General Public Licence (LGPL), which permits use in proprietary applications. It supports a number of charts, including combined charts. Charts in GUI automatically have the capability to zoom in with the mouse and change some settings through a local menu.

10.4.57 Jolicharts [88]

Jolicharts is a web-based service that helps to turn stored data in spreadsheets, JSON, or databases into charts, graphs, and maps. Chart color and number formats can be changed. It connects many data sources, it can upload files in any format (XLS, XLSX, and CSV) and import data from Google Spreadsheets, and it can be connected directly to any database (MySQL, PostgreSQL).

10.4.58 JpGraph [89]

JpGraph is a 2D graph plotting library for PHP5 and higher. It is meant to significantly simplify the creation of dynamic graphs using PHP scripting. The library can be used on its own or as an embedded part of a large

Web development project. It is released under a dual license. For noncommercial usage the library is released under the QPL 1.0 (Qt-License) and for professional use it is released under the JpGraph Professional License. It supports several plot/chart types.

10.4.59 JqPlot [90]

JqPlot is a jQuery plugin to generate pure client-side JavaScript charts on web pages. It is currently available for use in all personal or commercial projects under both the MIT and GPL version 2.0 licenses. It is an open source project.

10.4.60 jQuery Visualize [91]

jQuery Visualize is a jQuery plugin whose native JavaScript drawing API allows us to dynamically draw bitmap images on the page. The Visualize plugin parses key content elements in a well-structured HTML table and leverages that native HTML5 canvas drawing ability to transform them into a chart or graph. The Visualize plugin code is open source and available in a git repository. It also automatically checks for the highest and lowest values in the chart and uses them to calculate x-axis values for line and bar charts. Finally, the plugin includes two different CSS styles

10.4.61 JSter [92]

JSter is a catalog of frontend JavaScript libraries. It offers a categorization of 1573 frameworks. The catalog is divided into the following categories: Essential frameworks, UI, Multimedia, Graphics, Data, Development, Utilities, and Applications.

10.4.62 Kartograph [93]

It is a simple and lightweight framework for building interactive map applications without Google Maps or any other mapping service. It has two libraries: a powerful Python library for generating beautiful, illustrator-friendly SVG maps, licensed under AGPL, and a JavaScript library for creating interactive maps based on SVG maps, licensed under LGPL.

10.4.63 Knoema [94]

Knoema is a knowledge platform. The basic idea is to connect data with analytical and presentation tools. It is a free-to-use web-based public and open data platform launched for the purpose of statistical analysis. It is a search engine for data seamlessly connecting public and private sources and making data discoverable and accessible to information workers. It does for data what Google did for websites and the Internet overall.

10.4.64 Leaflet [95]

Leaflet is the leading open source JavaScript library for mobile-friendly interactive maps. It is designed with simplicity, performance, and usability in mind. It works efficiently across all major desktop and mobile platforms, can be extended with lots of plugins, and has a beautiful, easy-to-use and well-documented API and a simple, readable source code that is a joy to contribute to. It has core support (GeoJSON) for few GIS standard formats, with others supported in plugins.

10.4.65 LiveGap Charts [96]

LiveGap Charts is a free and online chart generator. It supports various different chart types. It can easily create charts from data.

10.4.66 Many Eyes [97]

IBM's Many Eyes is a web-based tool with a website where users can upload datasets, select a visualization type, and then visualize the data. This is a good example of sophisticated visualization tools. It is a public website where users may upload data, create interactive visualizations, and have discussions. The goal of the site is to support collaboration around visualizations at a large scale by fostering a social style of data analysis in which visualizations serve not only as a discovery tool for individuals but also as a medium to spur discussion among users. To support this goal, the site includes novel mechanisms for end-user creation of visualizations and asynchronous collaboration around those visualizations.

10.4.67 Mapbox [98]

Mapbox is an open source mapping platform for developers. It is available through public repositories on GitHub, most licensed under BSD. Large sources include OpenStreetMap, USGS, Landsat, Natural Earth, and OpenAddresses. It adopts existing specifications like GeoJSON and other new standards for new purposes. It is a large provider of custom online maps for websites. The technology is based on Node.js, CouchDB, Mapnik, GDAL, and Leafletjs.

10.4.68 Mapchart.Net [99]

With this anyone can make custom maps of the World, Europe, the Americas, the United States, the UK, and more with colors and descriptions of their own choice.

10.4.69 Maps Marker WP Plugin [100]

The Maps Marker WP Plugin is the most comprehensive and user-friendly mapping solution for WordPress. It can organize customized icons in tidy layers on a variety of maps and even in augmented reality browsers. It is an individual geo-content management system (Geo-CMS) that features the highest security standards and a moral code. While the free version of WP Google Maps allows to create a Google map with as many markers as one likes, the Pro version allows to create custom Google maps with high-quality markers containing locations, descriptions, images, categories, links, and directions.

10.4.70 Miso [101]

Miso is an open source toolkit designed to expedite the creation of high-quality interactive storytelling and data visualization content. It consists of Dataset, a JavaScript client-side data management and transformation library, Storyboard, a state- and flow-control management library, and d3.chart, a framework for creating reusable charts with d3.js. It is in active development. It can handle a variety of data sources such as JSON files, CSVs, remote APIs, and Google Spreadsheets.

10.4.71 Modest Maps [102]

Modest Maps is a small, extensible, and free library for designers and developers who want to use interactive maps in their own projects. It provides a core set of features in a tight, clean package. It is a BSD-licensed display and interaction library for tile-based maps in JavaScript.

10.4.72 Mr. Data Converter [103]

Mr. Data Converter takes CSV or tab-delimited data from Excel and converts them into several web-friendly formats, including JSON and XML. It is available under the MIT License. It is a conversion tool to take tab- or comma-delimited data and convert them into a variety of formats, including XML, JSON, ActionScript, and PHP.

10.4.73 Mr. Nester [104]

Mr. Nester is a simple open source console for learning and experimenting with d3.js data. It is released under the MIT License.

10.4.74 Myheatmap [105]

Myheatmap was designed for publication and presentation, that is, to zoom in on figures without impacting resolution. Color-coded heat maps are extremely easy to understand. Maps are not cluttered with markers, flags, contour lines, or growing blobs, and data are as simple to distinguish as hot and cold. It is completely interactive. Viewers are able to display data at any zoom level. Users can easily switch between different datasets within the same map. CSV files can be uploaded with data and the map is instantly viewable. There is no need to rummage through complicated API documentation or write complex computer code; the user can just upload and view data.

10.4.75 Networkx [106]

Networkx is based on Python language, for the creation, manipulation, and study of the structure, dynamics, and function of complex networks. With this, networks can be loaded in standard and non-standard data formats, many types of random and classic networks can be generated, network structures can be analyzed, network models can be built, new network algorithms can be designed, networks can be drawn, and much more. It provides an interface to existing numerical algorithms and code written in C, C++, and FORTRAN. It is a free software program available under the terms of the BSD License. It is suitable for operation on large real-world graphs. It is integrated into SageMath.

10.4.76 Nevron Vision [107]

Nevron Vision is an advanced data visualization tool for .NET end-to-end desktop and web applications. It offers the most comprehensive set of components for building enterprise-grade data visualization applications. The components in this suite feature coherent 2D and 3D data visualization effects that have a great visual impact on the audience. Moreover, a large set of data visualization techniques and innovations has been implemented to maximize the clarity of the visualized data and to make the data more comprehensive for the viewer.

10.4.77 NodeBox [108]

NodeBox is a node-based software application for creating generative art using procedural graphics and a new way to approach graphic design. The software uses a non-destructive workflow where every operation is represented by a visual block of code. It is open to extension. Nodes can be written in popular dynamic programming languages (Python/Clojure). With this data visualization, generative design, and complex production are easy. NodeBox is built from the ground up by designers to be easy-to-use, efficient, and fast. It is ideal for rapid data visualization. It can import many data formats. NodeBox for OpenGL is a free, cross-platform library.

10.4.78 NVD3 [109]

This project is an attempt to build reusable charts and chart components for d3.js without taking away the power that d3.js gives. This is a very young collection of components, with the goal of keeping these components very customizable, staying away from standard cookie cutter solutions. It is recommended to go with d3.js. It runs best on WebKit-based browsers. It is available under the Apache License.

10.4.79 OpenLayers [110]

OpenLayers is a high-performance, feature-packed library for all mapping needs. It makes it easy to include a dynamic map on any web page. It can display map tiles, vector data, and markers loaded from any source. It is completely free, open source, JavaScript-based, and released under the FreeBSD license. It can be used to process vector data from GeoJSON, TopoJSON, KML, GML, Mapbox vector tiles, and other formats. It leverages Canvas 2D, WebGL, and all the latest benefits from HTML5. It runs on all modern browsers.

10.4.80 OpenRefine [111]

OpenRefine (formerly Google Refine) is a powerful tool for working with messy data, cleaning them, transforming them from one format into another, and extending them with web services and external data. It is a web application. This architecture has emerged from our experience building similar systems such as Simile Longwell CSI, a faceted browser for RDF data. It provides a good separation of concerns (data vs. UI) and also makes it quick and easy to implement user interface features using familiar web technologies. The server-side part is implemented in Java whereas the client-side part is implemented in JavaScript and uses jQuery and jQuery UI to simplify portability across modern browsers. It is open source software and is licensed under the BSD license.

10.4.81 Paper.Js [112]

Paper.Js is an open source vector graphics scripting framework that runs on top of the HTML5 Canvas. It offers a clean Scene Graph/Document Object Model and a lot of powerful functionalities to create and work with vector graphics and Bezier curves, all neatly wrapped up in a well-designed, consistent, and clean programming interface. It is not simply a wrapper around the Canvas; it offers much more.

10.4.82 Peity [113]

Peity is a jQuery plugin that converts an element's content into an SVG mini pie donut line or bar chart and is compatible with any browser that supports SVG. Custom chart types can be added. It is available under the MIT License.

10.4.83 Piktochart [114]

Piktochart is a web-based design program that creates infographics, reports, presentations, and posters. It also provides data visualization features such as adding static or dynamic charts and maps. It provides options ranging from open access for a single user to multi-user subscription. It allows for export to JPEG, PNG, or PDF file formats. Data can be imported from a Microsoft Excel file, a Google Spreadsheet, or a SurveyMonkey account.

10.4.84 Plot [115]

Plot is loaded asynchronously so it will not affect website performance. The script itself is also superfast to download as it is served from the Amazon Cloudfront, a CDN which caches the content at various locations around the world. The content is served from the nearest location to each of the users. It works on all browsers. However, some browsers support more advanced and cooler features like video.

10.4.85 Polymaps [116]

Polymaps is a free JavaScript library for image- and vector-tiled maps using SVG, generating "slippy" maps in the style of Google Maps, Modest Maps, CloudMade, and OpenLayers. It is used for making dynamic, interactive maps in modern web browsers. The vector geometry is loaded as GeoJSON via asynchronous XMLHttpRequest.

10.4.86 Processing and Processing.Js [117,118]

Processing is an open source computer programming language and IDE built for the electronic arts, new media art, and visual design communities. It is free, licensed under the GNU General Public License. It includes interactive programs with 2D, 3D, or PDF output and OpenGL integration for accelerated 2D and 3D. Processing.js is the sister project of the popular Processing visual programming language, designed for the web. It makes data visualization, digital art, interactive animations, educational graphs, video games, etc., work using web standards and without any plugins. Processing.js takes this to the next level, allowing Processing code to be run by any HTML5 compatible browser.

10.4.87 Protovis [119]

Protovis composes custom views of data with simple marks such as bars and dots. It defines marks through dynamic properties that encode data, allowing inheritance, scales, and layouts to simplify construction. It is free and open source, provided under the BSD License. It uses JavaScript and SVG for web-native visualizations; only a modern web browser without plugins is required. It is no longer under active development.

10.4.88 Q Research Software [120]

Q Research Software is easy for a novice and potent for an expert. It quickly turns data into smart insights and clever chart-based reports. It uses the most advanced analysis methods, like correspondence analysis, logit, latent class analysis, regression, max-diff, random parameters, Kruskal, Shapley, TURF, etc. It is highly efficient by exporting editable charts to Office.

10.4.89 Qlik Sense and Qlikview [121,122]

Qlik Sense is a Windows application that gives individuals the power to create personalized, flexible, interactive data visualizations, reports and dashboards from multiple data sources with drag and drop ease. QlikView is very different from traditional BI software. It is simple and easy, and puts the user in total control. With just a few clicks, QlikView lets consolidate, search, visualize, and analyze all data sources for unprecedented business insight.

10.4.90 Quadrigram [123]

Quadrigram is a powerful drag and drop visual programming environment for visualizing data without the need for code. Using this, anyone can share interactive data visualization projects quickly, easily, and without any programming skills. It is located between the paradigms of standard programming and spreadsheets.

10.4.91 R [124]

R is a language and environment for statistical computing and graphics. It is a GNU project. It provides a wide variety of statistical and graphical techniques, and is highly extensible. It provides an open source route to participation in that activity. It is available as free software under the terms of the GNU General Public License. It is an integrated suite of software facilities for data manipulation, calculation, and graphical display. Another strength of it is static graphics, which can produce publication-quality graphs, including mathematical symbols. Dynamic and interactive graphics are available through additional packages.

10.4.92 Raphael [125]

Raphael is a cross-browser JavaScript library that draws Vector graphics for websites. It will use SVG for most browsers. It currently supports all modern web browsers. The source code is available on GitHub.

10.4.93 RAW [126]

RAW is an open web tool to create custom vector-based visualizations on top of the amazing d3.js library. Its aims at providing the missing link between spreadsheet applications and vector graphics editors. It works with tabular data as well as with copied-and-pasted texts from other applications based on the SVG format. It is also highly customizable and extendable, accepting new custom layouts defined by users. It is provided under the Apache License 2.0. It allows to export visualizations in vector (SVG) or raster (PNG) format and embed them in web pages.

10.4.94 Recline.Js [127]

Recline.Js is a simple but powerful library for building data applications in pure JavaScript and HTML. It is open source and easy to embed in other sites and applications. The used can view and edit his/her data in a clean grid interface, update/clean bulk data using an easy scripting UI, and visualize data.

10.4.95 Rickshaw [128]

Rickshaw is a JavaScript toolkit for creating interactive time series graphs. Graphs are drawn with standard SVG and styled with CSS. It is free and open source, available under the MIT License. It is a simple framework for drawing charts of time series data on a web page, built on top of the D3 library. These charts can be powered by static historical datasets or living data that are continuously updated in real-time. This library works in modern browsers. It relies on the fantastic D3 visualization library to do lots of the heavy lifting for stacking and rendering to SVG. Some extensions require jQuery and jQuery UI, but for drawing some basic graphs these are not essential. It uses jsdom to run unit tests in Node to be able to perform SVG manipulation.

10.4.96 SAS Visual Analytics [129]

SAS Visual Analytics is a web-based product that uses SAS high-performance analytic technologies to explore huge volumes of data quickly in order to see patterns and trends. It has now fully integrated the DataFlux suite of data quality, data integration, data governance, and master data management solutions.

10.4.97 Shield UI [130]

Shield UI specializes in the design and production of specialized highly functional and flexible UI components for pure JavaScript development. It offers a fully functional set of web development jQuery components, ranging from smaller input controls to large components such as the Shield UI jQuery Grid. It is licensed under the MIT License, supports numerous chart types, runs on legacy and newer web browsers, and is platform-independent.

10.4.98 Sigma.Js [131]

Sigma.Js is a JavaScript library dedicated to graph drawing. It has been designed as an engine that can be customized and used to develop highly interactive Web applications that show graph visualizations. It makes it easy to publish networks on Web pages and allows developers to integrate network exploration in rich Web applications. It provides a lot of built-in features, such as Canvas and WebGL renderers or mouse and touch support. It runs on all modern browsers that support Canvas and works faster on browsers with WebGL support.

10.4.99 Silk [132]

Silk sllows to create interactive data visualizations, publish websites, and tell interactive stories.

10.4.100 Smart Data Report [133]

This software minimizes manual development efforts. It transforms raw data into meaningful and comprehensive information by generating charts, graphs, pivot tables, and PowerPoint reports. It is a perfect solution for individuals and small businesses. No downloads and no HTML skills are required. Easy plug and play solutions are integrated.

10.4.101 StatSilk [134]

StatSilk is software for creating user-friendly interactive dashboards and visualizing data and maps (desktop, web-based, and mobile apps). Anyone can easily produce interactive data visualizations. It is completely free for use by local non-profit organizations and government institutions.

10.4.102 SVG Crowbar [135]

SVG Crowbar is a Chrome-specific bookmarklet that extracts SVG nodes and accompanying styles from an HTML document and downloads them as an SVG file. It was created with d3.js in mind, but it should work fine with any SVG.

10.4.103 Tableau Public [136]

Using this, anyone can create and share interactive charts and graphs, stunning maps, live dashboards, and fun applications in minutes and publish them anywhere on the web. It is very easy and free.

10.4.104 Tabula [137,138]

Tabula is a simple and user-friendly tool to create interactive data visualizations quickly and embed them on websites. It allows to extract those data into a CSV or Microsoft Excel spreadsheet using a simple, easy-to-use interface. It only works on text-based PDFs, not scanned documents. It is open source. It has bindings for JRuby and R.

10.4.105 Tangle [139]

Tangle is a JavaScript lightweight library that provides a simple API for tangling up the values in documents. It has no dependencies. It has an optional collection of UI components that let readers adjust values and visualize the results. It also includes and depends on a few helpful libraries, such as MooTools, sprintf, and BVTouchable.

10.4.106 Teechart [140]

This cross-platform charting component library offers hundreds of graph styles in 2D and 3D for data visualization and 56 mathematical, statistical, and financial functions. It can easily create and connect to an existing database or dataset in the project. A Web source component to retrieve Internet charts and data is included, as well as database charting with Summaries, Sorting, Crosstabs, and record level. Lots of third party reporting components and other applications are compatible with this library, such as IntraWeb VCL, ReportBuilder, QuickReport, FastReport, RAVE, etc.

10.4.107 Timeline [141,142]

The main function of this is to communicate time-related information, either for analysis or to visually present a story or a view of history. This allows the viewer to see any patterns appearing over any selected time period or how events are distributed during that time period. All code and data are processed and rendered in the browser. No data are sent to any server.

10.4.108 TimelineJS [143]

TimelineJS is an open source tool that enables anyone to build visually rich, interactive timelines. Novices can create a timeline using nothing more than a Google Spreadsheet, as described above for Timeline. Experts can use their JSON skills to create custom installations, while keeping TimelineJS's core functionality. It works on any site or blog.

10.4.109 Unfolding [144]

Unfolding is a library to create interactive maps and geo-visualizations in Processing and Java. It is a tile-based map library. It comes with various map providers, such as OpenStreetMap or TileMill. It can be used under the terms of the MIT License.

10.4.110 Ushahidi [145]

Ushahidi is an open source web application for information collection, data visualization, and interactive mapping. It helps to collect info from SMS, Twitter, RSS feeds, and email. It helps to process that information, categorize it, geo-locate it, and publish it on a map.

10.4.111 Vancharts [146]

Vancharts is a JavaScript chart library for Web-based and mobile applications. It provides a revolutionary tool: a chart maker which is provided for visualized design and JS code export. It has more wide-ranging chart types. It perfectly supports various platforms and browsers. HTML5-compliant cross-platform development and application are supported. It is based on Canvas but is compatible with all existing browsers.

10.4.112 Vega [147]

Vega is a visualization grammar, a declarative language for creating, saving, and sharing interactive visualization designs. With this, anyone can describe the visual appearance and interactive behavior of visualization in a JSON format and generate web-based views using Canvas or SVG. It provides basic building blocks for a wide variety of visualization designs. It defines an interactive visualization in JSON format.

10.4.113 Vida [148]

It is an open source, flexible, and extendable data visualization tool to build, reuse, and customize visualizations with D3.JS in the cloud. It includes basic charts, such as Line, Bar, Area, Pie, Bubble, GeoMap, Scatter Plot, and TreeMap.

10.4.114 Visage [149]

Visage is a new Web-based platform that transforms the uninspired data in reports into beautiful, branded visualizations that make messages more impactful and make work look good. The easy-to-use software helps to create high-quality, professional visualizations that are accurate, effective, and elegant.

10.4.115 Visualize Free [150]

Visualize Free is a free cloud-hosted, zero-client app that combines data preparation and visualization. It is an analytic tool that allows data exploration and discovery intuitively.

10.4.116 Weka [151]

Weka is a collection of machine learning algorithms for data mining tasks. The algorithms can be either directly applied to a dataset or called from your own Java code. It contains tools for data pre-processing, classification, regression, clustering, association, and visualization. It is also well suited for developing new machine learning schemes. It is open source software issued under the GNU General Public License. It is possible to apply it to Big Data.

10.4.117 WolframAlpha [152]

WolframAlpha is a computational knowledge engine or answer engine. It is an online service that answers factual queries directly by computing the answer from externally sourced "curated data." It is a computational platform or toolkit that encompasses computer algebra, symbolic and numerical computation, visualization, and statistics capabilities. Additional data are gathered from both academic and commercial websites. Users submit queries and computation requests via a text field. It then computes answers and relevant visualizations from a knowledge base of curated, structured data that come from other sites and books.

10.4.118 Yazoo Easydata [153]

Yazoo Easydata is a free database query and reporting tool that helps you quickly access, extract, and visualize your database data. Its main features include a Connection Wizard, Query Builder, SQL Editor, Results Viewer, Export Wizard, and Chart Designer.

10.4.119 Zebra BI [154]

Zebra BI is an Excel add-in that helps to create best-practice business reports in just a few clicks. Charts can be created from Excel values and formulas, Pivot tables, PowerPivot, or third party add-ins. Zebra BI visualizations automatically update to changes in Excel data.

10.4.120 ZingChart [155]

ZingChart is a declarative, efficient, and simple JavaScript library for building responsive charts with integrations in Angular, React, JQuery, PHP, Ember, and Backbone. ZingChart is wrapped in a variety of ways for easy consumption with popular JS libraries and frameworks. It includes a build tool that allows the user to create a custom library build for the client-side version.

10.4.121 ZoomCharts [156]

ZoomCharts is a JavaScript/HTML library that helps users to add visually rich and interactive charts to applications by using a minimal amount of code. It is a cross-platform HTML5 charts library for creating interactive visual data interfaces optimized for touchscreen devices and web applications. It bridges the gap between Big Data and mobile devices. It is free to use. It provides various chart families like NetChart, TimeChart, PieChart, FacetChart, GeoChart, and various new chart types.

10.4.122 Weave [157–159]

Weave is an open source, cross-platform, community-driven software platform that can be used with any modern browser. It is the only platform that automatically generates descriptions of visualizations in real-time as data or views change. It connects to a wide variety of relational and non-relational data sources. Some of these include CSV, SQL, GeoJSON, SHP/DBF, CKAN, and census servers.

10.4.123 Dundas Dashboard [160]

Dundas Dashboard gives full control over data so anyone can create stunning dashboards, embedded analytics, and a personal user experience. It provides a central location for users to access, interact with, and analyze up-to-date information so they can make smarter, data-driven decisions. It enables the user to monitor and measure performance and metrics in real-time and on the go. It can visualize and analyze data and focus on key performance indicators (KPIs) from across the organization.

10.4.124 Simile [161]

Simile is an open source web widget that is mostly used for data visualization. It is maintained and improved over time by a community of open source developers. Web pages are created with support for sorting, filtering, and rich visualizations by writing only HTML and optionally some CSS and JavaScript code. No database or server is needed. Temporal information is visualized on an interactive dragable timeline. Time series can be plotted and temporal events can be overlaid. Images can be displayed in a Coverflow-like visualization.

10.4.125 Datawatch Desktop [162]

Datawatch Desktop is an easy-to-use, powerful BI solution focusing on real-time data visualization. It has the capability to handle any type of unstructured as well as structured data from Excel spreadsheets, pdf files, databases, HTML files, data warehouses, etc. It is cross-platform.

10.4.126 Prefuse [163]

Prefuse is an open source software framework/user interface toolkit to handle any type of unstructured as well as structured data and create dynamic/interactive visualizations. It provides 2D designs.

10.4.127 MangoDB Compass [164]

MangoDB Compass is a GUI for popular MongoDB. It explores and quickly visualizes data and is hence useful to make smarter decisions. Data can be modified with a powerful visual editing tool. It is a cross-platform software, supports JSON, and is extendable via plugins.

10.5 Conclusion

Visualization tools/techniques provide a countless interactive view into information/data. However, any effective information/data view, together with visualization, depends on the capabilities to access, transform, purify, and mash up information/data. Notwithstanding, whether or not data are unstructured, semi-structured, or structured, they have to be ready for data/information viewing. Data need to be first organized into a useful model. These data models actually form the basis for visualization. These modeled data themselves are a vital asset. As an analytical tool for scientific or business forecasting, data/information visualization is performed worldwide. Data visualization has an important role in making the massively accumulated data over the internet (shopping malls, data centers, etc.) usable for future prediction, strategic development, risk analysis, etc. The availability of good statistical visualization software is key to effectively perform data analysis and to explore and develop new methods for data visualization. Compared with static visualization, interactive visualization adds additional natural and powerful ways to explore data. With interactive visualization an analyst can dive into the data and quickly react to visual clues by, for example, refocusing and creating interactive queries of the data. The objective of any data visualization tool/platform is to reduce BI complexity, but this definitely comes at a cost. A particular visualization tool/technique for a particular case needs to be chosen carefully. This chapter presents an overview of 127 data visualization tools/techniques and several of their properties.

References

[1] S. Busking, Visualization of variation and variability, 2014.
[2] A. Waddell, Interactive visualization and exploration of high-dimensional data, 2016.
[3] Texas Advanced Computing Center, The University of Texas, Austin, Overview and introduction to scientific visualization, https://www.tacc.utexas.edu/c/document_library/get_file?uuid=2568ed22-13ff-49ba-8104-0804dbccf56a&groupId=13601.
[4] Jeff Solka, Jennifer Welle, Visualizing Data, Lecture Slides, 2006, http://www.ub.edu/stat/docencia/bioinformatica/microarrays/ADM/slides/3c_VisualizeData_solka.pdf.
[5] D. Scott, Multivariate Density Estimation, John Wiley & Sons, Inc., New York, NY, 1992.
[6] D.G. Kendall, Shape manifolds, procrustean metrics, and complex projective spaces, Bulletin of the London Mathematical Society 16 (2) (1984) 81–121.
[7] D. Asimov, The grand tour: a tool for viewing multidimensional data, SIAM Journal on Scientific and Statistical Computing 6 (1) (1985) 128–143.
[8] M.Y. Huh, K. Kim, Visualization of multidimensional data using modifications of the grand tour, Journal of Applied Statistics 29 (5) (2002) 721–728.
[9] E.R. Tufte, N.H. Goeler, R. Benson, Envisioning Information, vol. 126, Graphics Press, Cheshire, CT, 1990.
[10] A. Buja, D. Cook, D.F. Swayne, Interactive high-dimensional data visualization, Journal of Computational and Graphical Statistics 5 (1) (1996) 78–99.
[11] A.C. Telea, Data Visualization: Principles and Practice, CRC Press, 2014.
[12] F.H. Post, G. Nielson, G.-P. Bonneau, Data Visualization: The State of the Art, vol. 713, Springer Science & Business Media, 2002.
[13] A. Kirk, Data Visualization: A Successful Design Process, Packt Publishing Ltd., 2012.
[14] B.A. Price, R.M. Baecker, I.S. Small, A principled taxonomy of software visualization, Journal of Visual Languages and Computing 4 (3) (1993) 211–266.
[15] H. Hagen, H. Müller, G.M. Nielson, Focus on Scientific Visualization, Springer Science & Business Media, 2012.
[16] G.-P. Bonneau, T. Ertl, G.M. Nielson, Scientific Visualization: The Visual Extraction of Knowledge from Data, vol. 1, Springer, 2006.

[17] H. Wright, Introduction to Scientific Visualization, Springer Science & Business Media, 2007.

[18] Mike Reich, Visualizing data: one great opportunity with three common challenges, http://www.seabourneinc.com/visualizing-data-one-great-opportunity-with-three-common-challenges/.

[19] Amcharts, https://www.amcharts.com/. (Accessed 12 December 2019), online.

[20] Arbor.Js, http://arborjs.org/. (Accessed 12 December 2019), online.

[21] Better World Flux, http://www.betterworldflux.com/. (Accessed 12 December 2019), online.

[22] CartoDB, https://github.com/CartoDB/cartodb/. (Accessed 12 December 2019), online.

[23] Chart.Js, http://www.chartjs.org/. (Accessed 12 December 2019), online.

[24] Chroma.Js, https://gka.github.io/chroma.js/. (Accessed 13 December 2019), online.

[25] Chroma.Js, https://github.com/gka/chroma.js/. (Accessed 13 December 2019), online.

[26] Circos, http://circos.ca/. (Accessed 13 December 2019), online.

[27] Cola.Js, http://marvl.infotech.monash.edu/webcola/. (Accessed 13 December 2019), online.

[28] Cola.Js, https://github.com/tgdwyer/WebCola/. (Accessed 13 December 2019), online.

[29] Colorbrewer, http://colorbrewer2.org/. (Accessed 14 December 2019), online.

[30] ColorBREWER, https://github.com/tgdwyer/WebCola/. (Accessed 14 December 2019), online.

[31] Creately, https://creately.com/. (Accessed 15 December 2019), online.

[32] Crossfilter, https://github.com/square/crossfilter/. (Accessed 15 December 2019), online.

[33] CSV, https://en.wikipedia.org/wiki/Comma-separated_values/. (Accessed 15 December 2019), online.

[34] JSON, http://www.json.org/. (Accessed 15 December 2019), online.

[35] Cubism.js, https://github.com/square/cubism/. (Accessed 15 December 2019), online.

[36] Cubism.JS, https://square.github.io/cubism/. (Accessed 15 December 2019), online.

[37] Cytoscape, http://www.cytoscape.org/what_is_cytoscape.html/. (Accessed 17 December 2019), online.

[38] Cytoscape.js, http://js.cytoscape.org/l/. (Accessed 17 December 2019), online.

[39] Cytoscape.JS, http://cytoscapeweb.cytoscape.org/. (Accessed 18 December 2019), online.

[40] D3e.Js, https://d3js.org//. (Accessed 18 December 2019), online.

[41] Dance.Js, https://github.com/michael/dance/. (Accessed 18 December 2019), online.

[42] Dapresy, http://dapresy.com/. (Accessed 18 December 2019), online.

[43] Data.js, https://datajs.codeplex.com/. (Accessed 18 December 2019), online.

[44] Databoard.js, https://bynd.com/work/google-databoard/. (Accessed 5 January 2020), online.

[45] Wrangler, http://ilpubs.stanford.edu:8090/1005/1/wranglerPaper.pdf/. (Accessed 6 January 2020), online.

[46] WRANGLER, http://vis.stanford.edu/papers/wrangler/. (Accessed 6 January 2020), online.

[47] Degrafa, https://www.degrafa.org/. (Accessed 6 January 2020), online.

[48] Dhtmlxchart, https://docs.dhtmlx.com/. (Accessed 6 January 2020), online.

[49] DHTMLXCHART, https://dhtmlx.com/docs/products/dhtmlxChart/. (Accessed 6 January 2020), online.

[50] P. Mazur, Tools and APIs for Visualisation of Timelines, Retrieved 12 (02) (2008), 2010.

[51] Dipity, http://www.dipity.com/. (Accessed 6 January 2020), online.

[52] Dygraphs, http://dygraphs.com/. (Accessed 6 January 2020), online.

[53] BIRT, http://www.eclipse.org/birt/. (Accessed 6 January 2020), online.

[54] S. Sundaramoorthi, Eclipse BIRT Plug-ins for Dynamic Piecewise Constant and Event Time-Series, Arizona State University, 2015.

[55] Envision.J, http://www.humblesoftware.com/envision/. (Accessed 8 January 2020), online.

[56] Envision.JS, https://github.com/HumbleSoftware/envisionjs/. (Accessed 8 January 2020), online.

[57] Eurostat, http://ec.europa.eu/eurostat/about/overview. (Accessed 8 January 2020), online.

[58] Excel, https://msdn.microsoft.com/. (Accessed 8 January 2020), online.

[59] Excel Map/Power Map, https://support.office.com/en-us/article/Get-started-with-Power-Map-88A28DF6-8258-40AA-B5CC-577873FB0F4A/. (Accessed 9 January 2020), online.

[60] Exhibit, https://simile-widgets.org/exhibit3/. (Accessed 9 January 2020), online.

[61] Factmint, http://factmint.com/. (Accessed 9 January 2020), online.

[62] FF Chartwel, https://www.fontfont.com/fonts/chartwell/. (Accessed 9 January 2020), online.

[63] Flare, http://flare.prefuse.org/. (Accessed 9 January 2020), online.

[64] FLARE, https://github.com/prefuse/Flare/. (Accessed 10 January 2020), online.

[65] Flot Chart, https://github.com/flot/flot/. (Accessed 10 January 2020), online.

[66] FFlowingdatat, http://flowingdata.com/. (Accessed 10 January 2020), online.

[67] Fusioncharts Suite Xt, http://www.fusioncharts.com. (Accessed 15 January 2020), online.

[68] GeoCommons, http://geocommons.com/. (Accessed 15 January 2020), online.

[69] Gephi, https://gephi.org/. (Accessed 15 January 2020), online.

[70] Google Chart, https://developers.google.com/chart/. (Accessed 16 January 2020), online.

[71] Google Fusion Tables, https://developers.google.com/fusiontables/. (Accessed 16 January 2020), online.

[72] Google Maps, https://developers.google.com/maps/. (Accessed 18 January 2020), online.

[73] Google Public Data, https://www.google.com/publicdata/directory/. (Accessed 18 January 2020), online.

[74] Google's Spreadsheets, https://www.google.co.in/sheets/about/. (Accessed 18 January 2020), online.

[75] Highcharts, https://www.highcharts.com/products/highcharts/. (Accessed 18 January 2020), online.

[76] Highmaps, https://www.highcharts.com/products/highmaps/. (Accessed 18 January 2020), online.

[77] I Want Hue, http://tools.medialab.sciences-po.fr/iwanthue/index.php/. (Accessed 25 January 2020), online.

[78] IWantHue, https://github.com/medialab/iwanthue/. (Accessed 25 January 2020), online.

[79] Icharts, https://icharts.net/. (Accessed 25 January 2020), online.

[80] Inetsoft, https://www.inetsoft.com/. (Accessed 25 January 2020), online.

[81] Infoactive, https://infoactive.co/data-design/. (Accessed 3 February 2020), online.

[82] Infocaptor, http://www.infocaptor.com/. (Accessed 3 February 2020), online.

[83] Inkscape, https://inkscape.org/en/about/overview/. (Accessed 3 February 2020), online.

[84] InstantAtlas, http://www.instantatlas.com/. (Accessed 3 February 2020), online.
[85] JavaScript Infovis Toolkit, https://philogb.github.io/jit/index.html/. (Accessed 3 February 2020), online.
[86] JfreeChart, http://www.jfree.org/jfreechart/. (Accessed 4 February 2020), online.
[87] JFREECHART, https://github.com/jfree/jfreechart/. (Accessed 4 February 2020), online.
[88] Jolicharts, http://www.jolicharts.com/. (Accessed 4 February 2020), online.
[89] JpGraph, http://jpgraph.net/. (Accessed 4 February 2020), online.
[90] JqPlot, http://www.jqplot.com/. (Accessed 7 February 2020), online.
[91] jQuery Visualize, https://github.com/filamentgroup/jQuery-Visualize. (Accessed 7 February 2020), online.
[92] Jster, http://jster.net/about/. (Accessed 7 February 2020), online.
[93] Kartograph, http://kartograph.org//. (Accessed 7 February 2020), online.
[94] Knoema, https://knoema.com/. (Accessed 7 February 2020), online.
[95] Leaflet, http://leafletjs.com/. (Accessed 7 February 2020), online.
[96] Livegap Charts, http://charts.livegap.com/. (Accessed 10 February 2020), online.
[97] Many Eyes, https://www.ibm.com/developerworks/community/blogs/iic-san-mateo/entry/big_data_data_journalism_and_ibm_s_manyeyes?lang=en/. (Accessed 7 February 2020), online.
[98] Mapbox, https://www.mapbox.com/. (Accessed 10 February 2020), online.
[99] Mapchart.Net, https://mapchart.net//. (Accessed 10 February 2020), online.
[100] Maps Marker WP-Plugin, https://www.mapsmarker.com/. (Accessed 10 February 2020), online.
[101] Miso, http://misoproject.com/. (Accessed 14 February 2020), online.
[102] Modest Maps, http://modestmaps.com/. (Accessed 14 February 2020), online.
[103] Mr. Data Converter, https://github.com/fitnr/Mr-Data-Converter. (Accessed 14 February 2020), online.
[104] Mr. Nester, http://bl.ocks.org/shancarter/raw/4748131/. (Accessed 14 February 2020), online.
[105] Myheatmap, https://www.myheatmap.com/. (Accessed 14 February 2020), online.
[106] Networkx, https://networkx.github.io/. (Accessed 15 February 2020), online.
[107] Nevron Vision, https://www.nevron.com/. (Accessed 15 February 2020), online.
[108] NodeBox, https://www.nodebox.net/. (Accessed 15 February 2020), online.
[109] NVD3, http://nvd3.org/. (Accessed 15 February 2020), online.
[110] Openlayers, https://openlayers.org//. (Accessed 18 February 2020), online.
[111] Openrefine, http://openrefine.org/. (Accessed 18 February 2020), online.
[112] Paper.Js, http://paperjs.org/. (Accessed 18 February 2020), online.
[113] Peity, https://github.com/benpickles/peity/. (Accessed 18 February 2020), online.
[114] Piktochart, https://piktochart.com/. (Accessed 19 February 2020), online.
[115] Plot, http://www.plot.io/. (Accessed 19 February 2020), online.
[116] Polymaps, http://polymaps.org/. (Accessed 19 February 2020), online.
[117] Processing, http://processingjs.org/. (Accessed 19 February 2020), online.
[118] Processing. Js, https://github.com/processing-js/processing-js. (Accessed 19 February 2020), online.
[119] Protovis, http://vis.stanford.edu/files/2009-Protovis-InfoVis.pdf/. (Accessed 19 February 2020), online.
[120] Q Research Software, https://www.qresearchsoftware.com/. (Accessed 21 February 2020), online.
[121] Qlik Sense, http://www.qlik.com/us/products/qlik-sense/. (Accessed 21 February 2020), online.
[122] Qlikview, http://www.qlik.com/us/products/qlikview. (Accessed 21 February 2020), online.

[123] Quadrigram, http://www.quadrigram.com/. (Accessed 21 February 2020), online.
[124] R, www.r-project.org/. (Accessed 21 February 2020), online.
[125] Raphael.
[126] RAW, http://raw.densitydesign.org/features/. (Accessed 2 April 2020), online.
[127] Recline.Js, https://jspreadsheets.com/recline-js.html/. (Accessed 2 April 2020), online.
[128] Rickshaw, http://code.shutterstock.com/rickshaw/. (Accessed 2 April 2020), online.
[129] SAS Visual Analytics, https://www.sas.com//. (Accessed 2 April 2020), online.
[130] Shield UI, https://github.com/shieldui/shieldui-lite/. (Accessed 4 April 2020), online.
[131] Sigma.Js, http://sigmajs.org/. (Accessed 4 April 2020), online.
[132] Silk, https://www.silk.co/. (Accessed 4 April 2020), online.
[133] Smart Data Report, http://www.smartdatareport.com/. (Accessed 7 April 2020), online.
[134] StatSilk, https://www.statsilk.com/. (Accessed 7 April 2020), online.
[135] Sigma.Js, http://sigmajs.org/. (Accessed 7 April 2020), online.
[136] Tableau Public, https://public.tableau.com/. (Accessed 7 April 2020), online.
[137] Tabula, http://tabula.technology/. (Accessed 11 April 2020), online.
[138] TABULA, https://github.com/tabulapdf/tabula/. (Accessed 11 April 2020), online.
[139] Tangle, http://worrydream.com/Tangle/. (Accessed 17 April 2020), online.
[140] Teechart, https://www.steema.com/product/vc/. (Accessed 17 April 2020), online.
[141] Timeline, http://www.datavizcatalogue.com/methods/timeline.html. (Accessed 17 April 2020), online.
[142] TIMELINE, https://developers.google.com/chart/interactive/docs/gallery/timelin/. (Accessed 17 April 2020), online.
[143] TimelineJS, https://timeline.knightlab.com/. (Accessed 17 April 2020), online.
[144] Unfolding, http://unfoldingmaps.org/. (Accessed 24 April 2020), online.
[145] Ushahidi, https://www.ushahidi.com/. (Accessed 24 April 2020), online.
[146] Vancharts, http://www.vancharts.com/. (Accessed 17 April 2020), online.
[147] Vega, https://vega.github.io/vega/. (Accessed 24 April 2020), online.
[148] Vida, https://vida.io/. (Accessed 3 May 2020), online.
[149] Visage, https://visage.co/product/. (Accessed 3 May 2020), online.
[150] Visualize Free, https://visualizefree.com/. (Accessed 3 May 2020), online.
[151] Weka, http://www.cs.waikato.ac.nz/~ml/weka/. (Accessed 12 May 2020), online.
[152] WolframAlpha, https://www.wolframalpha.com/. (Accessed 12 May 2020), online.
[153] Yazoo Easydata, https://marketplace.eclipse.org/content/yazoo-easydata/. (Accessed 12 May 2020), online.
[154] Zebra BI, https://zebrabi.com/features/. (Accessed 21 May 2020), online.
[155] ZZingcharts, https://www.zingchart.com/. (Accessed 21 May 2020), online.
[156] Zoomcharts, https://zoomcharts.com/. (Accessed 21 May 2020), online.
[157] Weave, http://www.iweave.com/. (Accessed 23 May 2020), online.
[158] WEAVE, https://www.gislounge.com/weave-open-source-data-visualization/. (Accessed 25 May 2020), online.
[159] WEave, https://github.com/WeaveTeam/Weave/. (Accessed 15 June 2020), online.
[160] Dundas Dashboard, https://www.dundas.com/. (Accessed 16 June 2020), online.
[161] Simile, https://www.simile-widgets.org/. (Accessed 17 June 2020), online.
[162] Datawatch Desktop, http://www.datawatch.com/. (Accessed 18 June 2020), online.
[163] J. Heer, S. Card, J. Landay, Prefuse: a toolkit for interactive information visualization, in: CHI'05: Proceedings of the SIGCHI Conference on Human Factors in Computing Systems, 2005.
[164] MangoDB Compass, https://www.mongodb.com/products/compass/. (Accessed 7 August 2020), online.

CHAPTER 11

An intelligent agent to mine for frequent patterns in uncertain graphs

V. Kakulapati
Sreenidhi Institute of Science and Technology, Hyderabad, Telangana, India

11.1 Introduction

There is a considerable spectrum of real-life applications and a lack of certainty. For instance, in the context of social network interactions, it might not be possible to describe the connection between Bill and Matthew utilizing available evidence, such as "Bill cooperates well with Matthew." In this work, the interaction with probability p is identified, and the value of p is measured sequentially by the domain knowledge utilizing data or knowledge processing. The criteria for managing insecurity are noticeable in the Big Data period, where data of varying quality often emerge. This study focuses on vague graphs, which use knowledge as a graph of uncertainty-dependent edges. A previously discussed social network is an uncertain graphic model developed in communication networks, wireless sensor networks, biological defense networks, and more. Frequent graphs help recognize graph datasets, grouping, classification, clustering, and structural catalogs for development.

The expanding need to analyze multiple graph data implies that graph mining (GM) has become an active and relevant area of investigation [1]. GM intends to derive the hidden information from a single large graph or a series of small graphs [2]. GM research is further divided in the following subareas: graph indexing [3], frequent subgraph mining, graph assessment, graph searching, schematic clustering, schematic pattern mining, and optimal schematic pattern mining.

For a multitude of legitimate applications, both endogenous and foreign, uncertainty is characteristic. For example, with Bill and Matthew participating in an informal organism, the connection of the structure "Bill coordinates well with Matthew" may not be deemed to be viable, using available information. Confidence in this relationship is usually determined

Advanced Data Mining Tools and Methods for Social Computing
https://doi.org/10.1016/B978-0-32-385708-6.00018-7

219

by chance, indicated by a probability p, and p estimates are physically resolved by space specialists using the data available or automatically by extracting information and aging rules. In the current information era, in which additional performance knowledge increases significantly, the need to monitor susceptibility is becoming more and more crucial. Here, we focus on uncertain diagrams, where insight is introduced as a chart with vulnerability related to edges. Different communication systems, distance sensor systems, protein interaction systems, natural administration systems, and uncertain graph models of social organizations have not been analyzed previously. A subset of objects is defined as a selection [4] of the connected components resulting in non-empty attributes. A minimum limit on the number of vertices in the relevant data induces the item sequence S C A. A subgraph consists of vertices comprising each object of S. The itemset sharing subgraph does not have to be densely connected, which is appropriate.

Frequency pattern mining has been an engaging topic in information science since the 2010s, gaining strong momentum. Diagram designs, or continuous subgraphs, which are subgraphs found from an assortment of little charts or a single huge chart with help, not precisely a client-specified edge, are pretty compelling as of late. Frequency subgraphs are valuable when portraying diagram datasets, ordering and grouping graphs, and building essential lists.

While the idea of frequency subgraph and strategies for regular mining subgraphs on deterministic charts are indeed known, the case turns out to be increasingly fascinating. Little work related to the development of uncertain graphs has been conducted. An uncertain graph is a distinct edge-weighted illustration. The weight on each edge (u, v) is the presence likelihood of the association between vertices u and v. As of late, inquiry about exertion has been devoted to frequency subgraph mining (FSM) on an assortment of little dubious charts. Being similarly significant, the issue of single enormous unsure diagrams remains open, given that massive natural systems are progressively engaging with vulnerability in nature.

Despite the significance of subgraph design for a deterministic graph, estimates based on dubious charts do not perform well. The regulation relationship is unclear or undetermined because of the diagram functionality's probabilistic proximity.

The present analysis describes support for several little uncertain diagrams that summarize the table's contribution when subgraphs are included. There are two distinct meanings for assistance, which are defined separately as connotation and probabilistic connotation. FSM is desirable for predictions when studying themes, although it is increasingly sufficient to discern focuses in the probabilistic sense. Driven by these efforts, we extend the impressions and describe support for single extensive ambiguous diagrams under the two-connotation anticipation and probability. The accumulated probability of the suggested graphs larger than the corner defines the support for help with the probabilistic connotation. For support under expected semantics, the combined contribution is weighted by ultimately interpreted graphs to its rationality, such as the probability that help will be appropriated in completely inferred diagrams. At that point, subgraphs outperforming a given measure are considered frequent. The improvement of existing algorithms on an assortment of uncertain charts is never again relevant to its dubious graphs. Therefore, propose precise and accurate arrangements for ensuring the proper management of threshold and extremity-based support is ensured in the system assessment.

An intelligent agent uses stored intelligence about its activities and user requirements to achieve its objectives. A computerized information agent is a software agent identifying, collecting, and managing information processed in the information network on a distributed basis. An intelligent agent is an autonomous software agent or a computer program that carries out tasks on behalf of users without intervention. The agent has two parts: the code component, which compiles directions that describe the agent's actions and intellect, and the agent's current state of performance. Every agent is independent and controls their activities, and all agents are goal-oriented. Agents have a task and act under that task. An agent can coordinate their actions, cooperate with other agents, work on their ideas to achieve their tasks, and adapt their behavior based on the changing environment.

An agent must have the following features: (i) autonomous, (ii) social, (iii) pro-active, (iv) reactive, (v) self-organizing, (vi) communication, (vii) cooperation, (viii) negotiation, (ix) flexibility, (x) destruction resistance, (xi) adaptability, and (xii) learning.

Here, we propose an FSM on the only uncertain graph and analyze connected subgraphs on those particular graphs, the complexity of support estimation, and efficient mining advancement. To achieve these, we implement substantial enhancements. Along with anticipated interpretations, to discover subgraphs, sequential, to be sure, to estimate the probability of subgraphs significantly accurately, indicating the probability of the largest proportion of probable graphs. The cost of a predictable investigation of the computational method is recommended. To achieve this, we propose exploratory integration with the estimation of the input tree. We implemented some control points instead of the maximum limit for benefits of execution. Similarly, we set a lower bound by gathering individual graphs and obtain a better understanding of proposed techniques.

11.1.1 Objectives of the proposed model

• Incorporate potential real-world semantics into probabilistic graphs and develop algorithms for documented data mining techniques within this model.

• Develop an efficient algorithm for elegant mining.

• Approximate actual utility in an interval with a specific promise and computation sharing heuristics to maximize performance addressing the #P through additional calculations.

• Provide subgraphs at checkpoints and validate them at upper and lower boundaries.

Consumers cannot be sure if an object X in a transaction ti is present or absent in a probabilistic data set D of uncertain data in the probabilistic model for uncertain data. Users assume that x is present, but they cannot promise it. The unspecified presumption may be described in terms of existing probabilities P (x, ti), demonstrating the probability of x in D. The probability P (x, ti) varies from a positive value close to 0 (indicating a low risk of being in D) to 1 (indicating that x is present). With this definition, each object can be presented as a 100% likely item in any transaction in conventional databases containing specific details (e.g., an online shopper's basket information).

This chapter is organized as follows. Section 11.1 presents an introduction to the proposed investigation, subgroup exploration, an exemplary paradigm of mining, and integration of users into the role of pattern discovery. Section 11.2 presents relevant works, and Section 11.3 presents the new state-of-the-art of related topics: mining and vertex graphical graphs. The proposed method and two subgraph mining algorithms are shown in Section 11.4. The findings and viewpoints of this work are discussing in Section 11.5. Section 11.6 provides the conclusion of the proposed work. Future directions are proposed in Section 11.7. Minimum value for frequent items, all equally distributed deleted subgrams, and some subgraphs whose prevalent count exceeds the threshold value given.

11.2 Related work

Many association rule mining techniques and a systematic approach have been implemented by prevalent GM. The Breadth First Search and the corresponding Depth First Search tests were performed. A diversity of appropriate patterns, along with correlated frequent [5], ended and max in the process [6], and approximately frequent [7], are also extracted by graph mining. Similarly, frequent graph-based frequent itemset mining aims to find all graph patterns that meet the lowest support threshold in challenging graph data databases. One of their critical drawbacks is that analytical approaches such as vertices, borders, and graphical isomorphism are considering for graph design mining instead of conventional pattern mining, which always covers simple elements.

The Gaston algorithm [8], which is ideal for comparing the proposed SVE-RGM algorithm, is a well-known fundamental graphical mining algorithm such as Gaston, gSpan, and FFSM. Gaston has the highest accuracy between these methodologies as a state-of-the-art method. The procedure more effectively generates frequent graphics by dividing mining into three parts, path, available tree, and stochastic graphs, as well as conducting suitable work on every step. In the optimization algorithm, the encoding sequence, an additional data process, allows it to perform operations in the mining industry more quickly. These basic graph machine learning algorithms have constraints with a fixed pre-defined threshold condition irrespective of the different graphical attributes, like data models and graph pattern intervals.

To eliminate repetitive subgraph patterns [9], in close graphs the patterns of regularly closed subgraphs are discovered; [10] SPIN evolved for repeated maximum subsection patterns; [11] and the RP-GD and RP-FP algorithms for subgraph pattern syncretization were proposed. Furthermore, some versions of the frequent subgraph pattern mining problem, such as frequently closed clicks [12], frequently closed sets [13], quasi-click crossgraphs [14], associated subgraph patterns [15], and substantial subscription patterns [16], were investigated. All such methods are only intended for accurate graph data mining and cannot be extended to uncertain graphs.

The mining graph has become an inexorably significant exploration theme in data mining. In numerous reasonable applications, graph information is commonly dependent upon uncertainties because of clamor, inadequacy, and mistakes. Such sort of diagrams has uncertainty. Topologies of wireless networks predict the involvement by extracting the protein–protein interaction (PPI) network in an uncertain graph of a partially defined protein complex [17].

Frequent patterns on an uncertain graph dataset can be explored [18] semantically unique to a precise dataset of graphs. On these databases, the criticalness of a subgraph design is estimated by the subgraph pattern's help, i.e., the extent of the information graph comprising the subgraph pattern. The persistent issue is subgraph design search over graph streams, which utilizes numerous genuine applications. For instance, to examine social networks, it is frequently helpful to distinguish structures. Interpersonal organizations develop over time. As such, collaborations among individuals change over time; thus, it is critical to identify a specific network's lifetime.

In the methodology UApriori [19], the calculation of the supporters is determined. It remedies a leverage-based frequency set similar to conventional Apriori. The lower closure property [20] is fulfilled in uncertain datasets. Therefore, it can indeed prune every superset of anticipated random items depending on support.

In recent days, the mining graph has become an inexorably significant exploration concept in mining methods in numerous applications [21]. Graph information is commonly dependent upon uncertainties because of clamor, inadequacy, and mistakes – such diagrams have probabilities. Collaborations among proteins [22], widely called a graph, are known as PPI networks in bioinformatics, where vertices are proteins and edges are interactions among proteins [23]. Countless PPIs have been identified by an assortment of techniques, and all approaches yield a lot of boisterous connections which do not occur and a small number of genuine interactions.

Every vertex portrays [17] the DNA replication, recombination, and formation of a protein. The quantity on the distinctive edge is the ambiguity of the communication delivered by data. Other than PPI systems, different instances of unsure graphs incorporate administrative procedures. Topologies of the wireless network [24] forecast a protein's contribution partly identified as a multi-faceted protein by mining a PPI as an indeterminate graph. Biologists are frequently keen on distinguishing practical modules and developmentally monitored subnetworks from biological networks [25], for example, the PPI network. Frequent subgraph pattern mining (FSPM) has been demonstrated to be an effective method.

Mining FSPM on indeterminate graph data [26] is semantically unique on precise graph data. In contrast, the complexity of a subgraph design is estimated by the extent of the information graph containing the subgraph pattern. Due to the issue of persistent subgraph design quests, graph streams are utilized in numerous genuine applications. For instance, to examine online platforms, it is frequently helpful to distinguish networks. Interpersonal organizations develop all the time. As such, collaborations among individuals alter with time; thus, it is critical to identify a specific network period. Framework-based frequent uncertain subgraph mining [33] incorporates both conceptual and procedural limitations to construct a candidate subgraph. Using this practical approach to fit the graph and a hybrid graph matching method that integrates estimated or inconsistent matching of conceptual graphs with semantic graph analysis of possible similarities between graph vertices refers to using the principle of probability in GM.

The authors of [34] investigated frequent subgraph mining on uncertainty graphs in an enumeration assessment framework, which provides a robust algorithm for elegant mining performance. They designed an approximation algorithm with precision under probabilistic semantics and developed computational sharing strategies to increase the mining efficiency to improve the solution. The algorithm can explain the issue with the anticipated semantics of control-based pruning, and a similar validation technique is used. Calculation #P-hard assistance is resolving by approximating the actual value with a promise of precision within an interval. Promising subgraphs using structural upper and lower limits at check and experiments show that the processes offer an optimistic real-life graph solution for frequent mining subgraphs.

11.3 Mining graphs and uncertainty

Mining frequent subgraphs are a significant challenge for graphic design, and all subgraphs are characterized as either identified frequently in a dataset based on a frequency threshold or identified unfrequently. Although many existing methods suggest a dataset with a massive number of subgraphs is necessary, recent advances such as social platforms and citations are represented through one single graph.

11.3.1 Mining graph

Several technologies and techniques are used to evaluate real-world graphic features, predict specific structural characteristics that would affect applications, and develop models to graph trends that match the real-world graphics accurately. The goal of graph extraction is to generate subgraphs that represent the structural data.

A system can contain relevant associations, and a graph can effectively describe those links; network-structured data communication analysis provides a generic issue with organized mining techniques. The following classes are classified as GM techniques. (i) Graph clustering is the task of clustering the graph's vertices to evaluate the edge of the chart, involving multiple edges and a considerably small number of clusters in each cluster. The graphic clustering of the input graph vertices in the cluster [30] predicates an unsupervised learning method, which does not include the classes before clustering. The graph clusters are built based on certain similarities in the graph. (ii) In graph classification (graph categorization), the primary objective is to graph distinct graphs into two possible classes throughout the data source. Categorization depends on the supervised method of learning, in which data classes are initially identified. (iii) In subgraph extraction, a graph is generated in which edges and outlines are subsets of a specific graph. Subgraph mining is a significant issue in subsection mining, where the aim is to generate a set of subsets of the provided n input graphs until a certain threshold [31].

11.3.2 Vertex attribute graphs

The correlated labels of the graph, vertices, or edges are connected features, reflecting properties, details on how the graph was developing, the texture of vertices in plotted graphs, and the edges' intensity in a graph database.

11.3.3 Subgraph discovery

Alternatively, the use of disconnected labeled graphs to model each of the entities – the objects in conventional discovery – and the interaction between them is an alternative form of modeling different entities. Every vertex of the graph matches an item, and every edge matches an association between two entities. All vertices and edges in this system have names that do not have to be exceptional. Identifying frequent itemsets is a challenge using this kind of graph, which happens relatively often around the whole sequence of graphs.

The need for graphs to simulate objects [32] enables us to describe inaccurate positive relationships. For example, a bag of objects can be processed into a graph, and therefore more specific a click, whose vertices match the objects of the basket, and all items connect via an edge to one another. Each edge contains convergence of u and v, with each edge having a label composed of either of the vertex labels at its ends. The vertex label corresponds to the proper identifier of items. Subsections often occur in several bags that traditionally include everyday objects if the subsections are becoming subgroups.

11.3.4 Uncertain graph

Vagueness refers to unpredictable or uncertain epistemological conditions. It is ideal for forecasts or scientific advancements. Inconsistencies occur not only to concerns, profligacy, or processes within limited measurable and probabilistic systems.

11.3.4.1 Data mining uncertainty

The availability or lack of certainty in datasets is unpredictable when stochastic datasets of incomplete data are handled. The confidence level can reflect the probabilistic inventory of new analysis and the intrinsic likelihood of individual objects. In a transaction ti, the essential probability P (x, ti) of an object x means x is in ti.

The lack of certainty, the state of minimal knowledge in which the actual communication, probable outcome or several possible outcomes are complicated by good correlation.

Many potential states or results wherever possible are pointing to every conceivable form or outcome – this also incorporates the utilization of a likelihood thickness capacity to continuous factors.

In the financial world, second-request vulnerability refers to likelihood thickness over (first-request) probabilities. Assessments of abstract rationales convey this sort of exposure.

11.3.4.2 Risk

Some possible results can have an undesired impact, or critical misfortune can occur.

11.3.4.2.1 Estimation of hazard

Some potential results can be unfortunate – this also includes ceaseless misfortune.

11.3.4.2.2 Knighting risk

In the financial world, in 1921, Frank Knight recognized vulnerability from chance, with exposure being the absence of information that is incomprehensible and difficult to ascertain; this is currently alluded to as Knighting uncertainties.

Inconsistencies are continuously extracted from this general definition of risk to be intensely selective. The underlying reality is that "risk" implies an indefensible sum of valuations, but often things are not of that subject. Among the wonders in which they are currently present and employed, there are sweeping and vital comparisons. It would leave the illusion of a genuine "threat" or measurable susceptibility, because we are using the word. It is not as much an unsurpassable resilience as it is by no mechanism a consequence (see Fig. 11.1).

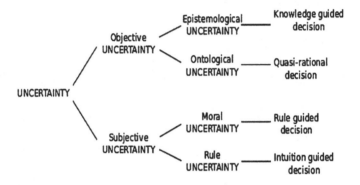

Figure 11.1 Categories of uncertainty.

In meteorology, material science, and building, the uncertainty or wiggle room of an estimation is given by a scope of qualities prone to encase the genuine truth, which might be signified by mistake bars on a diagram or by the accompanying notations:

estimated value ± uncertainty,

estimated value + uncertainty

− uncertainty,

estimated value (uncertainty).

11.4 Methodology

Graphs that accumulate uncertainties about vertices and edges are a specific group of graphs. There might not be an edge e between nodes u and v. We focus on the specific measures and actions. The occurrence of an edge depends on several factors. The response is transmitted with some probability in a social network. For instance, the edge refers to exchanging messages between two people.

Two broad categories of conventional subgraph mining exist: (i) the FSM-based graph transaction and (ii) single FSM-based graphs [27]. The input variables contain a series of small- and medium-sized diagrams in the graph transaction-based FSM: a graph database. The input data include the widest graph in a simple graph-based FSM. The FSM function lists all subsections of support above the pre-defined threshold limit. FSM-driven graph transaction utilizes transaction-based measuring support, so a single graph-based FSM drives the event. It is much more computationally complicated to mine frequent subgraphs in a single graph as most occurrences of similar subsections can be correlated.

Probability provides a way to describe our incompetence and insecurities accurately. A frequency of 0 indicates that a sentence is false, while 1 indicates that it is accurate. Chances of 0 to 1 are equal to optimal levels of objectivity of the sentence. In general, an expression is indeed either right or wrong. A varying value is then a moderate dimension of evidence. A certainty of 0.8 does not mean "80% true", but an 80% level of confidence – a reasonably high assumption. Suppose the objective evaluates a 0.8 probability sentence. The agent assumes the sentence is valid in 80% of instances, irrespective of the actual position, as the agent learns.

There are two types of frameworks in uncertainty:

- enumeration and
- evaluation.

11.4.1 Enumeration algorithm

An enumeration is a complete, ordered listing of all the items in a collection. The concept is commonly applied to the entirety of the components of a set in computation and systems development. For example, precise needs for a specification, whether the set must be restricted or inefficiencies, depend on the sequence of analysis and establishing a specific question.

A few sets can be identified by methods for a characteristic request (for example, 1, 2, 3, 4 or for the arrangement of positive numbers). Yet, in different cases, it might be essential to force a (maybe discretionary) request. In these cases, enumerative word recognition uses a more descriptive term rather than creating a detailed listing of these components to ensure the number of elements in a set. Some significant outcomes here incorporate the accompanying.

The quantity of named n-vertex detailed undirected diagrams is 2n(n − 1)/2.

The quantity of named n-vertex detailed coordinated diagrams is 2n(n − 1).

The number Cn of associated named n-vertex undirected charts fulfills the repeat relation

$$C_n = 2^{\binom{n}{2}} - \frac{1}{n}\sum_{k=1}^{n-1} k\binom{n}{k}2^{\binom{n-k}{2}}C_k.$$

One can be effectively ascertained n = 1, 2, 3, ..., where Cn's qualities are 1, 1, 4, 38, 728, 26704, 1866256, ... (classification A001187 in the OEIS). The quantity of marked n-vertex unrestricted trees is nn − 2 (Cayley's equation).

The quantity of unlabeled n-vertex coauthors is

$$2^{n-4} + 2^{\lfloor (n-4)/2\rfloor}.$$

11.4.2 Evaluation algorithm

Assessing probabilistic assistance, filter old, registering is a clear technique. The exact estimate and the limited probabilistic support. Take the specific estimate of the probabilistic support and contrast it and the limit. Processing probabilistic help legitimately by equations (1) and (3) is unnecessarily intricate; for every applicant subgraph, compute support in a probabilistic exponential number of graphs, wherever repetitive subgraph strength assessment takes much time. We will, without further ado, see that it is #P-finished to the evaluation algorithm.

Although expected help is defined uniquely in contrast to probabilistic support, we find that the techniques mentioned in Section 11.4 could be targeted to help evaluate under anticipated semantics. Due to the claim to fame of anticipated semantics, the example size required usually becomes a lot bigger. First, we show the association between the two definitions and present an assessment strategy with a checkpoint system for applicant pruning and approval.

First take a gander at the solidity of the issue. Hypothesis 1 is #P-finished to register psup(g).

Evidence from statement 1 illustrates that the psup(g) registration is #P done if resin's assistance on every graph is provided and the relationship of uncertainties predominantly carries the exceptionally high diversity of the concept. Also, at the end of the round, psup(g) care is even more complicated than the stochastic graph of help. In contrast, consider an approximation evaluation measurement in order to avoid rigorous improvements of extra reliability, and to complement the probability of g in FSM on stochastic graphs.

It is fascinating to have a subgraph returned in case of an unaffectedly complimentary session; to achieve this, we have to negotiate the results set with the rare subgraphs (false positive). Therefore, decipher the output of the evaluation as proximity [psup(g), psup(g)], which incorporates the legitimate psup(g) estimate and manages the supporting instances sensitively, analyzing subgraph g and mean square error sensitivity $\in$ (see Fig. 11.2).

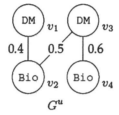

Figure 11.2 The subgraph of edges and vertices.

Statement 1 informs us that the standard mean for N sample expectations provides a precise p approximation.

In the above single graph, we can get three subgraphs based on edges:
Subgraph1 connectivity = v1, v2,
Subgraph2 connectivity = v2, v3,
Subgraph3 connectivity = v3, v4.

So, from the above single large graph, we got three subgraphs, and both algorithms find the same subgraphs by checking they are frequent or infrequent with the help of the threshold value. If we got frequent data, we could make better business decisions by knowing with which item users are engaging.

There are many things the author has described, but all are related to the abovementioned matter. The author has used three datasets, but we got only the DBLP dataset and used the same dataset. The DBLP dataset contains information about authors who publish papers. Sometimes, the primary author and coauthors work combined to make one paper of a single form. All authors are vertices of the graph, and edges are specified between the principal author and coauthors.

Jens Hofmann, Norbert Th. M.ller, Kasyap Natarajan
Friedemann Leibfritz, El-Sayed M. E. Mostafa
R. J. Gardner, Peter Gritzmann, D. Prangenberg

In the above bold data, the names are author names; the first name belongs to the first author, and other names belong to coauthors. Using the above dataset, we form a graph and generate frequent subgraphs by running probabilistic and estimate algorithms.

Therefore, all prediction assertions shall show the proof for the prediction. With the innovative precepts given to the agent, their assessment of probability reflects new evidence. We speak of pre- or absolute uncertainty before the proof is gathered; we talk about intermediate or predicted probability after collecting evidence. In some instances, an investigator has facts and laws and is involved in estimating the probability distribution of the findings applied in light of the proof. In specific examples, the criteria for evidence may still need to be calculated, plus evidence the investigator hopes to receive in the process.

An intelligent agent defines a sensor, an identifier or description that decides what happened, a logical collection of programs, rule-based interpretation, and a method to take action [28,29]. In the sense of an intelligent agent, a sensor can also be defined. Communication and training are some other qualities essential to the agent model. A portable agent can access a network and execute specific tasks. A learner assimilates the needs of the customer and variations in behavior automatically to dynamic environments.

11.5 Implementation

There are many things we have to describe but all related to the above matter. In this work, we utilize the DBLP dataset for implementation purposes. The DBLP dataset contains information about authors who publish papers. Primary authors and coauthors cooperate to make one paper, and the list of authors is shown in Fig. 11.3. All authors are vertices of the graph, and edges are specified between the principal author and coauthors.

Jens Hofmann, Norbert Th. M.ller, Kasyap Natarajan
Friedemann Leibfritz, El-Sayed M. E. Mostafa
R. J. Gardner, Peter Gritzmann, D. Prangenberg

In the above bold data, the names are author names; the first name belongs to the first author, and other names belong to coauthors. Using the above dataset, we form a graph and generate frequent subgraphs by

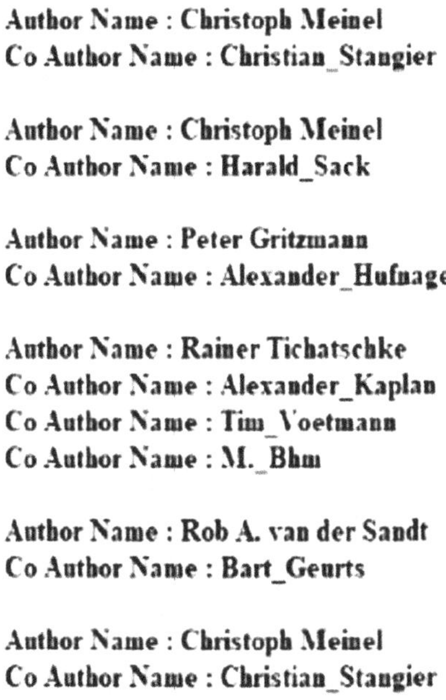

Author Name : Christoph Meinel
Co Author Name : Christian_Stangier

Author Name : Christoph Meinel
Co Author Name : Harald_Sack

Author Name : Peter Gritzmann
Co Author Name : Alexander_Hufnagel

Author Name : Rainer Tichatschke
Co Author Name : Alexander_Kaplan
Co Author Name : Tim_Voetmann
Co Author Name : M._Bhm

Author Name : Rob A. van der Sandt
Co Author Name : Bart_Geurts

Author Name : Christoph Meinel
Co Author Name : Christian_Stangier

Figure 11.3 The list of author and coauthor names.

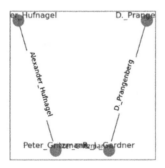

Figure 11.4 Frequent patterns of uncertain graphs for a threshold value of 3.

running probabilistic and estimate algorithms, as shown in Figs. 11.4 and 11.5.

A threshold value of 3 means that from a large graph, subgraphs are obtained whose number of edges is greater than or equal to 3. With a threshold value of 3, 13 graphs are received, and each graph is displayed with a pause of 3 seconds. If the given threshold value is 1 or 2, many subgraphs are generated, as shown in Fig. 11.8.

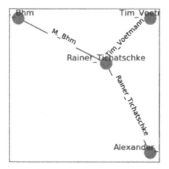

Figure 11.5 Efficient mining of frequent patterns of the uncertain graph.

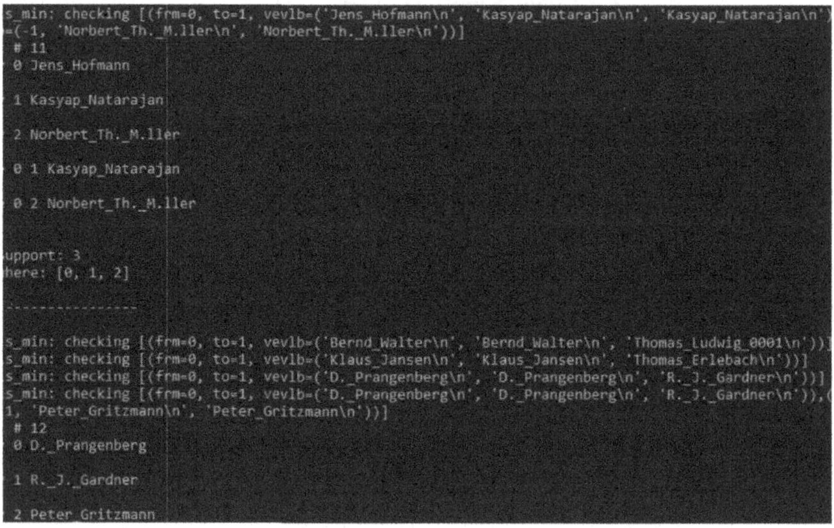

```
s_min: checking [(frm=0, to=1, vevlb=('Jens_Hofmann\n', 'Kasyap_Natarajan\n', 'Kasyap_Natarajan\n'
=(-1, 'Norbert_Th._M.ller\n', 'Norbert_Th._M.ller\n'))]
 # 11
 0 Jens_Hofmann

 1 Kasyap_Natarajan

 2 Norbert_Th._M.ller

 0 1 Kasyap_Natarajan

 0 2 Norbert_Th._M.ller


upport: 3
here: [0, 1, 2]
------------------
s_min: checking [(frm=0, to=1, vevlb=('Bernd_Walter\n', 'Bernd_Walter\n', 'Thomas_Ludwig_0001\n'))]
s_min: checking [(frm=0, to=1, vevlb=('Klaus_Jansen\n', 'Klaus_Jansen\n', 'Thomas_Erlebach\n'))]
s_min: checking [(frm=0, to=1, vevlb=('D._Prangenberg\n', 'D._Prangenberg\n', 'R._J._Gardner\n'))]
s_min: checking [(frm=0, to=1, vevlb=('D._Prangenberg\n', 'D._Prangenberg\n', 'R._J._Gardner\n')),
1, 'Peter_Gritzmann\n', 'Peter_Gritzmann\n'))]
 # 12
 0 D._Prangenberg

 1 R._J._Gardner

 2 Peter_Gritzmann
```

Figure 11.6 Representation of subgraphs on the console for a threshold value of 3.

One after another, all subgraphs are shown.

The vertex contains the first author's name in the above graph, and the edge link connects two vertices if both authors work together to complete one paper. After getting the total subgraph value below, we can click on the Run Estimate Sub Graph Mining button.

The number of frequent probabilistic subgraphs is 13.

Thirteen frequent subgraphs are generated, and each subgraph's connectivity is detailed in Fig. 11.6.

We provide a threshold value of 3; now we click on the OK button to get all subgraphs one after the other, and after getting all subgraphs and the

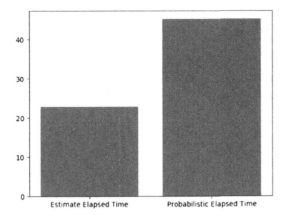

Figure 11.7 Comparison between estimated elapsed time and probabilistic elapsed time for a threshold value of 3.

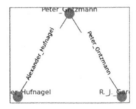

Figure 11.8 Frequent patterns of uncertain graphs for a threshold value of 2.

estimate algorithm, we also get 13 subgraphs. Now we click on the Elapse Time Comparison Graph button to compare both algorithms, as shown in Fig. 11.7.

In the above graph, the *x*-axis shows the algorithm's name and the *y*-axis shows the graph's generation. We conclude that the estimate algorithm is 20% faster. The probabilistic algorithm is 40% faster, i.e., 50% faster than the estimation algorithm.

The number of frequent probabilistic subgraphs is 254.

The number of estimate frequency subgraphs is 254.

Fig. 11.9 shows a comparison between estimated and probabilistic elapsed time. The probabilistic elapsed time is shorter than the estimated time.

Fig. 11.10 represents the console for a threshold value of 2.

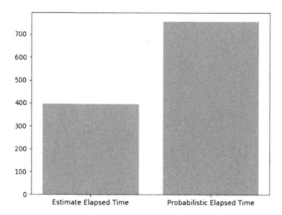

Figure 11.9 Comparison between estimated elapsed time and probabilistic elapsed time for a threshold value of 2.

```
Support: 2
where: [0, 1]

-------------------

is_min: checking [(frm=0, to=1, vevlb=('Subhendu_Bikash_Hazra\n', 'Volker_Schulz\n', 'Volk
is_min: checking [(frm=0, to=1, vevlb=('Markus_Casper\n', 'Markus_Casper\n', 'Rita_Ley\n')
is_min: checking [(frm=0, to=1, vevlb=('Markus_Casper\n', 'Markus_Casper\n', 'Rita_Ley\n')
lf_Merz\n', 'Ralf_Merz\n'))]
t # 253
v 0 Markus_Casper

v 1 Rita_Ley

v 2 Ralf_Merz

e 0 1 Markus_Casper

e 1 2 Ralf_Merz


Support: 2
where: [1, 2]

-------------------

Read:     0.02 s
Mine:    395.985 s
Total:   791.99 s
```

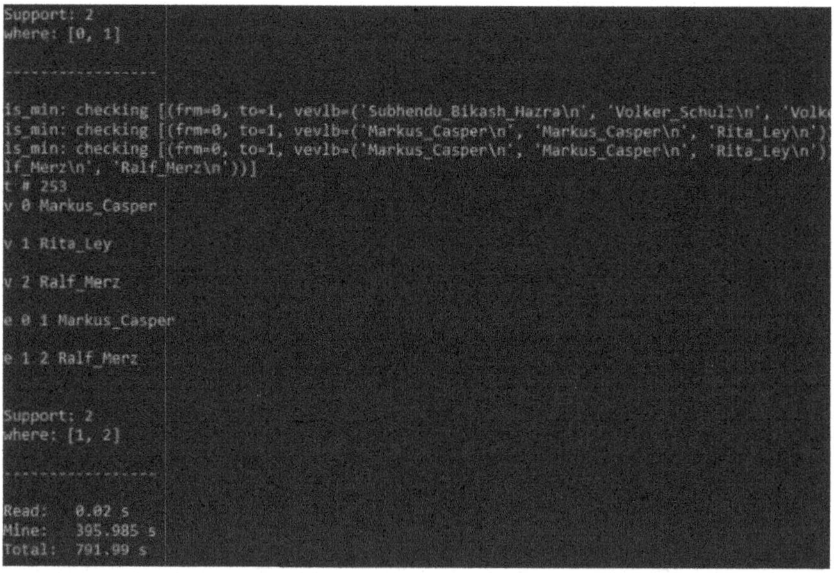

Figure 11.10 Representation of subgraphs on the console for a threshold value of 2.

11.6 Conclusion

This chapter discussed uncertain graphs. We generated the frequent subgraphs from the uncertain graph, using enumeration evaluation, probabilistic evaluation, estimation evaluation, and a minimum support threshold value to prune out all irregular subgraphs and take only those graphs whose frequent count is larger than the user-specified threshold value. By improving the estimate procedure, we obtained accurate subgraphs. Uncertain graphs are widely used for social networks and bioinformatics.

11.7 Future directions

Subconscious cognition detection can be used to identify malicious transactions on social networks, which is essential to secure online media services. Identifying different trends corresponding to deceptive practices can help to ensure the safety of social network applications.

References

[1] S. Thomas, et al., A survey on extracting frequent subgraphs, in: Int. Conf. Adv. Comput., Commun. Inform. (ICACCI), 2016, pp. 2290–2295.

[2] E. Abdelhamid, et al., Incremental frequent subgraph mining on large evolving graphs, IEEE Transactions on Knowledge and Data Engineering 29 (12) (Dec. 2017) 2710–2723.

[3] S. Ma, et al., Big graph search: challenges and techniques, Frontiers of Computer Science 10 (3) (2016) 387–398.

[4] Jun Sese, et al., Mining networks with shared items, in: Proceedings of the 19th ACM Conference on Information and Knowledge Management, CIKM 2010, Canada, October 26-30, 2010, pp. 1681–1684.

[5] Ozaki, et al., Closed and maximal subgraph mining in internally and externally weighted graph databases, in: Proceedings of the 25th IEEE International Conference on Advanced Information Networking and Applications Workshops, Singapore, 22–25 March, 2011.

[6] A. Bifet, et al., Mining frequent closed graphs on evolving data streams, in: Proceedings of the 17th ACM SIGKDD, USA, 21–24 August, 2011, pp. 591–599.

[7] S. Zhang, et al., Approximate graph mining based on spanning trees, in: Proceedings of the 23rd International Conference on Data Engineering, Istanbul, Turkey, 11–15 April, 2007.

[8] Nijssen, et al., The gaston tool for frequent subgraph mining, Electronic Notes in Theoretical Computer Science 127 (2005) 77–87.

[9] X. Yan, J. Han, Close graph: mining closed frequent graph patterns, in: KDD, 2003, pp. 286–295.

[10] J. Huan, W. Wang, J. Prins, J. Yang, Spin: mining maximal frequent subgraphs from graph databases, in: KDD, 2004, pp. 581–586.

[11] Y. Liu, J. Li, H. Gao, Summarizing graph patterns, in: ICDE, 2008, pp. 903–912.

[12] J. Wang, Z. Zeng, L. Zhou. Clan, An algorithm for mining closed cliques from large dense graph databases, in: ICDE, 2006, p. 73.

[13] Z. Zeng, J. Wang, L. Zhou, G. Karypis, Out-of-core coherent closed quasi-clique mining from large dense graph databases, ACM Transactions on Database Systems 32 (2) (2007) 13.

[14] J. Pei, D. Jiang, A. Zhang, On mining cross-graph quasi-cliques, in: KDD, 2005, pp. 228–238.

[15] Y. Ke, J. Cheng, W. Ng, Correlation search in graph databases, in: KDD, 2007, pp. 390–399.

[16] X. Yan, H. Cheng, J. Han, P.S. Yu, Mining significant graph patterns by leap search, in: SIGMOD, 2008, pp. 433–444.

[17] J. Ghosh, et al., On a routing problem within probabilistic graphs and its application to intermittently connected networks, in: INFOCOM, 2007, pp. 1721–1729.

[18] M. Kuramochi, et al., Finding frequent patterns in a large sparse graph, Data Mining and Knowledge Discovery 11 (3) (2005) 243–271.

[19] C.K. Chui, et al., Mining frequent itemsets from uncertain data, in: The Pacific-Asia Conference on Knowledge Discovery and Data Mining (PAKDD), 2007, pp. 47–58.

[20] R. Agrawal, et al., Fast algorithms for mining association rules in large databases, in: Proceedings of the Twentieth International Conference on Very Large Databases, Santiago, Chile, 1994, pp. 487–499.

[21] E. Adar, et al., Managing uncertainty in social networks, IEEE Data Engineering Bulletin 30 (2) (2007) 15–22.

[22] P. Boldi, et al., Injecting uncertainty in graphs for identity obfuscation, Proceedings of the VLDB 5 (11) (2012) 1376–1387.

[23] S. Biswas, R. Morris, Exor: opportunistic multi-hop routing for wireless networks, in: SIGCOMM, 2005, pp. 133–144.

[24] D. Chu, et al., Approximate data collection in sensor networks using probabilistic models, in: ICDE, 2006, p. 48.

[25] S. Asthana, et al., Predicting protein complex membership using probabilistic network reliability, Genome Research 14 (6) (2004) 1170–1175.

[26] D. Rhodes, et al., Probabilistic model of the human protein-protein-interaction network, Nature Biotechnology 23 (8) (2005) 1–9.

[27] C. Jiang, et al., A survey of frequent subgraph mining algorithms, Knowledge Engineering Review 28 (2013) 75–105.

[28] J.P. Bigus, Data Mining with Neural Networks - Solving Business Problems – from Application Development to Decision Support, McGraw-Hill, 1996.

[29] T. Dean, et al., Artificial Intelligence: Theory and Practice, The Benjamin/Cummings Publishing Co. Inc., 1995.

[30] H. Motoda, What Can We Do with Graph-Structured Data? A Data Mining Perspective, Springer, 2006, pp. 1–2.

[31] N.S. Ketkar, et al., Empirical Comparison of Graph Classification Algorithms, IEEE, 2009.

[32] Kuramochi, et al., Frequent subgraph discovery, in: Proceedings - IEEE International Conference on Data Mining, ICDM, 2001, pp. 313–320.

[33] Mohamed Moussaoui, et al., A new framework of frequent uncertain subgraph mining, in: 22nd International Conference on Knowledge-Based and Intelligent Information & Engineering Systems, in: Procedia Computer Science, vol. 126, 2018, pp. 413–422.

[34] Yifan Chen, et al., Efficient mining of frequent patterns on uncertain graphs, IEEE Transactions on Knowledge and Data Engineering (2018) 1, https://doi.org/10.1109/TKDE.2018.2830336.

CHAPTER 12

Mining challenges in large-scale IoT data framework – a machine learning perspective

Gaurav Mohindru[a], Koushik Mondal[b], Paramartha Dutta[c], and Haider Banka[a]

[a]Department of Computer Science and Engineering, IIT (ISM), Dhanbad, India
[b]Computer Centre, IIT (ISM), Dhanbad, India
[c]Department of Computer and System Sciences, Visva Bharati University, Santiniketan, India

12.1 Introduction

The next generation of smart computing generates data at an unprecedented rate due to advancements of social media, web crawling, and mobile and sensing Internet of Things (IoT) devices. The IoT, at times also referred to as the fourth industrial revolution, is a new frontier in information and communication technologies. It was estimated, by 2020, around 30 billion devices will be connected to the internet [2]. By the end of 2020, there are around 12 billion IoT connections and total no of connected devices are around 22 billion. IoT would augment and enable existing applications and bring in telling changes in different domains and human lives in the future. The future would entail the integration of these ubiquitous devices into the internet to realize the concept of smart environments. It is and will increasingly be helping the monitoring of health, the environment, supply chains, transportation, infrastructure, and our homes (smart homes). IoT and the data it generates need to be considered together for effective outcomes in areas where it is used [108]. Data generated need to be integrated, stored, processed, analyzed, and presented. Data analytics is critical and there is a dependence on machine learning techniques [3]. Exploratory Data Analysis (EDA) along with visualization techniques helps understand and build data analytics environments for heterogeneous and voluminous datasets [4]. Data can be present in different formats and can be of different types: structured, unstructured, or semi-structured and live or historic. The sources could be archives or connected objects. Such data when analyzed can provide useful insights for business gains [5]. The data and the information gained

239

from the connected object thus can be an important constituent to effect transformational changes in business and factors benefitting human lives. As more objects are connected in the digital domain, the data generated to be analyzed would also increase. Tools and algorithms such as machine learning will help create a model for analysis and prediction. Machine learning algorithms are categorized based on the learning style, the model structure, and how they work. They can be grouped as supervised, semi-supervised, unsupervised, and reinforcement models. Similarly, they can be categorized as regression, decision trees, ensembles, regularization, deep learning, neural network, dimensionality reduction, Bayesian, instance-based, clustering, etc. The goal is to create models to effectively get hidden insights and actionable knowledge from captured data for enhancing the efficiency of the application and provide better services to end-users. Researchers aim to effectively use the current data mining techniques and to develop new ones and to execute them on optimal frameworks to achieve this end.

Betsy et al. [6] have presented a model to address the challenges associated with mining and representation of high-volume and high-frequency data by creating spatio-temporal sensor graphs (STSGs) for modeling and mining sensor data. Such models are effective in addressing storage and memory issues and understanding present anomaly patterns and the potential hotspots in the future. It finds application in healthcare, monitoring environment and traffic, etc. Parisa Rashidi et al. [9] developed a novel adaptive data mining framework for pattern mining from sensor data. Creation of data happens easily but their analysis needs some effort. The explosion of data will present challenges.

The main focus is to consolidate all new machine learning-related algorithms under some experimental frameworks that are mainly designed to handle large datasets so as to enable researchers to offer conclusive results in an effective time frame. These frameworks of different scientific modeling will help governments, industry, research, and different other communities for their decision making and strategic planning.

Knowledge discovery and data mining (KDD) to analyze large datasets has a hardware and a software element and both need to be optimized to address the challenge. In terms of addressing hardware challenges, cloud and distributed computing can be leveraged. For addressing latency, resources and bandwidth challenges in real-time scenarios computation needs to be moved to the edge. The use of Intel neural compute stick (NCS) to deploy and run such operations on the edge is discussed in [110]. In terms of software, most of the mining technologies run on a single system and the algorithms cannot be applied as-is to analyze the data. To address the large data challenge and get effective results, the pre-processing operator of KDD needs optimization.

The chapter is organized as follows. Section 12.2, Review of literature, provides an in-depth survey on the related works pertaining to data classification and mining available in the literature. The focus of this chapter is mentioned in Section 12.3, Proposed work. Section 12.4, Application framework, elucidates the requisites of the basics of different important algorithms relevant to this chapter, viz. deep learning, gradient boosting machine (GBM), including extreme gradient boost (XGBoost), random forest, the generalized linear model (GLM), K-means, and naive Bayes. The principle of operation of the H_2O environment is highlighted in Section 12.5, H_2O work flow environment. The experimental results of application of the proposed methods are illustrated in Section 12.6, Experimental results. Section 12.7, Discussion and conclusion, concludes the chapter with future directions of research.

12.2 Review of literature

The applications of Big Data frameworks are all pervading. With the ever-increasing growth of volume of data every moment, it is a formidable research challenge. Article [50], discusses HACE theorem to outlines the determining factors in big data and proposed a Big Data processing model for data mining which meets the objectives of aggregating heterogeneous data sources on demand, performing mining and analysis, user interest modeling with considerations such privacy and security. The proceedings of International Conference on Data Mining and Big Data [72] discusses different Big Data applications to offer valuable insights. The edited volume contains reports on data mining algorithms [76] [62] [104] [82] [90], frequent itemset mining [92] [98], spatial data mining [64] [53] [91], prediction [68] [94] [86] [59] [96], feature selection [93] [58] [101], information extraction [100] [61] [55], classification [69] [57] [54] [89], anomaly pattern and diagnosis [73] [67] [106], data visualization [97] [81] [51] [105], privacy policies [84] [75] [70], social media [102] [88] [103] [87] [78], query optimization and processing [63] [56],

Big Data [66] [65] [85] [71] [95], and pattern recognition and computer vision [52] [60] [77] [83] [74] [80] [99] [79]. Another impressive survey is [35]. Furthermore, a good exposure on business analytics may be found in [38]. One may be interested in consulting [47] to have a meaningful exposure, though a bit outdated, about tracing the course of development of research initiatives on information extraction from Big Data.

One of the major thrust areas of research efforts is graph mining and related problems, such as [49] reporting mining closed frequent graph patterns, [34] addressing distributed graph mining, [45] offering data partitioning strategies in large graph mining, [39] and considering subgraph mining. In [46], authors explore pattern mining from big graphs after providing a comprehensive study on existing and emerging frameworks and methods used in Big Data analytics focusing graph data. The focus of this contribution is the discussion on several graph processing frameworks and pattern mining approaches for different inputs and the patterns produced. Apart from graph mining, there are significant research initiatives of mining challenges in a Big Data framework in general. While [44] provides a comprehensive review on efficient machine learning in Big Data, [48] discusses the significance and challenges in Big Data mining. One of the emerging trends in this space is parallel machine learning and data mining. An enabling set up on MapReduce for the same is discussed in [31]. Whereas [32] presents a high-level language for writing machine learning which then gets compiled and executed on MapReduce, [40], stresses on the need of a parallel and random approach when performing association rules mining to reduce time and storage space and proposes an algorithm to achieve the same in MapReduce.

More extensive computing requirements can be realized using an optimized architecture. Article [43] discusses the advantages of a hybrid architecture using optical interconnections for handling load distribution in data centers offering a better throughput with power reduction and low latency.

The novelty of [42] is how Machine Learning can be used with Big Data in solving complex scenarios such as predicting power generation. The challenge lies in forecasting electricity generation from a large dataset typically affected by noise.

The reference [36] offers an excellent review how the issue of frequent itemset mining in large scale data can be addressed in scalable algorithms based on Hadoop-and Spark. The authors theoretically as well as through experimental comparative analyses justify how the computation-hungry task of itemset mining is achieved through its distribution and parallelization strategies, thereby addressing the issues of memory usage, load balancing, and communication costs.

Keeping in view the effectiveness of deep learning-based artificial neural network models in extracting information from complex datasets, authors in [33] offer stepwise instructions on building a Deep Learning application capable on executing both on GPU and CPU clusters. The tools used primarily are Python, R, and Spark in streamlining complex, voluminous and increasing data.

Multilevel association rule compared to single level is more suitable to discover significant insights and hierarchical information in the hierarchical dataset. Thus authors in [37] have explored the mining effectiveness of multi-level association rules in a distributed set in deciding marketing strategies.

The article [41] considers an application about health informatics, where the vast amount of data produced opens up the possibility of analysis of these Big Data in a reliable manner, inducing gain in knowledge, not to speak of such information ensuring the improvement of the quality of healthcare offered to the patients.

12.3 Proposed work

Highly sensitive analysis like optimizing steel manufacturing schedules, heart transplant studies, mobile and data communications technology, hedge fund portfolios, etc., are fully dependent on complex combinations of techniques of data mining and data analysis. One can create significant new opportunities for stakeholders with the help of derived information from raw data. It gives enough mileage by ensuring efficiency and bringing quality by yielding richer results, personalized products, and services with deeper insights. It also helps us to integrate unstructured, semi-structured, quasistructured, and structured data with real-time inputs and queries for better insights. As per [1], datasets which are voluminous, distributed, diverse and have special and temporal attributes need setups and algorithms to extract insights and opportunities for business and optimization. The rate of data creation from different sources like mobile sensors, video surveillance, video rendering, geophysical exploration, smart cities, smart grids, gene sequencing, social engineering, etc., is accelerating manifold in recent years [11]. If we place dimension and volume along the x- and y-axes, respectively, with high and low (small) divisions along each axis, then we can easily classify the data in four sub-domains, viz. small datasets (low-

low), high-dimensional data (high-low), large data (low-high), and massive datasets (high-high). This massive data together with velocity and volume aspects and other V's, qualify as Big Data, which offers new challenges of handling the data ecosystem.

Data Analytics life cycle, basically a defined approach for managing and executing analytical projects, describes the whole process in six phases viz. Data Discovery, Data Preparation, Model Planning, Model Building, Communicating the results and Operationalize the model for real-life data [108]. The life cycle involves collecting, classifying, summarizing, analyzing, organizing and interpreting scientific and non-scientific information for better decision making and conclusion drawing [18]. There are, in general, two types of data used in general data analytics: qualitative (which cannot be measured on a natural numerical scale) and quantitative (which can be measured on a natural numerical scale).

Before Hadoop or similar architectures arrived into the picture, raw data moved through the ETL process stored into a database or data warehouse for further processing through known data models [10]. But now Hadoop-like architectures not only support relational data models, but are also able to handle dynamic formats and data layouts based on their local features or properties. Sometimes the occurrence of certain event grows as the size of the data grows. But those positive responses will not always be significant in selecting crucial features in the large data sets. This characteristic of data is popularly known as "Bonferroni's principle."

Over the years, data mining has evolved from basic statistical modeling to knowledge discovery, accommodating different machine learning algorithms with some efficient mathematical models for successfully categorizing linear and non-linear relations prevalent among datasets [12] [13] [28]. Data mining activity generally includes descriptive modeling, predictive modeling, exploratory data analysis, pattern discovery, and content retrieval. Initial data mining algorithms were known to be slow and memory inefficient. Such faults were largely not noticed until the recent advancement of large data sets computation, where datasets with millions or billion records or more could the limit. Even if the entire dataset fits into the memory, an additional memory chunk is required for processing and manipulating the data. Presently some open source softwares like R, Python, etc., are available in the market to efficiently deal with such situations. In the present chapter, we have consolidated all popular data mining techniques under a modern machine learning framework, viz. H_2O.

12.4 Application framework

An optimum application framework is critical to the success of a project and a robust framework should be capable to handle changes in data patterns and volumes over some time. The mathematical data expansion model is an important model for Big Data simulation. It helps study the data characteristics, simulate and study changes (evolution and deformation) of patterns. Evolution is attributed to changes in Big Data applications which impact results over time. Deformation can occur due to imbalance [109], incompleteness and inaccuracy in the datasets. Data expansion is used to create models. The generalized model leveraging standardization uses the standard score formula, also known as Z score defined by Berry and Lindgren [7]:

$$z = \frac{(x - \mu)}{\sigma}, \qquad (12.1)$$

where μ and σ represent mean and standard deviation, respectively, and z is generally assumed to observe a Gaussian/normal distribution when the parameter values of σ and μ are available. If we replace population parameters μ and σ with respective mean (sample) $\tilde{x}$ and standard deviation (sample) s_x from standardization, then Eq. (12.1) can be updated as:

$$t = \frac{(x - \tilde{x})}{s_x}, \qquad (12.2)$$

where t represents the standard score, following a Student's t-distribution mentioned in [8]. We can interpret the above equation for Big Data scenarios. Assuming n observations $x_{1j}, x_{2j}, ..., x_{nj}$ of the feature x_j, where value of $j = 1...p$. Assuming the mean μ and standard deviation σ of the population are unknown and with $(1 - \alpha)\%$ confidence, we can write the equation

$$\tilde{x}_j - ts_{x_j} \leq \mu_j \leq \tilde{x}_j + ts_{x_j}. \qquad (12.3)$$

This may be interpreted as: the values x_j are closely inclined to the mean μ_j that is representative of features and dispersed by ts_{x_j}, and thus $(1 - \alpha)\%$ of the features fall inside the range. Now we divide the confidence interval range into n values: $\tilde{x}_j + t_{1j}s_{x_j}, \tilde{x}_j + t_{2j}s_{x_j}, ..., \tilde{x}_j + t_{nj}s_{x_j}$. If we use the divided values to score the n observations, then we may write the following:

$$x_{ij} = \tilde{x}_j + t_{ij}s_{x_j}, \qquad (12.4)$$

where i is $1...n$ and j is $1...p$. Re-arranging, we will get the following:

$$t_{ij}s_{x_j} = x_{ij} - \tilde{x}_j. \qquad (12.5)$$

Now we divide the above equation by $1 + s_{x_j} \neq 0$. We get the following:

$$\frac{s_{x_j}}{1 + s_{x_j}} t_{ij} = \frac{x_{ij} - \tilde{x}_j}{1 + s_{x_j}}. \tag{12.6}$$

The weighted score may be taken for equating with the right-hand side as approximation standardized score w_{ij} for any large dataset application domain:

$$w_{ij} = \frac{x_{ij} - \tilde{x}_j}{1 + s_{x_j}}. \tag{12.7}$$

Using the above, researchers may expand the model for data with necessary parameters, where the approximation with standardized score is extended using a parameter β and mean shift by putting α:

$$x' = \alpha \tilde{x} + \beta \frac{x - \tilde{x}}{1 + s_x}. \tag{12.8}$$

The values of α and β are normalized. We need to select proper values of α and β to ensure orthogonalized properties between the classes. Gaussian and Uniform distribution can be leveraged to create a data expansion model for Big Data applications.

The results collected based on the available information patterns may not be valid after a certain amount of time. There are several attributes in Big Data projects that require proper care so as to smoothly sail through all the processing steps before generating desired outcomes. The framework of any Big Data project largely depends upon high performance with low latency, in-memory processing capacity, stateful computational semantics, fault tolerance capability, real-time stream processing power, and scalability of the ecosystem. The framework must handle full data mining suites with a strong focus on all machine learning algorithms so as to build suitable models for complex Big Data problems. Considering all the above factors, the following frameworks are widely used: (i) Hadoop, (ii) Spark, (iii) Flink, (iv) Storm, and (v) Samza. Out of the above, Hadoop and Spark are the most preferred frameworks for general Big Data applications. Nowadays, researchers are working on a combined model of Hadoop and Spark where Hadoop provides a distributed storage facility and Spark provides analytical processing engine for incorporating better machine learning algorithms. Spark allows in-memory processing with non-linear data pipeline construction, thereby reducing processing time to a greater extent. Apache Storm is used when distributed real-time processing of high-volume and unbounded streaming data is required. It follows a directed acyclic graph topology for its applications. Flink is another distributed, continuous, unbounded real-time stream processing framework though certain features such as high-level API, advanced features, and auto-adjustment, make it stand out in the space. Samza is another similar framework, an extension of Kafka, and executes on YARN clusters. Hive, Pig, Mahout, and Hbase are Apache projects which work on the Hadoop framework. Hive and Pig are used for batch processing use cases. Hive additionally with its SQL like structured language, Hive Query Language (abbreviated as HiveQL), enables users to fetch answers without writing low-level code. The query is translated to MapReduce jobs thus it combines the simplicity of SQL together scalability derived from Hadoop cluster. After Hadoop processing, analytical techniques can be executed in the scalable cluster using Apache Mahout executable java libraries. Apache Mahout contains algorithms grouped in categories of classification, clustering and recommenders or collaborative filtering. The algorithms in the Mahout library are listed. The algorithms in classification are Random Forests, Logistic Regression [27], Naive Bayes [26] and Hidden Markov models. Clustering contains K-means, Expectation-Maximization, Canopy and Fuzzy K-means. Distributed and non-distributed recommenders are present in Recommenders category. Yahoo's SAMOA and MLlib are similar data mining library packages available in the research domain with all machine learning algorithms for processing. HBase is modeled to be similar to Google's Bigtable. With different data structures and expanding data store requirements, there is another concept of Not only Structured Query Language (abbreviated as NoSQL). It stores unstructured data. The additional advantage with such storage is they can easily scale by addition of hardware to the multi-layer clustered platform. Some types of No SQL data stores are Key/Value (an example is Redis), document (an example is MongoDb), Columnar (an example is Hbase) and Graph (an example is social Neo4j).

12.4.1 Concept of deep learning

The framework of multi-layer neural networks [14] can be used to design basic deep learning-related solution space. It is used in designing models for hierarchical feature extraction with multiple levels of non-linearity. It is found to work well with labeled and unlabeled data. Deep learning models in the modern era are not limited to neural networks. The design is a composition of more than one level of learning where different machine learning algorithms are used, not necessarily neural network, to mine different features of any large dataset [15]. There exist four basic building blocks of any deep learning algorithms in the machine learning domain: data aggregation, cost function, optimization method or algorithm, and a model for the data. Deep learning provides a powerful framework of supervised learning and can be used in analyzing big datasets by training linear and non-linear models. Besides, the introduction of convolution and recurrent deep learning neural networks have helped to scale it to heterogeneous, large, and recurrent long temporal sequences [16]. With the advancement of the Big Data frameworks, some of the considerations in designing deep learning algorithms for different use cases are addressed. The generalization of statistical methods with reduced degree of freedom for sufficiently big datasets remains a great challenge for neural networks. Neural networks have evolved and become large with advancements in computation hardware and software algorithms [17] [18]. The apparent question is the choice of the algorithm for optimization. Different authors compared multiple optimization algorithms for their effectiveness in different learning scenarios. The results indicate that compared to any single algorithm to be best suited, a collection of algorithms with adaptive learning rates have a better performance. Broadly speaking, neural networks with many layers are the basis for deep learning. The number of layers in some cases might vary from 16 to 152 based on the requirements of actual feature extraction. Deep learning provides a robust, generalized, and scalable architecture for generating solutions from very complex target functions handling large datasets.

Different learning methods are available in this domain [19] [20]. They may be purely supervised, semi-supervised, or purely unsupervised. Logistic regression, multi-layer perceptron, and deep convolutional network are popular in the supervised domain, whereas auto-encoders, de-noising auto-encoders, stacked de-noising auto-encoders, deep belief networks, and restricted Boltzmann machines are more used popular in the unsupervised or semi-supervised domains. Standard datasets are available in the deep learning domain for cross-checking the robustness of any proposed algorithms. Those datasets [24] [25] are mainly divided in three categories: image processing, natural language processing, and speech/audio processing. CIFAR-10, ImageNet, MNIST, MS-COCO, etc., are popular in the image processing domain. Wordnet, Yelp reviews, Sentiment140, etc., are often used in natural language processing, and LibriSpeech, Million Song, VoxCeleb, etc., are popularly used in speech/audio processing.

12.4.2 Concept of gradient boosting machine

Primarily bias, noise, and variance are the possible factors for error in the predicted values from the actual ones and therefore machine learning techniques focus on reducing them [28] [29]. At times noise may be treated as an irreducible error but the other two components are crucial in effective prediction. Most of the practitioners employ ensemble methods for predicting the output variable with different predictors. In general, there are two groups of ensemble methods, parallel and sequential. Depending on whether the ensemble technique is focusing on reducing bias, variance, or in general improve predictions, they can be categorized as Bagging, Boosting, or Stacking techniques. Unlike Bagging where predictors work in parallel or independently, in Boosting they work in a sequence. In Boosting, the subsequent predictors adjust their weights learning from the error of the previous predictors. The most effective boosting technique is Gradient Boosting Machine (abbreviated as GBM) and its different variants.The basic idea behind the development of the Gradient Boosting Machine is to turn relatively "poor hypotheses" into "good hypotheses". It is achieved with the help of either of the following: using Adaptive Boosting (AdaBoost) and/or Generalization of AdaBoost using Adaptive Re-weighting and Combining techniques.

Gradient boosting generally works with three basic elements, viz. loss function, weak learners to predict, and a composite model that adds weak learners in a bid to improve the target outcome and minimize the prediction error. One has to select the loss function considering the specific problem requirement and characteristics of the desired model. Examples of loss functions are logarithmic loss function for classification and least squared error for regression. One can also define a custom loss function. Broadly, decision trees are used as a weak learner in gradient boosting. The gradient descent procedure is generally used to minimize loss functions. To enrich GBM to reduce the problem of overfitting, the following factors are considered for enhancement viz. Shrinkage, Tree constraints, Random Sampling, and Penalized Learning.

12.4.3 Concept of random forest

Random Forest (abbreviated as RF) is a generally used and effective bagging machine learning ensemble method. Bagging or Bootstrap aggregation is a basic ensemble technique where predictions from multiple models are combined using some model averaging techniques such as majority vote, weighted average, or normal average to decide the result instead of one model. It creates multiple decision trees with randomness in sampling and feature selection. The uncorrelated trees together result in more accurate predictions and reduce variance using the value-added through an ensemble. In the first stage of Random Forest, we need to create a random forest of decision trees while in the second we make a prediction using the models created. The Random forest can handle overfitting issues of boosting algorithms efficiently. Random Forest algorithm can be used for classification as well as a regression task. It also helped in reducing variance. Because of its in-built ensemble capacity, the task of building a generalized model for all datasets turns out much easier. It is capable of effectively handling large datasets with a lot of variables. The average decrease in impurity using each feature can help determine the importance of the feature.

The concept of the bootstrap method with its aggregation, popularly known as bagging, is the key behind this predictive modeling. Bootstrap is a common yet effective statistical technique for estimation from a data sample by using resampling to create multiple samples. There are algorithms [21] [22] which though are quite potent but have a high variance such as Classification and Regression Trees (abbreviated as CART). Bootstrap aggregation can be used to reduce the variance using the collective prediction of the group. Decision trees' structure and prediction vary based on the training dataset. Here, when we create multiple decision trees with less or no correlation and use ensemble and aggregation we can get better accuracy. Less correlation is important for varied tree structures and randomness is used to achieve it. There is another area where we use randomness in Random Forest. In the case of decision trees for selecting a feature for the split, we use all the available features [23]. In contrast in Random Forest, we select a random set of features from the available set. Randomness in RF mainly is in selecting random observations for growing the tree and random features for splitting the nodes.

12.5 H_2O work flow environment

Different machine learning and predictive analytic modeling algorithms require an integrated platform for efficient data handling and decision making. H_2O is one such platform. It is an open-source, linearly scalable, distributed in-memory platform and is capable of processing large data sets without issues. It is efficient mixing of massively scalable Big Data munging and analysis with all datatypes and databases having real-time data score with WebUI interfaces. Leading brands like Cisco, Comcast, PayPal,

Transamerica etc. are using H_2O platform for effective predictive modeling. Approximately, almost 9000 and more organizations are using H_2O platform for different applications. H_2O offers advanced and automated features as:

1. adaptive learning rates;
2. standardization of predictors;
3. initialization of model parameters;
4. handling of categorical and missing data;
5. cross-validation techniques; and
6. ability to handle complex and large datasets.

The H_2O framework uses Big Joins, which is almost seven times faster than R data table and it can scale linearly to 10 billion × 10 billion joins. H_2O efficiently handles Hadoop environments like CDH, HDP, etc., for managing and processing large datasets. H_2O can be launched on Hadoop with a prerequisite of a minimum 6 GB memory where each H_2O node is used as a mapper. In the H_2O environment there is no need of reducers for combining the results. There exist two communication paths, viz. mapper-to-driver and mapper-to-mapper, for efficient connection binding. It is recommended to open at least 20 ports for adaptive binding for successful H_2O communications. H_2O supports launching on YARN. The H_2O framework also provides options for CPU allocation, default queues for job submission, and specifying output directories for handling output data. The H_2O package for R lets R users control an H_2O cluster using R script which acts as a REST API client of the cluster. It is almost easy for non-experts to experiment with machine learning with some key tasks such as parameter tuning and selection of target models for setting efficient model deployment for further processing of preprocessed data. In the H_2O environment, with the help of different deep learning techniques, experts can handle high-cardinality class membership data and unlabeled data.

12.6 Experimental results

We have executed the in-built programs in the H_2O environment along with some standalone R programs to evaluate and compare the results. Standard datasets like MNIST, PML and Prostate Cancer Data are used in evaluating different machine learning algorithms in the Big Data framework [24] [25]. Nowadays, data analysis approach is not limited to a specific machine learning algorithm and instead is a collection of techniques which help in training efficiently using the dataset.

PML [30] [107], a popular human activity recognition dataset, is used in the environment to predict the best suitable model for each dataset. While pre-processing and plotting the predictors against the response classes, one can hardly notice any linearity prevalent in the dataset. Instead, the data

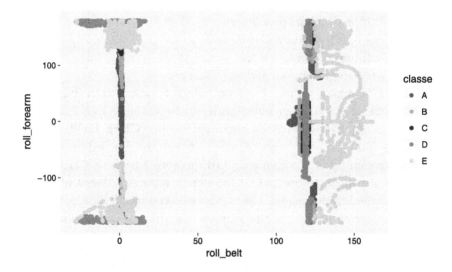

Figure 12.1 Class representation roll-belt vs. roll-forearm of PML data.

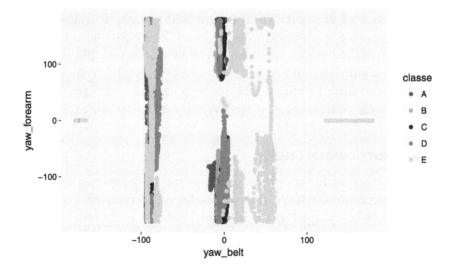

Figure 12.2 Class representation yaw-belt vs. yaw-forearm of PML data.

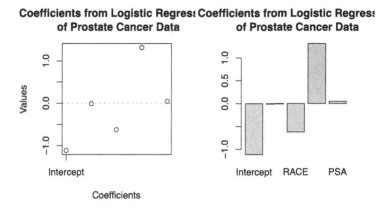

Figure 12.3 Prostate cancer data values comparison.

seem to be clustered around many gravity points. Therefore a model based on trees rather than on a linear regression appears more sensible. This indicates to use random forest to classify and predict weight lift performances out of five possible classes labeled "A" through "E". Different possible outcomes are shown in Figs. 12.1 and 12.2. Similarly, a comparison of different prostate cancer data is depicted in Fig. 12.3. Similarly, we have run the generalized linear model (abbreviated as GLM) and a deep learning algorithm on the prostate cancer data in the H_2O environment. We have compared the mean square error (abbreviated as MSE), the root mean square error (abbreviated as RMSE), LogLoss, the accuracy (abbreviated as AUC), Gini index of both algorithms and presented the indicators in Table 12.1.

Table 12.1 Basic statistics comparison of prostate cancer data.

Algorithm	MSE	RMSE	LogLoss	AUC	Gini
GLM	0.2027036	0.4502261	0.5914634	0.717601	0.435202
Deep learning	0.01448951	0.1203724	0.05684173	0.9986179	0.9972359

12.7 Discussion and conclusion

Gini index is a measure to find the purity of a node. A small value of the index indicates high purity of the node. In Random Forest scenario, the split criteria is the Gini index of the parent and child nodes, with the value of the child nodes being less than its parent.

In this chapter, we have tried to discuss the emerging changes in the machine learning techniques extensively used in Big Data environment with required optimizations. We have leveraged advanced and scalable computing environment to build efficient models for realizing our goal of efficient and improved predictive analytics with generalization capability.

References

[1] C. Manyika, Big Data: The Next Frontier for Innovation, Competition and Productivity, McKinsey and Co global report, 2011.
[2] A.B.I. Billion, Devices will wirelessly connect to the Internet of everything in 2020, ABI research, available: https://www.abiresearch.com/press/more-than-30-billion-devices-will-wirelessly-conne/, 2013.
[3] K. Mondal, Big data parallelism: issues in different X-information paradigms, Procedia Computer Science 50 (2015) 395–400.
[4] K. Mondal, Different visualization issues with big data, in: 1st International Conference on Information and Communication Technology for Intelligent Systems, in: Smart Innovation, Systems and Technologies, vol. 51 (2), Springer, 2016, pp. 555–562.
[5] K. Mondal, Design issues of big data parallelisms, in: Information Systems Design and Intelligent Applications, in: Advances in Intelligent Systems and Computing, vol. 434 (2), Springer, 2016, pp. 209–217.
[6] Betsy George, James M. Kang, Shashi Shekhar, Spatio-temporal sensor graphs (STSG): a data model for the discovery of spatiotemporal patterns, Intelligent Data Analysis 13 (3) (2009) 457–475.
[7] D.A. Berry, B.W. Lindgren, Statistics: Theory and Methods, second edition, International Thomson Publishing Company, 1996.
[8] L.C. Alwan, Statistical Process Analysis, Irwin/McGraw-Hill Publication, 2000.
[9] Parisa Rashidi, Diane J. Cook, An adaptive sensor mining framework for pervasive computing applications, in: Proceedings of the Second International Conference on Knowledge Discovery from Sensor Data, 2008, pp. 154–174.
[10] H. Ishibuchi, T. Murata, I.B. Turksen, Single-objective and multiobjective genetic algorithms for selecting linguistic rules for pattern classification problems, Fuzzy Sets and Systems 89 (1997) 135–150.
[11] K. Mondal, P. Dutta, Big data parallelism: challenges in different computational paradigms, in: IEEE Third International Conference on Computer, Communication, Control and Information Technology, 2015, pp. 1–5.
[12] X. Hou, L. Zhang, Saliency detection: a spectral residual approach, IEEE Conference on Computer Vision and Pattern (2007).
[13] H. Yu, J. Li, Y. Tian, T. Huang, Automatic interesting object extraction from images using complementary saliency maps, in: Proc. MMA 10, Firenze, Italy, October 25–29, 2010.
[14] S. Haykin, Neural Networks: A Comprehensive Foundation, second edition, Prentice Hall, Upper Saddle River, NJ, 1999.
[15] Lars Graening, Bernhard Sendhoff, Shape mining: a holistic data mining approach for engineering design, Advanced Engineering Informatics 28 (2) (April 2014) 166–185, 1995.
[16] J. Kacprzyk, S. Zadrozny, Data mining via linguistic summaries of data: an interactive approach, in: T. Yamakawa, G. Matsumoto (Eds.), Methodologies for the Conception, Design and Application of Soft Computing-Proceedings of 5th IIZUKA'98, 1998, pp. 668–671.

[17] Ian H. Witten, Frank Eibe, Mark A. Hall, Data Mining: Practical Machine Learning Tools and Techniques, The Morgan Kaufmann Series in Data Management Systems, ISBN 978-0-12-374856-0, 2011.

[18] Brian Caffo, Jeff Leek, Roger D. Peng, Data Science Specialization Course, Johns Hopkins University, 2014.

[19] Miao Chong, Ajith Abraham, Marcin Paprzycki, Traffic accident data mining using machine learning paradigms, in: Fourth International Conference on Intelligent Systems Design and Applications (ISDA'04), Hungary, ISBN 9637154302, 2004, pp. 415–420.

[20] Shu-Hsien Liao, Pei-Hui Chu, Pei-Yuan Hsiao, Data mining techniques and applications: a decade review from 2000 to 2011, Expert Systems with Applications 39 (2012) 11303–11311.

[21] S. Bhattacharyya, P. Dutta, U. Maulik, Binary object extraction using bi-directional self-organizing neural network (BDSONN) architecture with fuzzy context sensitive thresholding, Pattern Analysis & Applications 10 (2007) 345–360.

[22] S. Bhattacharyya, U. Maulik, P. Dutta, A parallel bi-directional self-organizing neural network (PBDSONN) architecture for color image extraction and segmentation, Neurocomputing 86 (2012) 1–23.

[23] Merrill Warkentina, Vijayan Sugumaranb, Robert Sainsburyd, The role of intelligent agents and data mining in electronic partnership management, Expert Systems with Applications 39 (18) (2012) 13277–13288.

[24] R.A. Fisher, Iris data set, machine learning and intelligent systems, https://archive.ics.uci.edu/ml/datasets/Iris, 1936.

[25] Datasets for Data Mining and Data Science, http://www.kdnuggets.com/datasets/index.html.

[26] S. Benferhat, K. Tabia, On the combination of naive Bayes and decision trees for intrusion detection, in: IEEE International Conference on Computational Intelligence for Modelling, Control and Automation, 2005, pp. 211–216.

[27] A. Gelman, J. Hill, Data Analysis Using Regression and Multilevel/Hierarchical Models, Cambridge University Press, 2006.

[28] F. Ramsey, D. Schafer, The Statistical Sleuth: A Course in Methods of Data Analysis, Duxbury Press, 2002.

[29] J.C. Platt, Probabilistic outputs for support vector machines and comparison to regularized likelihood methods, in: A.J. Smola, P. Barlett, B. Schölkopf, D. Schuurmans (Eds.), Advances in Large Margin Classifiers, MIT Press, 2000.

[30] Morent, et al., Comprehensive PMML preprocessing in KNIME, in: ACM SIGKDD, 2011, pp. 1–4.

[31] A. Ghoting, P. Kambadur, E. Pednault, R. Kannan Nimble, A toolkit for the implementation of parallel data mining and machine learning algorithms on MapReduce, in: 17th ACM SIGKDD International Conference on Knowledge Discovery and Data Mining, KDD'11, ACM, New York, USA, 2011, pp. 334–342.

[32] A. Ghoting, R. Krishnamurthy, E. Pednault, B. Reinwald, V. Sindhwani, S. Tatikonda, Y. Tian, S. Vaithyanathan SystemML, Declarative machine learning on MapReduce, in: 27th International Conference on Data Engineering, ICDE'11, IEEE Computer Society, IEEE, Washington DC, USA, 2011, pp. 231–242.

[33] Alcides Fonseca, Bruno Cabrali, Prototyping a GPGPU neural network for deep-learning big data analysis, Big Data Research 8 (2017) 50–56.

[34] C.H.C. Teixeira, A.J. Fonseca, M. Serafini, G. Siganos, M.J. Zaki, A. Aboulnaga, Arabesque: a system for distributed graph mining, in: 25th Symposium on Operating Systems Principles, SOSP'15, ACM, New York, USA, 2015, pp. 425–440.

[35] Chun-Wei Tsai, Chin-Feng Lai, Han-Chieh Chao, Athanasios V. Vasilakos, Big data analytics: a survey, Journal of Big Data 2 (21) (2015) 2–32.

[36] Daniele Apiletti, Elena Baralis, Tania Cerquitelli, Paolo Garza, Fabio Pulvirenti, Luca Venturini, Frequent itemsets mining for big data: a comparative analysis, Big Data Research 9 (2017) 67–83.
[37] Dinesh J. Prajapati, Sanjay Garg, N.C. Chauhani, MapReduce based multilevel consistent and inconsistent association rule detection from big data using interestingness measures, Big Data Research 9 (2017) 18–27.
[38] Hsinchun Chen, Roger H.L. Chiang, Veda C. Storey, Business intelligence and analytics: from big data to big impact, MIS Quarterly/Special Issue: Business Intelligence Research 36 (4) (2012) 1165–1188.
[39] L.T. Thomas, S.R. Valluri, K. Karlapalem, Margin: maximal frequent subgraph mining, ACM Transactions on Knowledge Discovery and Data Mining 4 (3) (2010) 10.
[40] M. Riondato, J.A. DeBrabant, R. Fonseca, E. Upfal, PARMA: a parallel randomized algorithm for approximate association rules mining in MapReduce, in: 21st ACM International Conference on Information and Knowledge Management, CIKM'12, ACM, New York, USA, 2012, pp. 85–94.
[41] Matthew Herland, Taghi M. Khoshgoftaar, Randall Wald, A review of data mining using big data in health informatics, Journal of Big Data 1 (2) (2014) 1–35.
[42] Mohammad Naimur Rahman, Amir Esmailpour, Junhui Zhao, Machine learning with big data an efficient electricity generation forecasting system, Big Data Research 5 (2016) 9–15.
[43] Mohammad Naimur Rahman, Amir Esmailpour, A hybrid data center architecture for big data, Big Data Research 3 (2016) 29–40.
[44] O.Y. Al-Jarrah, P.D. Yoo, S. Muhaidat, G.K. Karagiannidis, K. Taha, Efficient machine learning for big data: a review, Big Data Research 2 (3) (2015) 87–93.
[45] S. Aridhi, L. d'Orazio, M. Maddouri, E. Mephu Nguifo, Density-based data partitioning strategy to approximate large-scale subgraph mining, Information Systems 48 (2015) 213–223.
[46] Sabeur Aridhia, Engelbert Mephu Nguifo, Big graph mining: frameworks and techniques, Big Data Research 6 (2016) 1–10.
[47] Fan Wei, Albert Bifet, Mining big data: current status, and forecast to the future, ACM SIGKDD Explorations Newsletter 14 (2) (2012) 1–5.
[48] X. Jin, B.W. Wah, X. Cheng, Y. Wang, Significance and challenges of big data research, Big Data Research 2 (2) (2015) 59–64.
[49] X. Yan, J. Han, CloseGraph: mining closed frequent graph patterns, in: Ninth ACM SIGKDD International Conference on Knowledge Discovery and Data Mining, KDD'03, ACM, New York, USA, 2003, pp. 286–295.
[50] Xindong Wu, Xingquan Zhu, Gong-Qing Wu, Wei Ding, Data mining with big data, IEEE Transactions on Knowledge and Data Engineering 26 (1) (2014) 97–107.
[51] Ying Tan, Yuhui Shi (Eds.), A Data Mining and Visual Analytics Perspective on Sustainability-Oriented Infrastructure Planning, LNCS, vol. 9714, Springer, Bali, Indonesia, June 2016.
[52] Ying Tan, Yuhui Shi (Eds.), A First Attempt on Online Data Stream Classifier Using Context, LNCS, vol. 9714, Springer, Bali, Indonesia, June 2016.
[53] Ying Tan, Yuhui Shi (Eds.), A Geo-Social Data Model for Moving Objects, LNCS, vol. 9714, Springer, Bali, Indonesia, June 2016.
[54] Ying Tan, Yuhui Shi (Eds.), A Hybrid Model Combining SOMs with SVRs for Patent Quality Analysis and Classification, LNCS, vol. 9714, Springer, Bali, Indonesia, June 2016.
[55] Ying Tan, Yuhui Shi (Eds.), A Linear Regression Approach to Multi-Criteria Recommender System, LNCS, vol. 9714, Springer, Bali, Indonesia, June 2016.
[56] Ying Tan, Yuhui Shi (Eds.), A Range Query Processing Algorithm Hiding Data Access Patterns in Outsourced Database Environment, LNCS, vol. 9714, Springer, Bali, Indonesia, June 2016.

[57] Ying Tan, Yuhui Shi (Eds.), A Sequential k-Nearest Neighbor Classification Approach for Data-Driven Fault Diagnosis Using Distance- and Density-Based Affinity Measures, LNCS, vol. 9714, Springer, Bali, Indonesia, June 2016.

[58] Ying Tan, Yuhui Shi (Eds.), A Supervised Biclustering Optimization Model for Feature Selection in Biomedical Dataset Classification, LNCS, vol. 9714, Springer, Bali, Indonesia, June 2016.

[59] Ying Tan, Yuhui Shi (Eds.), Advanced Predictive Methods of Artificial Intelligence in Intelligent Transport Systems, LNCS, vol. 9714, Springer, Bali, Indonesia, June 2016.

[60] Ying Tan, Yuhui Shi (Eds.), An Effective Semi-Analytic Algorithm for Solving Helmholtz Equation in 1-D, LNCS, vol. 9714, Springer, Bali, Indonesia, June 2016.

[61] Ying Tan, Yuhui Shi (Eds.), An FW-DTSS Based Approach for News Page Information Extraction, LNCS, vol. 9714, Springer, Bali, Indonesia, June 2016.

[62] Ying Tan, Yuhui Shi (Eds.), An Improved Algorithm for MicroRNA Profiling from Next Generation Sequencing Data, LNCS, vol. 9714, Springer, Bali, Indonesia, June 2016.

[63] Ying Tan, Yuhui Shi (Eds.), Ant Colony-Based Approach for Query Optimization, LNCS, vol. 9714, Springer, Bali, Indonesia, June 2016.

[64] Ying Tan, Yuhui Shi (Eds.), Application of the Spatial Data Mining Methodology and Gamification for the Optimisation of Solving the Transport Issues, LNCS, vol. 9714, Springer, Bali, Indonesia, June 2016.

[65] Ying Tan, Yuhui Shi (Eds.), Big Data Meaning in the Architecture of IoT for Smart Cities, LNCS, vol. 9714, Springer, Bali, Indonesia, June 2016.

[66] Ying Tan, Yuhui Shi (Eds.), Big Data Tools: Haddop, MongoDB and Weka, LNCS, vol. 9714, Springer, Bali, Indonesia, June 2016.

[67] Ying Tan, Yuhui Shi (Eds.), Bigger Data Is Better for Molecular Diagnosis Tests Based on Decision Trees, LNCS, vol. 9714, Springer, Bali, Indonesia, June 2016.

[68] Ying Tan, Yuhui Shi (Eds.), Bulk Price Forecasting Using Spark over NSE Data Set, LNCS, vol. 9714, Springer, Bali, Indonesia, June 2016.

[69] Ying Tan, Yuhui Shi (Eds.), Classification of Power Quality Disturbances Using Forest Algorithm, LNCS, vol. 9714, Springer, Bali, Indonesia, June 2016.

[70] Ying Tan, Yuhui Shi (Eds.), Cloud-Based Storage Model with Strong User Privacy Assurance, LNCS, vol. 9714, Springer, Bali, Indonesia, June 2016.

[71] Ying Tan, Yuhui Shi (Eds.), Data Models in NoSQL Databases for Big Data Contexts, LNCS, vol. 9714, Springer, Bali, Indonesia, June 2016.

[72] Ying Tan, Yuhui Shi (Eds.), Data Mining and Big Data, LNCS, vol. 9714, Springer, Bali, Indonesia, June 2016.

[73] Ying Tan, Yuhui Shi (Eds.), Detecting Variable Length Anomaly Patterns in Time Series Data, LNCS, vol. 9714, Springer, Bali, Indonesia, June 2016.

[74] Ying Tan, Yuhui Shi (Eds.), Efficient Multidimensional Pattern Recognition in Kernel Tensor Subspaces, LNCS, vol. 9714, Springer, Bali, Indonesia, June 2016.

[75] Ying Tan, Yuhui Shi (Eds.), Efficient Probabilistic Methods for Proof of Possession in Clouds, LNCS, vol. 9714, Springer, Bali, Indonesia, June 2016.

[76] Ying Tan, Yuhui Shi (Eds.), Enhance AdaBoost Algorithm by Integrating LDA Topic Model, LNCS, vol. 9714, Springer, Bali, Indonesia, June 2016.

[77] Ying Tan, Yuhui Shi (Eds.), Ensemble of One-Dimensional Classifiers for Hyperspectral Image Analysis, LNCS, vol. 9714, Springer, Bali, Indonesia, June 2016.

[78] Ying Tan, Yuhui Shi (Eds.), Environment for Data Transfer Measurement, LNCS, vol. 9714, Springer, Bali, Indonesia, June 2016.

[79] Ying Tan, Yuhui Shi (Eds.), Extraction of Dynamic Nonnegative Features from Multidimensional Nonstationary Signals, LNCS, vol. 9714, Springer, Bali, Indonesia, June 2016.

[80] Ying Tan, Yuhui Shi (Eds.), Fingerprint Reference Point Detection Based on High Curvature Points, LNCS, vol. 9714, Springer, Bali, Indonesia, June 2016.

[81] Ying Tan, Yuhui Shi (Eds.), High-Dimensional Data Visualization Based on User Knowledge, LNCS, vol. 9714, Springer, Bali, Indonesia, June 2016.

[82] Ying Tan, Yuhui Shi (Eds.), Implementing Majority Voting Rule to Classify Corporate Value Based on Environmental Efforts, LNCS, vol. 9714, Springer, Bali, Indonesia, June 2016.

[83] Ying Tan, Yuhui Shi (Eds.), Industrial Internet of Things: an Architecture Prototype for Monitoring in Confined Spaces Using a Raspberry Pi, LNCS, vol. 9714, Springer, Bali, Indonesia, June 2016.

[84] Ying Tan, Yuhui Shi (Eds.), Key Indicators for Data Sharing – in Relation with Digital Services, LNCS, vol. 9714, Springer, Bali, Indonesia, June 2016.

[85] Ying Tan, Yuhui Shi (Eds.), Linear TV Recommender Through Big Data, LNCS, vol. 9714, Springer, Bali, Indonesia, June 2016.

[86] Ying Tan, Yuhui Shi (Eds.), Link Prediction by Utilizing Correlations Between Link Types and Path Types in Heterogeneous Information Networks, LNCS, vol. 9714, Springer, Bali, Indonesia, June 2016.

[87] Ying Tan, Yuhui Shi (Eds.), Local Community Detection Based on Bridges Ideas, LNCS, vol. 9714, Springer, Bali, Indonesia, June 2016.

[88] Ying Tan, Yuhui Shi (Eds.), Malay Word Stemmer to Stem Standard and Slang Word Patterns on Social Media, LNCS, vol. 9714, Springer, Bali, Indonesia, June 2016.

[89] Ying Tan, Yuhui Shi (Eds.), Mining Best Strategy for Multi-View Classification, LNCS, vol. 9714, Springer, Bali, Indonesia, June 2016.

[90] Ying Tan, Yuhui Shi (Eds.), Model Proposal of Knowledge Management for Technology Based Companies, LNCS, vol. 9714, Springer, Bali, Indonesia, June 2016.

[91] Ying Tan, Yuhui Shi (Eds.), Optimization on Arrangement of Precaution Areas Serving for Ships' Routeing in the Taiwan Strait Based on Massive AIS Data, LNCS, vol. 9714, Springer, Bali, Indonesia, June 2016.

[92] Ying Tan, Yuhui Shi (Eds.), Oracle and Vertica for Frequent Itemset Mining, LNCS, vol. 9714, Springer, Bali, Indonesia, June 2016.

[93] Ying Tan, Yuhui Shi (Eds.), Partitioning Based N-Gram Feature Selection for Malware Classification, LNCS, vol. 9714, Springer, Bali, Indonesia, June 2016.

[94] Ying Tan, Yuhui Shi (Eds.), Prediction and Survival Analysis of Patients After Liver Transplantation Using RBF Networks, LNCS, vol. 9714, Springer, Bali, Indonesia, June 2016.

[95] Ying Tan, Yuhui Shi (Eds.), Probabilistic Mining in Large Transaction Databases, LNCS, vol. 9714, Springer, Bali, Indonesia, June 2016.

[96] Ying Tan, Yuhui Shi (Eds.), Range Prediction Models for E-Vehicles in Urban Freight Logistics Based on Machine Learning, LNCS, vol. 9714, Springer, Bali, Indonesia, June 2016.

[97] Ying Tan, Yuhui Shi (Eds.), Real-Time Data Analytics: an Algorithmic Perspective, LNCS, vol. 9714, Springer, Bali, Indonesia, June 2016.

[98] Ying Tan, Yuhui Shi (Eds.), Reconstructing Positive Surveys from Negative Surveys with Background Knowledge, LNCS, vol. 9714, Springer, Bali, Indonesia, June 2016.

[99] Ying Tan, Yuhui Shi (Eds.), Study of the Harmonic Distortion (THD) and Power Factor Oriented to the Luminaries Used in the Traffic Light System of Bogotá City, Colombia, LNCS, vol. 9714, Springer, Bali, Indonesia, June 2016.

[100] Ying Tan, Yuhui Shi (Eds.), Term Extraction from German Computer Science Textbooks, LNCS, vol. 9714, Springer, Bali, Indonesia, June 2016.

[101] Ying Tan, Yuhui Shi (Eds.), Term Space Partition Based Ensemble Feature Construction for Spam Detection, LNCS, vol. 9714, Springer, Bali, Indonesia, June 2016.

[102] Ying Tan, Yuhui Shi (Eds.), The Role of Social Media in Innovation and Creativity: the Case of Chinese Social Media, LNCS, vol. 9714, Springer, Bali, Indonesia, June 2016.

[103] Ying Tan, Yuhui Shi (Eds.), Two-Phase Computing Model for Chinese Microblog Sentimental Analysis, LNCS, vol. 9714, Springer, Bali, Indonesia, June 2016.

[104] Ying Tan, Yuhui Shi (Eds.), Utilising the Cross Industry Standard Process for Data Mining to Reduce Uncertainty in the Measurement and Verification of Energy Savings, LNCS, vol. 9714, Springer, Bali, Indonesia, June 2016.

[105] Ying Tan, Yuhui Shi (Eds.), Visual Interactive Approach for Mining Twitter's Networks, LNCS, vol. 9714, Springer, Bali, Indonesia, June 2016.

[106] Ying Tan, Yuhui Shi (Eds.), Waiting Time Screening in Diagnostic Medical Imaging – a Case-Based View, LNCS, vol. 9714, Springer, Bali, Indonesia, June 2016.

[107] E. Velloso, A. Bulling, H. Gellersen, W. Ugulino, H. Fuks, Qualitative activity recognition of weight lifting exercises, in: Proceedings of 4th International Conference in Cooperation with SIGCHI (Augmented Human '13), ACM SIGCHI, Stuttgart, Germany, 2013.

[108] G. Mohindru, K. Mondal, H. Banka, IoT and Data Analytics: a current review, Wiley Interdisciplinary Reviews: Data Mining and Knowledge Discovery 10 (3) (2019) 1–27.

[109] G. Mohindru, K. Mondal, H. Banka, Different hybrid machine intelligence techniques for handling IoT based imbalanced data, CAAI Transactions of Intelligence Technology (2021).

[110] N. Tiwari, K. Mondal, NCS based ultra low power optimized machine learning techniques for image classification, in: IEEE Region 10 Symposium (TENSYMP), 2019, pp. 750–753.

CHAPTER 13

Conclusion

Sourav De[a], Sandip Dey[b], Surbhi Bhatia[c], and Siddhartha Bhattacharyya[d]

[a]Department of Computer Science & Engineering, Cooch Behar Government Engineering College, Cooch Behar, India
[b]Department of Computer Science, Sukanta Mahavidyalaya, Jalpaiguri, India
[c]Department of Information Systems, College of Computer Sciences and Information Technology, King Faisal University, Al Hasa, Saudi Arabia
[d]Rajnagar Mahavidyalaya, Birbhum, India

With the influx of huge amounts of data in the present-day digital world, the need for retrieval and analysis of relevant data has assumed paramount importance. Data mining [1][2][3] refers to the techniques and procedures to unearth relevant trends, patterns, and correlations in these huge amounts of data in order to extract meaningful information. Thus, data mining techniques typically resort to cluster analysis of the data under consideration with the aim to retrieve strikingly similar features along with dissimilar features.

With the advent of social media, the amount of data has exploded. These data possess enormous variety, given the fact that the data are generally generated based on different user sentiments. Not only do user-generated data vary in nature, they also exhibit ambiguity in content due to differences in human reasoning. Thus, machine intelligence is often called for in order to deal with this ambiguous information distribution. As far as the faithful analysis of these huge amounts of data is concerned, different clustering methods, viz. k-means clustering [4] and k-medoid clustering [5] methods, are found to yield efficient outcomes when it comes to handling ambiguous data. However, these clustering techniques fail to deliver appropriate results when it comes to handling the uncertainties and imprecision prevalent in the data.

As such, various fuzzy set theoretic techniques including the widely used fuzzy c-means [6][7] have come in vogue, which are efficient in the analysis of the inherent properties of data.

Social network data often contain irrelevant content; hence data mining techniques are required to retrieve relevant information out of these data. The mining procedures can be classified into the following categories:

Advanced Data Mining Tools and Methods for Social Computing
https://doi.org/10.1016/B978-0-32-385708-6.00021-7

1. Text mining: Text mining [3] is generally used to deal with unstructured data. Also referred to as text data mining, it is focused on deriving high-quality textual information by means of exploring unstructured data to recognize underlying patterns. Text mining uses the tools of data mining, information retrieval, statistics, and machine learning to handle natural language texts in any available format.

2. Image and video mining: Images and videos are different forms of continuous data associated with temporal information. As such, the data complexity is greater. Images/videos are acquired using cameras. Images may not only contain irrelevant information, but are generally affected by various types of noise, including channel noise and ambient noise, to name a few. Image mining [3] is a popular tool used for extracting implicit knowledge, relationships between image and data, or patterns. As such, it can be thought of as an extended part of data mining in the image domain involving database processing, machine learning, computer vision, image processing, and artificial intelligence. Video mining [3] can be thought of as the next level of image mining, which brings to light structures, knowledge, and patterns in video data.

3. Web data mining: Web data mining is an application area of data mining [7][8]. It is very useful to uncover patterns from the World Wide Web. Several automated techniques can be utilized for extracting data from web pages. Data can also be extracted from server logs and different link structures.

4. Mining of sequence patterns: Mining sequence patterns is a problem in which the association between distinct items in a database needs to be found. Mining sequence patterns encompasses itemsets, substructures, or subsequences which appear within a set of data and have frequency not below a user-specified limit. Frequent pattern mining [9][10] has been a requisite task in data mining, and researchers have been dedicated to this field for the last couple of years. Frequent pattern mining finds applications in recommender systems, bioinformatics, and decision making.

5. Mining time series data: In the last few years, mining time series data have gained utmost popularity among data mining researchers [9]. Different clustering, classification, indexing, and segmentation algorithms have been developed over the decades to find anomalies in time series.

This volume is a treatise on applications of data mining concepts to social network data. The interdisciplinary content of the volume is poised to provide immense benefits to the academic community, including researchers and practitioners.

References

[1] M. Injadat, F. Salo, A. Nassif, Data mining techniques in social media: a survey, Neurocomputing 214 (2016) 654–670.

[2] M. Adedoyin-Olowe, M.M. Gaber, F.T. Stahl, A survey of data mining techniques for social media analysis, CoRR, arXiv:1312.4617 [abs], 2013.

[3] G. Barbier, H. Liu, Data Mining in Social Media, Springer US, Boston, MA, 2011, pp. 327–352.

[4] J.B. MacQueen, Some methods for classification and analysis of multivariate observations, in: Proceedings of 5th Berkeley Symposium on Mathematical Statistics and Probability, vol. 1, University of California Press, 1967, pp. 281–297.

[5] L. Kaufman, J.P. Rousseeuw, Partitioning Around Medoids (Program PAM), Wiley Series in Probability and Statistics, John Wiley & Sons, Inc., Hoboken, NJ, USA, 1990, pp. 68–125.

[6] J.C. Dunn, A fuzzy relative of the ISODATA process and its use in detecting compact well-separated clusters, Journal of Cybernetics 3 (3) (1973) 32–57.

[7] J.C. Bezdek, Pattern Recognition with Fuzzy Objective Function Algorithms, 1981.

[8] I.-H. Ting, H.-J. Wu, Web Mining Techniques for On-Line Social Networks Analysis: An Overview, Springer, Berlin Heidelberg, Berlin, Heidelberg, 2009, pp. 169–179.

[9] D.L. Olson, Data mining in business services, Service Business 1 (2007) 181–193.

[10] J. Han, H. Cheng, D. Xin, X. Yan, Frequent pattern mining: current status and future directions, Data Mining and Knowledge Discovery (2007).

Index

Printed in the United States
by Baker & Taylor Publisher Services